An Introduction to Gregorian Chant

# An Introduction to Gregorian Chant

Richard L. Crocker

Yale University Press
New Haven & London

MW  $27.90  4/23/02  (3)

Set in Ehrhardt by Fakenham Photosetting Ltd, Norfolk
Printed in Great Britain by Biddles Ltd, Guildford and Kings Lynn

Library of Congress Cataloging in Publication Data

Crocker, Richard L.
  An introduction to Gregorian chant/by Richard L. Crocker.
  Includes bibliographical references and index.
  ISBN 0-300-08310-6 (cloth: alk. paper)
    1. Chants (Plain, Gregorian, etc.)—History and criticism. I. Title.

ML3082. C73 2000
782.32'22—dc21                                        99–88603

A catalogue record for this book is available from the British Library.

# Contents

# Compact Disc Tracks

Tracks 1 and 26: The Orlando Consort: Robert Harre-Jones, Countertenor; Charles Daniels, Tenor; Angus Smith, Tenor; Donald Greig, Baritone; used by permission. The Orlando Consort appears by kind permission of Deutsche Grammophon GmbH.
Tracks 2, 6, 22, 23, 24, 25: Marika Kuzma and Richard Crocker.
Tracks 3, 4, 5, 7–21: Richard Crocker.

# Illustrations

## Plates

## Figures

# *Acknowledgements*

This book's introductory nature and scope seemed to render inappropriate a comprehensive scholarly apparatus of sources and authorities. I can acknowledge here only in general the many people who have taught me what I know about writing, about singing, about singing chant, along with the many more who have sung it with me. It is nonetheless obvious, I trust, that in scholarship as well as musical performance I depend in essential ways on long traditions. Full documentation of the scholarship that has informed me will by itself require a book at least as big as this one (given strength and time I hope to provide it). In the meantime I believe that most questions can be referred to David Hiley's now-standard work, *Western Plainchant*. For the rest – conclusions of my own that depart from conventional wisdom – I can take refuge in no one else's scholarly authority.

Les Éditions de Solesmes kindly gave permission to reproduce a page from the *Graduale Triplex*. Chant scholarship and also performance depend directly on a millennium of chant books and – while most of them seem to be in the common domain – it is a pleasure to acknowledge their availability due to creation by publishers such as Solesmes as well as to their maintenance as historic sources by libraries such as those of St Gall and Einsiedeln along with the Bibliothèque Nationale, the British Library, and many more.

Yale University Press, in particular Robert Baldock and Malcolm Gerratt of the London office, provided enthusiastic encouragement at the start of the project and throughout its development. I am grateful to the Press for allowing me a CD with my own (also idiosyncratic) interpretation of the chant. To put that in proper context, the Orlando Consort kindly provided a benchmark of received British tradition of chant performance, and Marika Kuzma contributed her own beautiful witness of the sound made by the other half of humanity.

Books these days are written on computers, and I would be barely able to turn mine on but for my beloved Gloria. For her help in this and other ways I am deeply grateful.

# I

# *Chant, Chanting and Gregorian Chant*

> We listened to the Gregorian chant echoing through the vast shadowy recesses of the Gothic cathedral. The rich sound seemed to blend with the glowing, nearly palpable light filtering through the stained-glass windows. We could not see who was singing, but we knew it was the monks chanting their ancient liturgy; and even though we could not make out the words of the chant, we knew it was the Latin Psalms, chanted since time immemorial as part of the sacred ritual. We felt we could partake of the meditation, that we could be borne up in the mystic ascent to eternity, to serenity.

This is one person's report of a musical experience. It is a frequent experience: any one of us may have had it, and many have. It is a highly valued experience, and we would not be without it. Many features of the experience are indistinct; indeed, that indistinctness may be essential. Heard from the back of the cathedral, the mystical chanting seems an inner experience, and that is because much of it comes from inside the listener.

The experience just reported was my own, more than a half-century ago. People then were much more apt to encounter Gregorian chant as I did, in a cathedral, rather than on sound recordings, which were rare. It is different at the end of the twentieth century, for recordings of Gregorian chant on compact disc seem to be everywhere. In hearing chant for the first time on disc, we may not experience the cathedral context – the sound and light, and possibly also incense, that made the 'chanting' a mystical experience.

I observe, however, that a curious thing often happens: when Gregorian chant is sounding on an audio system, even if unannounced, listeners sometimes suddenly take notice of it with delight and surprise – 'Oh, that must be chanting!' Just as remarkable as the recognition of the experience is the identification by the word 'chanting', as if this special experience could be evoked by the word, without a context.

These two encounters with Gregorian chant intersect in the music, in spite of the fact that each strongly evokes another realm of experience that eludes definition. Coming from afar, the chant seems to be greeted (not so much in the listening ear as in the mind) with recognition, as music known but not remembered. In my own experience, I knew from the back of the cathedral what the chanting *had to be,* although I could not see who was actually singing, and what; and I was not entirely correct in some of the external details. My conviction came from some other source.

'Chanting – it is so beautiful! What is it?' This book begins with the fact that many people in the modern world respond to 'chanting' as if they knew what it was, and would like to know more. Knowing more involves on the one hand getting to know it better, on the other hand learning more about it – *about* it, that is, learning of the circumstances in which chanting is sung and heard, its context. These are two different kinds of knowledge, and both will be pursued here. It is important, however, to be aware of what you can expect from reading about music in a book.

The path to knowing any kind of music better is listening more, and listening more closely; a teacher, or a book such as this one, can only direct your attention, and encourage you to receive what you hear and to respond to it. This kind of knowledge is direct perception; in the case of music it is 'ears-on' perception, even though, like other kinds of sense perception, it is processed by the mind in important ways that we do not understand very well.

There may be a difficulty along that route, since one of the predictable results of becoming more familiar with this or any repertory of music is a loss of any sense of mystery that the music might have had when heard indistinctly. This result is very likely in the case of Gregorian chant: those who know Gregorian well find it not only familiar but natural; it feels like their kind of music. Some readers may look forward to that result; others may be wary of it. To both kinds of readers I want to say that in my experience the initial sense of beautiful vagueness is indeed replaced by a keen awareness of sharply focused detail, which in turn evokes a different kind of mystery, much more musical and much more poignant.

Listening more closely from the back of the cathedral has another curious and seemingly inescapable result. 'Chanting' is a rich experience, one whose features are as difficult to identify individually as to comprehend as a totality. (I shall continue to refer to it as 'chanting' in quotation marks in order to keep in mind the unique quality of this experience.) As soon as we focus on *one* feature, such as the sound, then suddenly the light and the incense, along with the singers and other listeners, the occasion, the place – all become *contexts* of the sound, and we perceive them in a different way. We can read (and write!) about them in a book, understand them intellectually, learn facts and configure them in our imagination, develop a picture of how all the features fit together.

Such a picture, however, may end up obliterating the experience of 'chanting', for, as everyone knows, the paradox of knowledge is that conceptualization can overlay experience. What we get from information about context is a prompt – a great many prompts – about what we might hear if we listened more closely with the context in mind. Using the knowledge of context, this book tries to show what chant can *become* in the musical experience of any listener.

The impression of 'chanting' as just described is a very widespread experience, and furthermore can be produced by any one of a number of different types of chant and manners of singing it. Gregorian chant is only one of these types. Some of the other types will be listed at the start of chapter 4, but there is not room in this book to discuss them at any length, nor can the experience of 'chanting' be explored in general.

Gregorian chant itself is a very specific but highly important musical repertory, requiring a close definition. Before attempting such a definition, however, I want to show what can be expected of a definition in these matters. I can show this more easily with a visual image, and it may be helpful to use the image of a cathedral, since that is one of the most important contexts of Gregorian chant.

What is a cathedral? Here is this huge pile of masonry in front of us, but *what is it*? A cathedral can be defined as the head office of the bishop. Even though exact and precise, this by itself may not be helpful, since most people visiting a cathedral are not aware of the bishop's presence. It may be even less relevant why the building is called a cathedral. It is because the bishop's throne, where he sits to make important pronouncements, is called his *cathedra*; the cathedral as a building houses the cathedra. Most visitors, again, will not be aware of the cathedra.

So, what is a cathedral *really*? People viewing a cathedral outside and inside may see only what matches their hopes and expectations. Those who come to participate in a traditional service – a Mass – may not see much in the exterior, except for soaring spires that point heavenwards, where the worshippers hope their consciousness can ascend. In the interior of the cathedral these same worshippers may find dark echoey spaces, conducive to meditation. But some may have a different idea of worship, and may see the interior of the cathedral as a beautifully decorated and brilliantly lit open space, ideal to accommodate the elaborate ceremonial in which the celebrant, attended by deacons and a dozen or more sacred ministers and acolytes surrounding the altar, performs the Sacrifice of the Mass.

Still others who come to worship, however, may not want to witness such a spectacle, but desire instead to participate in close communion with an intimate group; these people will see the open spaces as vast and barren. Indeed, over the centuries desperate attempts have been made to transform the interiors of the huge Gothic cathedrals so that they might be more suited to different ideas of Christian worship. And, of course, not everyone comes to worship: some want only to meditate alone.

In the Middle Ages the aisles and porches of the newly-built Gothic cathedrals served as central gathering-places for social interaction and small-scale commerce. In modern Europe and England the famous Gothic cathedrals are now apt to be filled with guided tour-groups as well as gift shops and cafeterias. As for non-religious appreciation, some observers seek only architectural beauty; they may focus on the long lines and balance or proportion among surfaces and volumes – and they may or may not find beauty, depending on their tastes.

The cathedral can be all of these different things to different people because it includes so many elements – more than can be easily listed, more than can be usefully summarized in one global concept. This constitutes a problem only if we try to complete the sentence, 'A cathedral *is* . . .'. So with Gregorian chant. And the definition I shall soon offer will not be much more helpful. Let me begin, rather, by describing a few of the most obvious kinds of Gregorian chant; for like a cathedral, chant's different aspects fulfil different needs for different people.

The first distinction to make is between simple and complex kinds of chant. This is not immediately apparent from the back of the cathedral, where everything tends to sound the same; but with a little close attention the difference will become apparent. There are some kinds of Gregorian chant simple enough to be sung by everyone in the congregation as they participate in the worship service. Because of their purpose, these kinds of chant will sound simple to any listener, and will be clearly different from the more complex kinds.

Much of the Gregorian repertory, however, is melodically too complex to be sung regularly by congregations – though, over the centuries, there have been individual congregations sufficiently motivated to learn how to do it. But even in monasteries, where most of the singing is done by everyone in the monastery, the most complex chant has often been sung by a select group of practised singers. And in cathedrals the usual practice, beginning from the time Gregorian chant first appeared, has been for the congregation to listen to it performed by a select group, the *choir*.

The difference between participating and simply listening leads to a more subtle distinction between functional and decorative chant. In music, as in architecture, there is an ancient tension between the needs of religion and those of aesthetics. From the beginning many Christians have been fussy about music – not so much about what kind they like, but rather about what kind seems appropriate for worship services. For some people, music is only a resource for worship; these people tend to use it only for congregational participation. Other people want music to be beautiful, either to enhance the service, or simply to be heard for its own sake. In early Christianity this was a basic difference in orientation, and resulted in bitter disputes. It still does.

### Recitation formulas and melodies

There is a special kind of functional Gregorian chant called a *recitation formula*. Each formula has a *reciting pitch*, a single musical tone on which the singer *intones* most of the syllables of the words to be sung; a few syllables of each sentence or verse are *not* sung on the reciting pitch but on other pitches, usually at beginnings and endings of phrases to *inflect* the intonation. These inflections are used to mark the syntax of the words, for instance lowering the pitch at the end of a sentence.

The sound of a reciting pitch is distinctive: it is unlike most other music that we hear. It is probably the sound by which we first identified 'chanting' from the back of the cathedral. Recitation formulas are used in Christian worship for the special purpose of communicating many words in a direct, efficient way. Typically they are used for singing prayers, or psalms, or reading lessons from the Bible. These selections are sometimes lengthy, and so the recitation may go on for a while; that is one reason why it seems as though recitation formulas were important in the Gregorian repertory.

If we pay closer attention, even from the back of the cathedral, we can soon tell that some of the singing does not use a reciting pitch. In Gregorian chant, in fact, it turns out that most of the repertory is characterized by an *avoidance* of reciting pitches; the pitches usually change from one to the next. Since this kind of change is normal in what we think of as melody, we can say that the greater part of the Gregorian repertory consists of *melodies*, not recitation formulas.

This difference between recitation formulas and melodies is easy to perceive in itself, but it may have confusing implications. While recitation formulas are in fact the simplest kind of Gregorian chant, they seem at first to be the most alien, the most unlike music we know. Yet they can lead the listening ear directly into a centre of musical experience, one which can be described as a centre of tonal space. Chapter 2 will begin to explore this tonal space; once we are there, we shall find – unexpectedly – that it is a space well known to the modern listener. And within that tonal space the most complex Gregorian melodies, those that seem so remote from modern experience, turn out to be strangely familiar in certain basic respects. Understanding how Gregorian chant can be both remote and at the same time familiar is the principal concern of this book.

*Unison singing*

One thing in general can be said about Gregorian chant that is true of many
other repertories of chant as well: it is all sung in *unison*, all the singers singing
exactly the same melody at exactly the same time. Unison singing is used in
recitation formulas and melodies, in simple melodies and complex ones.

Unison singing makes a very distinctive musical sound. Under certain
conditions it is a powerful kind of sound that shows the power of musical
tone to involve the listener vicariously in performance. To be in the presence of this sound is to participate in it: listening and singing become one.

Of importance to us here is that the unison sound of Gregorian chant
gives the listening ear – and the mind – direct access to the music in a way
that classical and popular music do not. Since in unison music only one
pitch is sounding at a time, the pitches of even the most complex chant are
on the surface for our perception. We can easily hear the relationship
between one pitch and the next. And it is in the relationships between
pitches that the inner meaning of Gregorian chant is to be found.

With such familiarity, however, there returns the nagging fear that we
might lose the mystery. As we get to know the relationships among individual pitches, will we lose the mystical experience of 'chanting'? This book
proceeds with the conviction, from my own experience, that close familiarity with Gregorian chant brings the listener to an ever keener appreciation
of the true mystery of the chant, which is not a function of its indistinctness
in a richly evocative context, but rather of its own deep musical nature.

*Gregorian chant as a historical style*

So far I have mentioned features that can be found in many different types
of chant. Chapter 4 will list some of these types, then sketch the historical
development of the type called Gregorian. This kind of historical definition
can be very precise but, like the definition of the cathedral, may not correspond to our immediate experience. Furthermore, the definition involves a
technical understanding of Christian liturgy, which will require chapters 5
and 6. The definition offered here does not seem to have much to do with
how the chant sounds or why it sounds that way. It is simply a working definition: it points at a certain collection or *repertory* of music in order to have
something specific to discuss.

We can say that *Gregorian* denotes a set of 500 to 600 chants called *Proper
chants of the Mass* that appeared in Europe north of the Alps around AD 900
and has been used in the context of the Catholic Mass on and off ever since
(the technical terms will all be explained later; or see the Glossary). This is
not only the strictest definition of Gregorian chant, it is also the narrowest;
but ultimately it is the easiest to understand.

The term Gregorian, however, is often applied in broader senses that include additional repertories of chant, repertories that are different even though related. For instance, the repertory of chants for the *Divine Office* (a religious practice separate from the Mass) is so closely related to the Proper chants for Mass that for most purposes it, too, can be called Gregorian (the technical terms, again, will all be explained later).

But another repertory commonly called Gregorian – the repertory of *Ordinary chants for the Mass* – is different enough in musical style for most specialists to agree in excluding it from Gregorian chant in a strict sense. While much of the music identified as Gregorian chant on compact disc recordings does indeed come from the core repertory of Proper chants of the Mass, much comes from these other related repertories.

The adjective Gregorian has ever since the ninth century seemed most interesting and most important, since it was once taken to mean that Pope Gregory the Great (who died in 604) composed the chant or at least caused it to be composed. Very few scholars now believe that this was the case. While there is no agreement about what the term actually meant, it seems to have been a function of the chant's original political context around 800, when it was first called Gregorian; this context will be described in chapter 4.

### Gregorian chant as both near and far

Defining Gregorian chant as a specific repertory produced out of a histori- cal process places it far in the past and in a seemingly remote culture – or at least a special subculture, the Christian community. How can we hope to understand music with such seemingly inaccessible origins? How can knowledge about the origins of the chant – who first sang it and why – help our understanding of the chant as we hear it performed in a modern context?

These questions have parallels, again, in the cathedral. The reason Gothic cathedrals are now so crowded with visitors seems to be a profound curiosity on the part of Europeans and Americans to rediscover the ancient places and sources of their traditions. The places seem strange, remote, unlike places normally frequented in modern life. At the same time they seem strangely familiar, or at any rate they evoke deep-seated responses in us.

It was a common idea in the Middle Ages that Gregorian chant was the music of the angels, that is, it seemed different from the ordinary music made by humans. We may still attribute an angelic or heavenly quality to the chant (or to any music) as a way of saying that it is uniquely beautiful – even though, upon close inspection, the music is clearly being produced by humans. While many people are curious about the different ways music was made in these remote circumstances, they seem also to want to know that the music was made by real people, that in spite of all these differences it was somehow like music we know.

The sources to which we go for more knowledge – the circumstances of original performance, of social context, of personal involvement – these are the stuff of history; this is what a study of the history of chant can provide. This book will supply as much historical information as possible within the space available, drawing on historical research, European and American, from throughout the twentieth century. This type of historical study is sometimes called *reception history*, for in it we can learn what the music meant to listeners in the past by the way they received it; then we can compare that meaning with what we find in the music by listening to it. Sometimes, however, we learn more about the listeners than we do about the music.

If Gregorian chant were in fact alien, then all we could do, as outsiders, would be to conclude from reception history what the music meant to the original listeners. But if, on the other hand, there are elements in the music which were operative for the original listeners *and are operative for us as well*, we can conclude that we hear and respond as they did. It seems to me that the reality involves a mix of some elements that are immediately familiar and others that are unfamiliar but can be learned. There may also be elements that are really alien and perhaps beyond our reach.

When music from another culture is studied by ethnomusicologists, there is a lively debate among them about whether it is possible for a musician from outside to learn to perform music from, say, Indonesia. Some American ethnomusicologists study music in Indonesia, with Indonesian teachers, and attempt to enter the culture as deeply as they can in order to perform its music authentically. This is called 'going native' by other ethnomusicologists, who doubt that it can be successful, and furthermore feel that the outsider who tries to get inside loses the status of an objective observer and can no longer perceive Indonesian music or culture accurately. To this the outsider-gone-inside replies that only by perceiving the music from the inside can its true meaning be understood.

There is controversy, too, in judging the success of the outsider in performance: inside critics would say, almost as an axiomatic prejudgement, that the performance does not sound authentic no matter how expert it may be – indeed, that it could never sound authentic simply because the outsider is not an insider. But in some cases critics from the outside as well as the inside have had to admit that certain performances have been so close to authentic as to be virtually indistinguishable from native performances. It is clear that some non-native performers have in fact learned to perform music from remote cultures, just as some musicians from remote cultures have become brilliant performers of music in, say, the European tradition.

What about listeners? It is obvious that a great many people have learned to appreciate music from cultures other than their own. Insiders can, of course, always insist that outsiders do not and cannot understand the *true* meaning – but we would have to take the insiders' word about that, since there is no way of checking on the inner experience of either outsider or insider. (The same kind of disagreement can sometimes be heard between a German and a non-German on the music of Beethoven, or a Lutheran and a non-Lutheran on the music of Bach.) Nonetheless, it is still legitimate and important to ask, Is our enthusiastic response appropriate to Gregorian chant itself, or are we hearing something that is not actually there in the music?

If there is a problem with Gregorian chant being remote, it is not going to be solved by historical information about its origins, simply because there is not enough specific, reliable information available from history. There is nothing that tells us what the chant sounded like or what it was intended to sound like until late in the Middle Ages. Historical sources are simply lacking in this case, and we are thrown back on much more general information and on our own musical response to what we hear in the chant as performed today.

Fortunately, there is one very solid piece of general information that guarantees us at least some access to the way Gregorian chant sounded when first developed. The chant uses the same tonal system that comes down to us in the tradition of European music. Whether simple or complex, Gregorian melody moves within a system of musical pitches called *diatonic* – essentially the white keys on the piano. We shall spend time with the use of this basic system; for now it is enough just to identify it as the system that underlies Gregorian chant and also classical and popular music.

The use of the diatonic system, by itself, can account for the familiarity of Gregorian chant. If Gregorian chant sounds strange (as it does to many listeners) its strangeness can be ascribed to its style of melodic movement *within* the diatonic system. This style of melodic movement will be discussed in chapter 3.

## *The words of Gregorian chant*

We might think that, since Gregorian chant is a completely vocal repertory (sung, not played on instruments), the words that are sung should tell us what the singing is about. The meaning of the words should bridge any cultural gap between modern ears and ancient singers.

There are, however, several reasons why this is not the case. First, there are some basic considerations having to do with the nature of music and of words. Music, everyone agrees, has essentially non-verbal meaning; hence, if there is a problem with understanding the purely musical meaning, the poetry will not help. On the other hand, even though music may not be a universal language, there seems to be no reason why ancient music should be harder for us to understand than ancient poetry; and there seem to be few complaints about our ability to understand ancient poetry.

Second, in the case of Gregorian chant several purely practical factors place distance between us and the meaning of the words. The words are in Latin, requiring for most listeners a translation in some form. (This book will provide Latin texts and English translations for all the pieces on the compact disc, and will discuss them.) Furthermore, in many performances, live as well as recorded, it is difficult just to make out the Latin words, either because the singers do not project them well, or because the words are blurred by an echoey ambient. So, as with opera when sung in a foreign language, listeners need to follow the words in a programme, or to have studied them ahead of time – or simply to ignore them and enjoy the music. This last, in fact, is what many people do when listening to Gregorian chant, and it seems to me that nothing musical is lost thereby.

The words of Gregorian chant are taken almost entirely from the Latin Bible (the Latin translation called the *Vulgate*, compiled and mostly translated by St Jerome shortly before AD 400 from the Greek Bible and other sources, including the Hebrew sacred writings). Jerome's Latin Bible is all in prose, not verse – even the psalms, which as Hebrew sacred poetry were originally in verse. Being in prose, the Latin words have no poetic rhythm: they have a fine sense of rhythm, but it is the free, irregular rhythm of prose. Thus, the words have little to contribute to any sense of regularity that the modern ear might listen for in the rhythm of the chant. Here again, the words do little to diminish the distance between the modern ear and Gregorian chant.

As it turns out, the modern ear does not need to get a sense of rhythm from the words of Gregorian chant, for it is perfectly capable of understanding free, irregular rhythm, having had at least some experience of this kind of rhythm in classical music. In any case, the rhythm that we hear in chant does not come from the words, but from the music. This requires some further discussion, but the principle is simple: in most Gregorian chant more than one pitch is sung to each syllable; some syllables, even in relatively simple chant, may have three, or four, or five pitches. These lengthen the syllable and break up the continuity of whatever rhythm might have emerged from the words when spoken. Compare these two performances (by speaking them) of one of the first chants we will study.

**Pu**-er **na**-tus est **no**-bis.
Pu-u-er na-a-a-tus e-e-est no-o-o-o-bis.

In the first line the accented syllables are printed in bold; we might hear a rhythm organized around the syllables *na-* and *no-*. The second line is printed so that the vowels are repeated for as many different pitches as are sung on that vowel. This stretches the distance between syllables, and whatever rhythm we hear is going to be heavily influenced by the several pitches that come on each syllable. In case you do not get the point by reading what I have written here about the rhythm, be assured that you will immediately understand when you hear the rhythms performed.

### Melismatic chant
Sometimes a syllable in Gregorian chant is sung to so many pitches – up to twenty or thirty, or more – that we lose track of what word the syllable was from, and are aware only of the vowel sound that is being prolonged. Not only is all trace of verbal rhythm lost, but the sense of the words may become lost, too.

The melody on the prolonged syllable is called a *melisma*, and it is of central importance in Gregorian chant. A piece of chant is said to be *melismatic* when at least one of its syllables has a melisma; usually several individual syllables will each have a melisma, longer or shorter, but most of the syllables in the piece will have only a few pitches – three or four, or even only one. Melismatic chants are by no means in the majority, but by their nature are usually the most elaborate and impressive of the repertory.

In a melisma we hear pure melody, music alone – just as we hear in instrumental music. A melisma interrupts the connectedness of the words, and intrudes into the verbal meaning with a musical meaning that may or may not mesh with the verbal one. The melisma reminds us that two different things, words and melody, are going on at the same time.

### Words and liturgy
If we read the words of Gregorian chant in translation (or if we can understand them in performance), their surface meaning is usually clear. The words of Gregorian chant are most often from the Book of Psalms (the *Psalter*) in the Hebrew Bible (Christians call it the *Old Testament*); many psalms are cast in the first person singular, and speak of the individual's relationship to his God – words of praise, petition, complaint, repentance, sometimes of exhortation to his fellow men to join in praise or petition.

It is true that the meaning of the psalms is occasionally obscure because of scholarly uncertainty in reading and translating the ancient Hebrew text. The words used for Gregorian chant, however, were taken selectively from the Latin translation and usually avoid the obscure passages, so the surface meaning of the words in Gregorian chant is almost always clear.

The surface meaning, however, does not always make sense in the context of Christian worship, and seems in fact to have been mistrusted by early Christians (and later ones, too). There is a continuing problem in what the words from the Hebrew Old Testament mean when sung in a Christian worship service. Many of the sentiments expressed in the psalms (as generally in the Old Testament), such as the invocations of divine retribution on enemies, seem inappropriate in the context of New Testament religion. Christian practice in public worship has avoided such language by using only selected psalms or verses. Much energy has been expended by Christian teachers, especially in the early centuries and in connection with singing psalms, in allegorizing the Old Testament words to show how they could be more appropriately understood by Christians.

Hence it is sometimes not obvious what the words of a given piece of Gregorian chant have to do with the occasion on which it is sung – Christmas, for instance, or Easter. Each piece of Gregorian chant, as we shall see, is assigned to a specific day in the church year, days that commemorate events in the life, death and resurrection of the Lord Jesus (the 'story of salvation') or that commemorate one of the many saints and martyrs in Christian history. The applications are often allusive and presumptive: they sometimes require laboured explanation. In fact, sometimes we have to know first what the Christian liturgical application is in order to 'read' the text, to discover or understand its Christian meaning.

## Gregorian chant and liturgy

The most important context for Gregorian chant is Christian worship service or *liturgy*, and in particular the liturgy called the *Mass*. This is the context in which we find it when it first appears in writing in ninth-century France. Gregorian chant has also appeared in the context of Mass throughout the twentieth century in Europe and America, and around the world. Gregorian chant is often described if not defined as liturgical, and in order to know what that means we need to know a little about the liturgy of the Mass.

As we shall glimpse in chapter 5, early Christian worship involved hard thinking and hard talking about what liturgy should include, and that discussion continues throughout the present age. Modern Christian observers differ radically in their opinions concerning the relevance of Gregorian chant to Mass in the Middle Ages, or the relevance of Gregorian chant to Mass in the modern age, or even the relevance of Mass itself to the modern age. We do not need to be involved in the controversial discussion, or even know very much about it. But since, under the heading of reception history, we are dealing with how the singers and listeners at Mass feel about Gregorian chant, that involves their feelings about Mass as well.

As to the immediate meaning of the word 'liturgical' and related terms, a simple set of definitions can be given; these progress from general to specific.

*Cult* is public devotion (which may or may not involve worship).
*Rite*, or *ritual* cult, is formalized cult, in which public devotion is expressed according to pre-arranged procedures, usually but not necessarily invariant.
*Liturgy*, or *liturgical* rite, is assigned rite, in which the various procedures are assigned to specific individuals, to be performed at certain times in certain ways.

In spite of its use by the news media especially for strange, potentially sinister groups, cult is a normal, neutral term from Latin for public devotion. A distinction was traditionally made in antiquity between devotion to gods, for whom devotion could include worship, and devotion to (human) heroes, for whom worship was not considered appropriate in Greco-Latin culture. Christians continued the distinction, and spoke of cult particularly in connection with *their* heroes – saints and martyrs. Or they spoke more generally of '*divine* cult', *cultus divinus*, by which they meant devotion to *their* God, not the pagan gods. Roman Catholics continue this use of the word down to the present.

*Ritual* is an adjective used very often as a noun. Cult, simply as public devotion, need not be ritual; it can be spontaneous, not pre-arranged. Rite, by definition, is worship performed according to prescribed forms. A prearranged form of cult is a rite. The *Roman rite* is the form of worship prescribed by Roman Catholic practice. Used as a noun, *ritual* means ritual worship.

The noun *liturgy* had a very specific meaning in Greco-Latin culture, designating various assigned tasks ranging from janitorial to financial support for civic temple activities. Christians again continued the use of the term, so that at the rite of Mass the bishop had his liturgy, the deacons their liturgy, the people theirs.

In English, *liturgy* and *ritual* are often used loosely and interchangeably. For Greek Christians, however, the rite of the eucharist is *the* liturgy; other worship services are identified by their individual names. In the Latin West, *liturgical* is applied loosely but not very helpfully to any kind of worship service controlled by ancient prescription. This application has led to the connotation of arbitrary restrictiveness that many people find objectionable. And liturgy has another connotation. A very wise, very well-informed historian of liturgy once made an apparently whimsical yet profound definition of liturgy : 'Liturgy', he said, 'is people doing things for which they have forgotten the reasons.'

*The bishop as liturgical authority*

In the conduct of Roman Catholic worship, formal initiative as well as final determination traditionally rests with the bishop – an essential point to which we shall return again and again. As head of his *diocese* (geographical area of jurisdiction) the bishop has ultimate responsibility for every member of his diocese (the Roman Catholic Church has not recognized women as bishops). One of the bishop's important functions is to decide on liturgical practice in his diocese.

If we were to ask, 'Is Gregorian chant liturgical?' the immediate answer would be, 'If the bishop says so'. This would have to be determined by survey, diocese by diocese, century by century.

From early on (the second century, perhaps), many bishops looked to the bishop of the city of Rome for ritual models, among other things; Roman bishops responded to this need of their brother bishops by recommending the rites in use in the diocese of Rome. Over the centuries this process resulted in the Roman rite as standard and universal for all dioceses that regard themselves as 'in communion' with the diocese of Rome. Hence, while a bishop of the Roman Communion determines liturgical practice in his diocese, the practice that he determines is – at least in principle – that of the Roman rite.

As far as the words and ceremonial actions of the Mass are concerned, the rite remained basically unchanged from the Middle Ages until the twentieth century. The words of Gregorian chant had been laid out, assigned to specific functions and occasions as a special part of Mass, early in the Middle Ages; the stability of assignment is a reason for calling them 'liturgical'.

The fact that the words were laid out, however, does not mean that their melodies were set down at the same time, with the same fixity and permanence. As we shall see, the melodies remained in general use for only a few centuries, being replaced in more recent times with very different music. As a part of Mass, the Gregorian repertory was sung at the direction of the bishop; but if singers or the congregations did not want to use the chant, and if the bishop took no action to have it sung, then it was not sung. This actually happened: slowly but inexorably, over the centuries between roughly 1400 and 1900, Gregorian chant stopped being heard at Mass throughout Western Europe. Since the words were written in the Roman Missal (the book that stood on the altar and contained everything that was to be said at the Roman Mass), bishops and priests of the Roman Communion continued to say the words of Gregorian chant at the altar, either out loud or to themselves, along with all the rest of the words for Mass. Sometimes the singers sang the Gregorian words to other music; sometimes they sang completely different words and music instead; but the

Gregorian melodies went out of use. They were still 'liturgical', because assigned in the book, but they were no longer music that people wanted to hear.

Starting in the middle of the nineteenth century, a few people became interested in the ancient forgotten Gregorian melodies as music; and some people, mostly in monasteries, became interested in their possible use in worship services – even at Mass. Slowly more and more people became interested; the story of how the Gregorian melodies came eventually to be used again will be sketched at the ends of chapters 4 and 8.

## Modern liturgical reform and Vatican II

The interesting phase of the story begins in the twentieth century. In retrospect we can make out two different attitudes at work: there was intense interest in Gregorian chant *as music*, and there was a need to confirm the Mass as the centre of Roman Catholic cult. The people interested in the chant made extreme efforts to get it sung at Mass. This involved persuading their bishops that it was a good idea and persuading the people that chant was what they wanted to hear at Mass. Some did, some did not; and on this point the bishops in general took careful account of the preferences of their people.

Towards mid-century, interest in Gregorian chant seemed to be on the increase. Those pushing hardest for the use of Gregorian chant at Mass buttressed their arguments by saying that it was the traditional music, already liturgical, and also the ideal music for the Mass – and we certainly want to do everything we can to make Mass meaningful for Roman Catholics and attractive to secular society, do we not?

Unfortunately, an affirmative answer to that question was not forthcoming. For while interest in chant might have been growing, interest in the Roman Catholic Mass was not. It began to appear to many Roman Catholic leaders that it was time to think the unthinkable, to decide which elements of the traditional Mass should be continued in use, and which should be relegated to history.

What made it thinkable at all was the increasingly problematic position of Mass in the whole range of Catholic activities in society. The problems were addressed at *Vatican II*, the Council of Roman Catholic bishops held at St Peter's in Rome, 1962–5. In 1959 Pope John XXIII had convoked the bishops of the Roman Communion to agree on fundamental recommendations affecting a broad spectrum of church polity, including basic matters of liturgy.

The bishops met, discussed and acted in committees, commissions and as a general assembly in several sessions during 1964 and 1965. Intense historical scholarship went into the preparation for the Council; the

discussions themselves were long and impassioned. In response to unprece-
dented pressure from parish priests and the people, the Council undertook
the most sweeping changes in ritual forms since Charlemagne had
attempted to install the Roman rite throughout Europe almost exactly 1200
years earlier – a process we shall survey in more detail in chapter 4.

A particular concern of Pope John XXIII, as well as of the bishops assembled at Vatican II, was the participation of the people in the ritual cult. It
was deemed essential to increase the extent and significance of the people's
liturgy in the rite. Judging by subsequent reactions, however, there was no
real agreement about how best to do this: some Roman Catholics wanted to
preserve traditional forms, some did not. The resolutions of the Council,
framed to represent agreement, seemed to include conflicting provisions, or
at any rate sent mixed messages to the people. Roman Catholics are still
trying to draw practical conclusions from the voluminous and complex recommendations of the Council.

The Council sustained Gregorian chant as a traditional model for liturgical music, but it also understood the exclusive use of Latin for Mass to be
incompatible with popular participation. The Council provided for Mass to
be said in a vernacular language, and that by itself eliminated Gregorian
chant in its traditional form – that is, with Latin words – as an assigned
element at Mass.

If, for the benefit of English-speaking peoples, say, the Mass as a whole
was to be translated into English, why could not the Latin words of
Gregorian chant also be translated into English, and sung as part of the
reformed Mass? (This had been done for a long time by those Anglicans
who used Gregorian melodies at Mass.) Such translation was not undertaken, apparently because the real obstacle to the continued use of
Gregorian chant was not that the words were in Latin, but that they no
longer seemed meaningful to the people; nor did the melodies.

It had long been difficult to find enough music with Latin words in a
musical style that was popular with Roman Catholic congregations. As soon
as the reformed Mass could be said in the vernacular – in English – church
musicians made immediate and extensive use of the several styles of popular music with guitar accompaniment, those styles being also vernacular,
and therefore a logical counterpart to the new liturgy; and they seemed to
be well received at Mass. Another style of music that turned out to be unexpectedly popular with Roman Catholics was that of the Protestant hymn.
Neither of these alternatives, however, can be reconciled easily with
Gregorian chant as a model. Lovers of Gregorian chant, insiders as well as
outsiders, watched in dismay as the process of reform worked itself out.

Our concern here is with reception history: what does the reception, or
non-reception, of Gregorian chant in modern liturgy tell us about the

chant? The most prominent aspects of the history are the drastic nature of the changes right after the Council, and then the subsequent complexity of Roman Catholic practice. For as decades go by, in various places Gregorian chant and even certain seemingly traditional features of the Roman rite are returning to use.

I find one important conclusion to be that the drastic liturgical changes taking place immediately after the Council were obviously not something foisted upon the people by the bishops; rather, they were an expression of what a substantial number of people wanted – and had wanted for a long time. A historian could observe in general that turbulence in our age was not so much a result of recently prevailing attitudes as a result of the willingness of our age, like the preceding Victorian age, to sit on a turbulent situation until the lid blew off. It is obvious to a historian that for centuries Europeans had not wanted to listen to Gregorian chant; and in fact, they did not listen to it. Gregorian chant, even though officially appointed to the Roman Mass, had suffered the same fate as the long procession of other European musical styles, namely, it lost meaning and went out of use. This can suggest to a historian that musical preference might also have had something to do with the original development of Gregorian chant, possibly as much as did liturgy.

The abrupt rejection of Gregorian chant immediately after the Council in favour of the guitar Mass showed that the growing enthusiasm for chant in the half-century *before* the Council did not represent as much of the Roman Catholic population as some had hoped. The multiple, conflicting points of view were and are represented at all levels of the hierarchy and throughout the Roman Catholic community. A historian, again, can observe that this may always have been the case. The image of one rite, one set of liturgical assignments, one body of liturgical music persisting throughout European history, is an image of uniformity propagated by a singularly single-minded administration. If the reception history of the twentieth-century Roman Mass reveals different and conflicting preferences, could not the same have been true in the ninth century?

Many liturgical scholars, in preparation for the Council, made the general recommendation to return to worship practices of an earlier stage of Christian liturgical development, and this recommendation was implemented by the Council in several specific ways. As we shall see in chapter 6, the presence of a select choir singing Gregorian chant was one of the distinctive features of the Roman Mass in the eighth century; this eighth-century form of the Roman Mass was the one that survived through the ages until Vatican II, and it was the form of Mass that had to be changed. The earlier stage was the one *before* Gregorian chant was added. In this way of seeing it, there seems to be more than one kind of liturgy; the early kind,

which is also the kind desired in the twentieth century for greater participation of the people, seems not to need or want Gregorian chant.

It is possible for an outsider to conclude from all this that acquaintance
with the context of the Mass is irrelevant to understanding Gregorian
chant. But I would conclude, rather, that the addition of Gregorian chant to
the Mass in the eighth century can alert us to the musical power the chant
may have had for at least some people at that time.

### Liturgical quality of Gregorian chant

My own experience began with a different sense in which Gregorian chant
is liturgical. As I stood at the back of the cathedral, listening to 'chanting'
for the first time, I had an impression that the chant *seemed* liturgical – even
before I knew exactly what 'liturgical' meant, how the Mass went, or how
chant was assigned to it. It did indeed seem that the singers were chanting
to fulfil their own solemn commitments to some ancient tradition of sacred
ritual; but the source of that impression was the music they were singing,
rather than anything I knew beforehand or that the singers told me.

Witnessing their collective mystic transport evoked in me an intense
desire to be a part of it. It was obvious that singing these words together
required initiation, learning, long participation; yet just standing there, listening, I could almost participate merely by virtue of the kind of singing I
heard. As I got to know both chant and liturgy, what each was and how each
was different from the other, I continued to find the chant an essential
access to the meaning of the activity in which I participated at Mass.

It seems to me that music makes a basic contribution to the sense of
liturgy, if not actually creating that sense. The sound of prayers being
intoned by the priest at the altar is very different from the sound of the same
words being spoken. The sound of the congregation singing together in
unison has a mystical quality completely lacking from the sound of the congregation *speaking* together. And, if liturgy is supposed to be a means of
spiritual ascent, the close encounter with Gregorian melody can guide the
spirit to mystic realms as nothing else can.

Could this have been true so long ago, in early Christian times? During
the formative period of Christian music and liturgy John Chrysostom, one
of the most prominent early Christian leaders around AD 400, and called
'golden (tongued)' because of his skill in oratory, wrote of 'mixing melody
with prophecy' to arouse the souls of the worshippers. His wording shows
that even he trusted music, more than words, to be immediately
meaningful.

The power of music is confirmed in a very different context by an early
report of the use of chant *outside* the liturgy. This report is from Gregory,
bishop of Tours in France in the late 500s, who wrote a very famous *History*

*of the Franks*. Gregory of Tours was a Gallo-Roman, a leading member of the old provincial population, who watched in fascinated horror as the members of the Merovingian dynasty, the ruling family in France, struggled with each other for power. Gregory's *History* is a simple unadorned account of one of the most unrelenting struggles in human history between blood relatives, a tale of vengeance wreaked on each other – and on anyone who got in the way – of treachery, violence, brutality, murder and not-so-sudden death. (They caught up with the wicked grandmother Brunnhild in the Jura mountains, tied her to the tail of a wild horse, and let the horse run.) Gregory's terrible story has little room for anything good or beautiful, and certainly does not show the Merovingians as devout or even religious. But in a brief vignette he tells how, when the Merovingian king Guntram was visiting Tours in 585, he requested that Gregory at dinner one night have his deacon sing the responsory he had sung at Mass the day before. And while it was being sung, the king told Gregory to have the other bishops (there were several present) order *their* deacons to do likewise.

This brief account is well known, being one of the earliest, perhaps *the* earliest mention of the type of chant eventually called *gradual responsory*, which we shall meet as the most important kind of Gregorian chant. Some historians of liturgy place great importance on Gregory's witness as evidence that something called 'responsory' was indeed sung at Mass by this date, 585. What seems to have gone unnoticed, however, is the point of Gregory's story: this most important kind of liturgical chant was *also* sung by a soloist on a purely secular occasion, with no liturgical context whatsoever, simply for the pleasure of this Merovingian king and the other powerful guests. This kind of hearing is the same as when we listen at home to a compact disc.

Appreciation of music for its own sake receives documentary witness in yet another way from a well-known story about the other Gregory, 'the Great', pope in Rome around 600. It has been shown that, far from being responsible for the chant that bears the same name, this Gregory had little interest in music. When it came to his attention that his deacons were turning vain from flattery received for the beauty of their singing, he forbade them to sing anything at Mass except the Gospel (which would be recited in a simple style). Once again, an anti-liturgical aspect of the story has been consistently ignored by liturgical historians. It is clear from Gregory's action that people derived great pleasure from hearing – in church – fancy music sung beautifully by a soloist.

*Gregorian chant in this book*
There are many different cathedrals as well as many different kinds of chant. What you hear from the back of the cathedral as vague but beautiful

'chanting' may not be Gregorian at all but rather some other kind, and then the descriptions in this book will not apply. Similarly, accounts in standard reference books, as well as current publications in liturgy, music history and criticism, may define Gregorian chant differently: while using that name, they may actually be discussing some other kind of chant, hence may give a description that differs from the one given here.

Then, too, there are very divergent ideas about the history of certain kinds of chant. In particular (to summarize briefly the different – and changing – ideas about Gregorian chant), there is also a kind called Old Roman, now usually considered to be a sister, or perhaps first cousin, to Gregorian. For a long time it was thought that both types came from Rome, although there was no agreement about which came first, or how they were related to each other. More recently, some scholars feel that only the Old Roman represents truly Roman practice, while Gregorian was a different musical style developed by French and English singers.

This divergence of historical interpretation can make a difference in musical interpretation, as when we say, for instance, that if Gregorian chant is from a northern European culture it must have a musical effect different from the Roman chant from a Mediterranean culture. Further differences of opinion result from the fact that since in this case we have no way of knowing how either Old Roman or Gregorian sounded when first developed, we can only judge their musical effects by much later evidence – or just from how they sound today. That, of course, depends largely on how today's performers think the music should sound. While we would like to be able to demonstrate from analytical or historical evidence how Gregorian chant sounded, or should sound, that seems in fact not possible; or at any rate, we cannot agree.

Musical performance, in Gregorian chant as in any music, seems to spring mainly from the inner conviction of the performer, and we would not have it any other way. Historical evidence, when available, has the important but still not decisive function of suggesting new and different ways of performing that might not occur to a modern performer.

In this book my ideas about Gregorian chant are represented by my performances on the compact disc. For me, this is the way Gregorian chant is. Other performances on other discs (even those by other singers on this disc) present Gregorian chant differently. But even performance – mine or some other – does not say what Gregorian chant *is*, for, like all music, it is the way you hear it. My way of singing, for instance, may seem to some observers to be indistinguishable from the twentieth-century tradition established by the Benedictine monks of Solesmes; the Benedictines themselves, on the other hand, might find my style different or even very different from theirs. (I shall sketch some of the reasons for such similarity or difference in chapter

8.) The best way, perhaps the only way, to know Gregorian chant is to listen as closely as possible to various performances, observing the different musical effects on you. The more extensive the listening experience, the greater becomes musical understanding and appreciation.

Since I am persuaded that it is consonant with the best scholarly and critical methods to begin with one's own response to Gregorian chant (as also to other kinds of music), I want to say here what my response is, if only to encourage each reader to begin, at least, with his or her own experience.

For me, Gregorian chant is first of all music to be sung: I find singing it to be a most rewarding musical experience. I love to sing it with others in chorus, I love to sing it solo. I love to sing it alone at home, or in concerts, but also at Mass and in the Divine Office, where I find it extremely appropriate – as appropriate as any other musical repertory I know. I sang Gregorian chant at Mass for forty years; still, that experience notwithstanding, I feel the Gregorian style to be in certain ways a very personal one, which is why I enjoy singing and listening to it outside a liturgical situation just as much. As a musical activity I find it so intrinsically meaningful that the question of *what* it means never comes up. I have no sense of distance from Gregorian chant, but still a profound sense of its mystery.

## 2

# Tone and Tonal Space for Gregorian Chant

From the back of the cathedral we perceived the chant being sung within a large volume of space. Everything about the sights and sounds was affected to some degree by the qualities of the architectural space – its dimensions, contours, surface materials. We could not be aware of all its specific qualities, and may have had only a vague impression; but the impression could be a strong one, with a strong effect on details that we did perceive.

Similarly, the listening ear locates specific pieces of music within a *tonal space*. It is common to speak of a 'world' that a composer such as Beethoven can create with a particular powerful work. Most of the music we hear does not create the effect of a world so strongly. Still, the listening ear seems to perceive, or construct, a world of tone for music habitually heard.

Describing such worlds of tone is the principal problem in writing about music. The usual solution, trusting in visual rather than auditory experience, uses words that refer to spatial rather than musical dimensions. The concepts of space, distance, high and low are all firmly embedded in the technical language of music, as in common understanding. Such concepts are very useful, as long as we keep in mind that they are metaphors. Listeners often think that they do not understand the music, when in reality what they do not understand is the metaphor.

It is difficult to be aware of the tonal space in which we hear much music in modern times, simply because that space is so diffuse, containing such a wide range of musical tones, often veiled or obscured. Nonetheless, that world has specific identifiable qualities that form an important part of the experience of any listener. We can become aware of these qualities when we hear a piece of music that seems to be in a completely unfamiliar style, or seems to come from another cultural world; that stylistic or cultural strangeness may be due simply to the use of an unfamiliar musical world, a different tonal space.

The remarkable aspect of Gregorian chant is that it does *not* move in a different tonal space, but in a part – a central part – of the tonal space with which we are most familiar in classical and popular music. This chapter will try to locate Gregorian chant within this familiar space.

In chapter I a basic distinction was made between Gregorian chant that used *recitation formulas* and Gregorian *melodies*. Recitation formulas, used for prayers, psalms and lections (readings), place most of the syllables on one pitch, moving to one or two alternative pitches only for punctuation. In contrast, melodies change pitch with almost every syllable, moving through a much greater number of pitches.

A melody generates a tonal space by moving through a range of pitches. A reciting pitch, in contrast, does not generate a space, but rather just a place to be, by dwelling on one pitch. The reciting pitch seems to be a point, a sharply defined location in an otherwise undefined expanse. In comparison, the tonal spaces generated by melodies are less well defined than a reciting pitch; still, they are readily audible. Awareness of tonal space is easily heightened; and even when we are not aware of it, tonal space is a principal source of the musical meaning of Gregorian chant.

## *Tone, pitch and note*

Musical tone is a given, a prime term, undefined; it is simple sense perception; nerve synapses fire away, and we know a tone. We do not even have to qualify it as *musical* tone; tone is musical, is the essence of music. Tone is what pierces the heart. No one needs to learn how to hear tone. And anyone can hear the essential relationships between individual tones – even very complex relationships – without reading anything about them. It is helpful, however, to learn how other people hear these complex relationships; the problem, which this chapter addresses, is understanding the words and concepts used to describe what we hear. But the words will not make much sense to the mind unless the sounds of the chant from the compact disc are sounding in the ear, or have just finished sounding.

The bare physical definition of tone is a sound of stable frequency (as opposed to one of unstable or varying frequency). This book always refers to tone in this sense by the common term *pitch*, simply because the term *tone* has some other very important, closely related, but distinct meanings.

Tone as in *whole tone* designates the standard interval in the diatonic scale, the normal distance from one pitch to the next higher or lower. Certain intervals in the diatonic scale, however, are smaller than the whole tone; they are called *half-tones* or *semitones*.

*Tone* is regularly used to refer to a recitation formula, consisting of a reciting pitch along with two or three adjacent whole tones or semitones; we speak of a *psalm tone*, or a *lection tone*, or a *prayer tone*.

*Ton* is used regularly in French for English *key* (in German *Tonart*), a certain collection of tones and semitones (either a *major key* or a *minor key*). From this use, the root *ton-* produces the widely used terms *tonic, tonal, tonality*. Not all of these terms need to be discussed here; their specific meanings will be identified as needed.

This book uses *pitch* instead of the more common term *note*, because *note* refers specifically to the graphic mark used to identify a pitch. The first singers of Gregorian chant, however, did not sing from notes, and it is of the greatest importance not to describe the earliest stage of Gregorian chant as if it was written down. When we discuss how the early singers *did* write it down (in chapter 8), we shall need to identify very carefully what they used for notes, and how these were distinct from pitches.

A single pitch is the basic element of music. Pitches can last for a longer or shorter time; but even when a sound is so short as to be barely perceptible, the ear registers the pitch, along with its similarity to and difference from the surrounding pitches. The rest of what we hear is in the mind, which locates the pitches in a configuration with musical meaning.

Individual pitches have several qualities besides frequency and duration, for instance *timbre* or tone quality. Such qualities are very prominent and need to be taken into account in interpreting the configuration; still, it is pitch that is at the centre of our musical experience. In Gregorian chant the range of other qualities is deliberately held at a minimum. Even in Gregorian chant, however, the pitch is not simple, the sound is not pure, and important complexities bear upon whatever we try to say about it.

(Throughout the following discussion, a few technical terms, and eventually the letter names of pitches, will be included in parentheses for the sake of readers who are accustomed to using them. Neither the technical terms nor the letter names, however, are essential to the discussion, and can be ignored. Listening to the examples, on the other hand, will be essential; the discussion may not make sense unless the sound of the example is in the reader's ear.)

## Unison singing

In music, unison means 'one sound'. As mentioned in chapter 1, Gregorian chant is sung in unison; hence, we can say that Gregorian chant comes to us 'one pitch at a time'. We must be aware, however, of what we are actually hearing. Since Gregorian chant is most often sung by a group, we are hearing sound from several sources, several mouths, and it is not automatic that they are all singing exactly the same pitch. If men and women, or men and boys, are singing together, they are definitely not singing the same pitch: the women and boys are singing higher than the men (an octave higher). Even a single voice on one pitch does not produce a single, simple frequency; under certain conditions the complexity of the pitch is clearly audible, and even when not perceptible, the complexity has important effects and implications.

The early Christians, profoundly concerned with the problem of singing, had the best and most pragmatic way of describing what they wanted. When Christians sing together (they said), all should sing 'as if with one voice', *quasi una voce*. The sound should be as if it came from a single mouth. That might not be a theoretically pure sound, but it was close enough, since as a model it effectively avoided the idea of two competing sounds being heard at the same time.

The expression 'as if with one voice' is useful to us because it both defines the ideal – a single sound source – and at the same time acknowledges the reality that most music involves more than one sound source. Since Christian worship necessarily involves more than one person, Christian music has always involved a group of people singing together. The words 'as if' are most important: the members of the worshipping group are to sing *as if* they were one person, even though they are not one, but many. The Christian paradox of the many being 'one in Christ' comes into play here; or, in more practical terms, the singing in unison can be a powerful symbol of the unanimity of spirit so desired in Christian worship. Just as St Paul expressed unity of spirit by vivid reference to 'one body' (1 Corinthians 12:12), so other early writers expressed unity of sound by reference to 'one mouth'.

Early Christian leaders rejected in principle all the ways in which people might sing *different* sounds at the same time, for instance using different words, or singing at slightly different times, or singing different pitches simultaneously. They also rejected all kinds of instrumental participation; for even if instruments were playing the same pitches that were being sung, the instrumental timbre would differentiate the sound sufficiently to count as more than one sound. And it is clear that in Greco-Latin culture instrumental accompaniment, which was in common use in music for cult or entertainment, could involve more than one pitch at a time.

The intent that music for Christian worship should consist of only one pitch at a time was effective through the period (seventh–eighth centuries) in which Gregorian chant was developed. After that, European music, including Christian music, intensively explored the use of more than one pitch at a time, in a broad spectrum of techniques we call *polyphony* ('many sounds'). Eventually European music became essentially polyphonic, which is the form in which we know it in the classical and popular repertories. This chapter will describe the kinds of relationships between single pitches found in Gregorian chant, then at the end will consider briefly some of the differences that present themselves when we hear more than one pitch at a time, as in most of the music we hear around us.

## Intonation and resonance

In discussing chant, reference is often made to *intonation*, which in its most general sense is 'putting into tone', or, in effect, making music. We say that a singer intones a prayer, in that he puts the words of the prayer into tone. It may be into a single tone, as a reciting pitch, or into a few pitches, as in a recitation formula, or into many pitches, as in a melody. Sometimes the word *intonation* is used in a very limited sense as referring to the first pitch, or the first two or three pitches, of the formula or melody, as when a soloist sings the intonation of a chant which the chorus continues; the soloist is also said to *intone* the chant. Intoning is what is different from speaking, and that difference is more important than the difference between intoning in a recitation formula (using one pitch repeatedly) and intoning in a melody (changing pitch by pitch).

The special quality of intonation is produced by *resonance*: in dwelling on the same pitch the sound can *re*-sound: the pulses of the sound travelling through the air can restrike the ear at a constant rate (frequency), reinforcing its effect in a marvellous way. Resonance is basic in many modes of human experience. A simple but vivid example is pushing a child in a swing: when the push exactly matches the momentum of the swing, the motion of the swing builds up much faster and greater than it would otherwise. Even more vivid, however, is resonance in sound, once you become sensitive to it: resonance is responsible for music's most common characteristics – as well as its most magical effects.

One of the most important aspects (although not the only one) of a chorus singing as if with one voice is that they are singing exactly the same pitch, so that the sound can resonate like the sound of a solo voice. But a chorus can never be exactly in tune, and the very slight discrepancies in pitch are what make a chorus sound different from a solo – slightly fuzzy, warmer, less distinct.

### Reinforcement of resonance

There are ways of reinforcing sound that are important for chant of all kinds; these ways sometimes increase the effect of resonance, but sometimes interfere with it. In any kind of building, the sound bounces off the walls and, depending on architectural configuration, this *reverberation* can re-inforce or confuse. In a large space such as a cathedral, the distance delays the reverberation by as much as three or four seconds, making it very noticeable. In some ancient churches large clay pots were installed in the walls behind the singers to act as resonators. Nowadays we use an electronic black box (a *reverb*) to produce the same effect – although not usually in liturgical music.

A reverberant acoustic space can reinforce certain components of a sound selectively, making these components much more noticeable. Under most conditions any intoned pitch produces *overtones*, certain other pitches that are higher but that blend in well with the *fundamental* [tone] – so well that they are usually not noticed. (These overtones occur at multiples of the fundamental frequency, beginning at twice the frequency, then at three times the frequency, and so on up, usually getting progressively weaker.) The first and second overtones are strong in the human voice, and are sometimes audible under ordinary circumstances; in a reverberant space they can be greatly magnified, increasing the power of the sound. A cathedral or other reverberant space may magnify the overtones selectively, producing remarkable effects (depending, again, on the configuration of the building and its materials). Our idea of Gregorian chant should include the possibilities of these dimensions of sound.

In performance, musicians of all kinds often reinforce the first overtone (it sounds the octave above the fundamental). Called *doubling*, this is done regularly in the orchestra and on the piano; and it happens in Gregorian chant whenever men and women or men and children sing together. In chant it is sometimes called 'singing in parallel', because the women (or children) sing the same melody as the men, only higher; yet the two parts blend so well that they still sound as if with one voice. The result is not two parallel melodies but rather one enriched melody. (In medieval practice, chant was sung in parallel at other intervals as well, in addition to or instead of the octave; smaller intervals made the sound even richer – but further away from the ideal of a solo voice.)

## Reciting pitch

When a solo voice intones a prayer, or a reading from Scripture, on a reciting pitch, the intonation on a single pitch can result in extreme resonance. The natural ability of the human voice to speak directly to our inner hearing is maximized with intonation and the resonance that it brings. This has a special application in Christian worship: when expressed by a strong clear solo voice, with the resonance reinforced by cathedral reverberation, this kind of intonation can penetrate the listener's heart, seeming to convey the truth of the words of doctrine.

While a solo voice on a reciting pitch has the power to penetrate the listener's understanding, the sound of a chorus does not so much penetrate as envelop, gathering up the listener into a larger unity. The sound of the whole congregation intoning in unison is like no other musical experience. Unison singing by everyone is not just a *symbol* of being together, it is an archetype, a primary experience of being together, one of which other experiences may be symbols.

When psalms are sung this way in a reverberant acoustic space such as a cathedral, the reciting pitch builds up very great resonance – especially if the singers find the reciting pitch specific to that building, the particular pitch that resonates most strongly in it. As the sound continues minute after minute, it permeates the whole space and everyone in it. The walls reverberate, the building itself seems to reproduce the tone. Certain medieval churches have this effect to a remarkable degree, and recordings have been made that show an extreme development of the overtones produced by such resonance.

## Hearing pitch relationships

The most important way to understand Gregorian chant is through awareness of the pitch relationships. Every listener hears these relationships, but because of their unfamiliar configuration in Gregorian melody, many listeners feel that they cannot understand their true meaning. In reality a great many modern listeners understand the meaning of Gregorian melody very well, as demonstrated by the popularity of the chant in the 1990s. But listeners may still need encouragement to acknowledge that what they are hearing is indeed the chant's meaning.

The reason why it is possible for a modern listener to understand Gregorian chant is that the pitch relationships in the chant are the same as those in classical and popular music; hence, they are perfectly familiar in modern experience. This identity, while by no means obvious, can be shown in principle by explanation in a historical context, which will be provided later in this chapter. First, however, a few simple exercises, using some of the chants on the compact disc, can lift pitch relationships to the top of your awareness.

In order to understand the meaning of a poem, we have to hear individual words. Of course, we also have to hear their configuration, how they go together, and that is so important that we may take the individual words for granted; but without perception of the words one by one we do not get much out of their combination. After we hear a line of poetry, we may find that one or two most important words of the line linger in the ear; these words have become imprinted in temporary memory, and are available, at least for a moment, for reflection. This same kind of activity can take place in listening to chant – or any music – and is the easiest access to the chant's musical meaning. (The basic difference between verbal and musical meaning, so important in other contexts, is not relevant here.) The following exercise depends on actually listening to Psalm 2 on track 20 of the compact disc.

Listen to a few verses of the psalm, from the beginning of the track. The reciting pitch will be obvious – inescapable, in fact. To a casual listener it will seem like the only pitch in the world, at least while the psalm is going on (other pitches sound occasionally, and will be mentioned in a moment). During the recitation on this one pitch, we experience it by itself, with no relationship to other pitches: it is tone, the basic element of music.

In learning a new word in a foreign language, or even an unknown word in our native language, we instinctively repeat the word immediately upon hearing it, as a way of confirming what we heard. In the same way we can hum a reciting pitch, just by reflex, after hearing a few verses. The purpose of this exercise is not to learn how to sing psalms, but rather to realize that musical sounds leave traces in the ear, and that pitches in chant, sounding one at a time, can leave especially clear traces. These traces form the context in which the ear hears and understands pitch relationships – even without paying attention.

Chant singers, after *singing* several psalms on the same reciting pitch, sometimes have the experience of hearing in memory that pitch for an hour or more (provided it is not obscured by some other pitch sounding in the meantime). Reciting pitches produce this effect simply because of the insistent reiteration of a single pitch, with relatively few other pitches competing with it. Any piece of music, however, produces this effect to a greater or lesser extent; any piece imprints the ear with its most prominent pitches. Untrained listeners can leave a concert humming the last tune of the last piece, if it was sufficiently prominent.

Listeners can be reassured that this temporary pitch memory is completely independent of so-called perfect pitch or absolute pitch, an apparently innate ability to identify pitches without reference to any context. Far from being required for understanding Gregorian chant or any other music, the faculty of perfect pitch is in some ways a real obstacle to proper perception of pitch relationships; those who possess it are more to be pitied than envied.

Recitation formulas always include, along with the reciting pitch itself, at least one other pitch, typically used to mark beginning and endings. Such additional pitches are shown in figure 2.1 for that particular psalm tone: there are two that are used at the beginning of each *group* of verses, one that is used in the middle of each verse, and two that are used at the end of each verse.

When I listen to a few verses of a psalm sung as on track 20, I find that, in addition to the reciting pitch, I can also hear in memory these other pitches of the psalm tone. 'Echoing' may be too strong a word to describe them; still, they have left enough trace for me to remember what they sounded like – as long as I do not interfere with too much effort. I do not actively *recall* them, but merely observe that they are there. And I can remember them *as a set* more easily than I can remember exactly how the formula went.

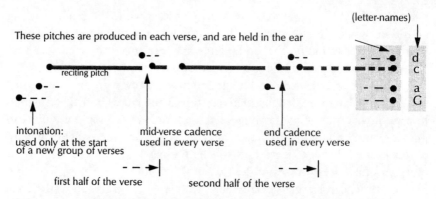

Figure 2.1 Recitation formula for a psalm tone. This is psalm tone 8, used for Psalm 2 as sung on track 20 of the compact disc. (This is one of two alternative endings for psalm tone 8 known as 8c; the other variety is 8G. The other psalm tones 1–7 also have alternative endings.)

In figure 2.1 the echo of the set of pitches as held in the ear is represented by the dots in the grey box to the right: there is one pitch higher than the reciting pitch, and two that are lower. If you pause your listening at the end of a verse and, without any distraction, consult your inner ear, you should find a sound image corresponding to the dots in the box. The second grey box to the right gives the letter names of these pitches, for the sake of readers who want to use them; but the letter names are not needed in order to hear or understand what is going on.

The imprint of pitches in memory is a complex and extremely important phenomenon: it forms the context in which we understand the melody. This context seems always to be present and operative when we listen to music. The ear can hear more than the pitch that is actually sounding; it can hear, in memory, the preceding pitches as well. This makes it possible to hear in Gregorian chant a network of *pitch relationships*, not just single pitches.

## Pitch relationships in a melody

In the case of the psalm tone there is a very great contrast between the strong reciting pitch and the other much weaker pitches, and so we may not be encouraged to notice relationships among these pitches. The reciting pitch is so strong that it seems to be the only pitch; the other pitches in the psalm tone are mere distractions, exceptions that emphasize the rule of the reciting pitch. We can explore pitch relationships of a chant more easily in the case of a Gregorian *melody*, as opposed to a recitation formula, since in a melody no one pitch is repeated over and over for long stretches without

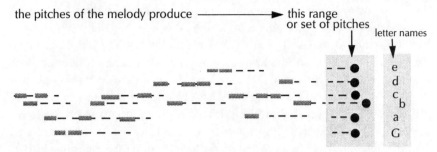

the pitches of the melody produce ⟶ this range
or set of pitches

letter names

Do-mi-nus dix- - it ad me fi- li-us me- us es tu

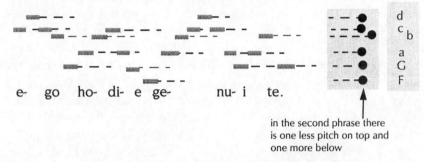

e- go ho- di- e ge- nu- i te.

in the second phrase there
is one less pitch on top and
one more below

Figure 2.2 Accumulation of pitches in the antiphon *Dominus dixit*. The horizontal black bands over the syllables represent the pitches. The dotted horizontal lines represent the imprint made in the ear. These imprints accumulate at the end of the phrase in a set or range of pitches, shown by dots in the first grey box. (The grey box further to the right shows the letter names of these pitches. The pitch dots are whole steps apart, except for the dot set off to the right, which is a half step below the one above.)

variation; instead, each successive pitch is usually different from the one immediately preceding.

An example of a short Gregorian melody is the antiphon *Dominus dixit* found on the same track (track 20) with Psalm 2. The antiphon can be heard sung several times in the course of this psalm, starting after the fifth verse. In listening straight through the whole psalm, including the antiphon as it returns, the ear will distinguish between psalm tone and antiphon. Identifying the antiphon as different from the psalm tone is the first step – and an important one – in hearing pitch relationships: the antiphon sounds different because it lacks the reiterated reciting pitch of the psalm tone. In the antiphon the imprint of each pitch will be weaker, but the pitches will be more equal in impact, and the ear can be more aware of their relationships. To put it another way, the ear will hear the pitches of a melody more globally, more as a set.

Figure 2.2 shows how the pitches of this melody accumulate at the end of each phrase. The pitches are represented by short thick horizontal bars.

This type of musical notation shows exactly what is sounding 'out there', and does not include anything that is added 'in here' by the way we listen. (This notation is derived from MIDI technology – Musical Instrument Digital Interface – used in audio recording.) Such a diagram does not look much like the melody sounds. We shall need this kind of diagram only as a graphic record here of how single pitches accumulate into a melody.

Figure 2.2 also shows thin black dashed lines starting in each thick bar, suggesting the subjective imprint that the pitch leaves in the ear after it sounds. These dashed lines do not go far, since conscious attention shifts to the following pitches, which are different. But the dashed lines suggest how each pitch, once sounded, remains in the background, and can be summoned up in memory when the phrase ends. The grey box at the right suggests the set of pitches that you can find in your head at the end of the phrase; humming, quickly and by reflex, will bring them up more clearly. (This type of diagram is used here only for the purpose of identifying the imprint.) The melody accumulates more pitches than the recitation formula in figure 2.1; the set in figure 2.2 is actually a segment of a familiar *scale*, which we shall identify. The letter names, again, are only for those who like to use them.

One important feature of the diagram is that it shows how, for this as for any specific Gregorian melody, there are only a limited number of pitches – maybe as few as five for a simple melody, or up to twelve or more for a flamboyant one. In phrase 1 of *Dominus dixit* (figure 2.2) there are six pitches, shown by the dots at the end of the first line; these constitute the *set* or *range* of pitches used in that phrase. Phrase 2 uses almost the same set of pitches – one less on top, one more below.

*Reference pitch and central tonal space*

Within a Gregorian melody almost all the pitches are used more than once, that is, almost every pitch returns at some point during the course of even the shortest piece. The more often a pitch returns, the more impact it has on the ear.

Even though in a Gregorian melody no single pitch is reiterated in the manner of a reciting pitch, frequently a single pitch is made to function as a *reference pitch*. The other pitches are heard in relation to it, sounding higher or lower. The reference pitch may in fact be frequently reiterated, or accented, or associated with important words, or made to stand out in some other way. Or, the reference pitch may simply be located relative to the other pitches so that it *feels* like a point of reference. Reasons can be produced from music theory to suggest why certain pitches come to feel like reference pitches, but with or without reasons these pitches do have this effect.

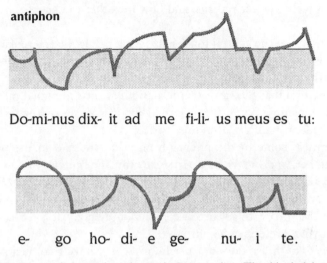

**antiphon**

Do-mi-nus dix- it ad me fi-li- us meus es tu:

e- go ho- di- e ge- nu- i te.

Figure 2.3 Reference pitches and tonal space in *Dominus dixit*. The thin dark horizontal lines show reference pitches. The grey rectangle shows the central tonal space.

In many Gregorian melodies the pitches *next* to a reference pitch are just as prominent, forming together with the reference pitch a band or zone of three, or four, or five pitches. It is as if a reference pitch had been broadened. This expanded zone of reference can be called a *central tonal space*. The other pitches of the melody may be above or below this central space.

The melody from figure 2.2 is shown again in figure 2.3 with a central tonal space shown by a long grey rectangle. The point of this kind of diagram is to show how a particular melody moves through its tonal space. In the first phrase some of the melody is within the grey rectangle representing the central tonal space, but some is above it; in the second phrase one pitch of the melody is below the box as well.

The way the pitches were indicated in the preceding example (figure 2.2), while objective and accurate, seems unattractive and does not match the subjective effect of the supple, flowing melodic line that we hear when the chant is sung. The short thick horizontal bars showing pitches in figure 2.2 have been replaced in figure 2.3 with curves that flow only approximately through the points of pitch but are (I hope) aesthetically more pleasing and thereby show the effect of the melodic line better. The curves do not represent the melody exactly, and should be referred to only to see how it fits into the grey rectangle.

In *Dominus dixit* (figure 2.3) a reference pitch emerges gradually during the first phrase. It sounds on the very first pitch and again on the third one, both on the syllable *Do-*; it reappears several times during the phrase, although with none of the insistence of a reciting pitch. More important is the way it feels when it returns, and how the other pitches feel in relation-ship to it.

The pitches of the central tonal space lying below the reference pitch are all sounded during the words *Dominus dixit*; the melody moves down and up through the central tonal space. The motion through this space seems so easy, so natural that the ear is scarcely aware of the individual pitches or of their relationships. They seem normal for this piece – which is what is meant by identifying a central tonal space.

In contrast, some of the pitches from *ad* to the end of the phrase are clearly higher, and higher in a particular way. The pitches on *ad* and *filius* lift up from the central tonal space, as if reaching out; their goal, however, is not a still higher pitch, but instead the reference pitch itself, which returns on *me-(us)* with a sense of completion; that is part of what is meant by identifying a reference pitch.

The second phrase does not reach out as far above the tonal space, but instead descends below it. The pitch on (*hodi-*)*e* is not just lower, but has a deeper feeling, a descent to a realm relatively remote from the tonal space marked out so far in this piece. Not only does it feel lower than its simple distance down, but also it suggests a melodic motion still further, a defini-tive departure from the central tonal space. That does not happen, however, and the melody returns up into the central space, perhaps with a sense of pulling itself out of a hole.

These are all subtle aspects of the melody, and not very obvious because this melody, being short, has but little time to develop its meanings. But such meanings are there, and the modern ear can find them. A rationale, again, can be produced by music theory. And historical reasons can be produced for believing that the same meanings were audible in the ninth century.

The pitch at the end of the first phrase on *tu* sounds just *below* the refer-ence pitch rather than on it. Clearly, the first phrase does not sound com-plete: it requires completion, which is supplied by the resumption of the reference pitch at the start of the second phrase on *ego*. This shows how a reference pitch can feel very central, very stable. One of the striking aspects of Gregorian melodic motion in tonal space is that a Gregorian melody seldom ends on a reference pitch. It may end on a pitch that is clearly related to the reference pitch, as in *Dominus dixit*, or it may end on a pitch that seems unrelated. In *Dominus dixit*, the ending pitch has been the lower boundary of the central tonal space, seemingly an integral part of this set of pitches normal for this piece. Yet this lower boundary seems not to provide completion for the melody, which could end much more conclusively on the reference pitch. If you find someone to sing or play the melody with an ending on the reference pitch, you can easily hear the difference in sound.

In *Adiutor*, a much longer chant on track 8 of the compact disc, the central tonal space is established early on and remains prominent, in spite of extravagant excursions above and especially below. The upper boundary of the central tonal space is given by a very strong reference pitch: the tonal space is marked out by the first two pitches, of which the higher one becomes the reference pitch. The melody often returns emphatically to this pitch throughout.

Towards the end of *Adiutor*, on the words *exsurge, Domine*, the melody comes to a sharp focus on the reference pitch in order to emphasize the point of the words, which implore God to vindicate the righteous – 'Arise, O God!' After this strong arrival on the upper pitch of the central tonal space, however, the melody ends in a place that seems to have no clear relationship to either the upper or lower boundaries of the space.

Inconclusive endings of this and other kinds are frequent or even normal in Gregorian chant. Their use does not betray a different tonal sensitivity (or, as was once thought, an ignorance of 'natural' tonal relationships) but rather, a different aesthetic sensitivity – different from that of classical music. Gregorian melody rarely resorts to an emphatic rhetoric in order to begin or end or reach a climax.

## The diatonic scale

The choice of ending pitches, then, can make Gregorian chant sound different. In contrast, the *interiors* of Gregorian melodies often move through tonal space in a way that sounds very familiar to the modern ear. Looking back at figure 2.2, the set of pitches that accumulated in that antiphon forms part of a scale called *diatonic*. The most vivid picture available of the diatonic scale is provided by the *white* keys on the piano (the black keys are something else). There are 52 white keys, and they embody the diatonic scale, but there could be more if the keyboard were wider – out to the limits of audibility.

This scale is the basis of any systematic explanation of classical music as found in any textbook. Furthermore, it is imprinted in the ear of anyone who listens to classical and popular music – or even just hears this music without listening consciously, and without any formal instruction in what to listen for. Listeners who have had formal instruction know this scale best in one particular *segment* of it called the *major scale* (on the white keys, the 'C-major scale'). That segment is closely identified with the conclusive sound of the kind of ending typically used in classical music (the 'dominant-to-tonic cadence'). Gregorian chant uses the major scale, along with other diatonic segments, but without giving it special prominence, or any connection to endings of the classical kind.

As far as pitch relationships are concerned, *there is only one diatonic scale*. The reason Gregorian chant sounds so familiar to us is that it uses this scale even more consistently than do the classical and popular repertories. The specific relevance of this fact to Gregorian chant is that even though the configuration of pitches – the melody – of a piece of chant is of an unfamiliar kind, the pitch relationships it uses are all extremely familiar, being the same ones used throughout classical and popular music.

Pitch relationships are what we hear in music. Like tone, they are intuitive; they involve immediate perception. Trying to describe a relationship between two pitches is like trying to describe a relationship between two colours. And, rather than focusing on the relationships, we tend to notice what seem like qualities of individual pitches. Some pitches, for example, may seem in repose, while others push on; some higher pitches may trumpet forth, while others, still higher, may only float, or even spin off from the melodic curve. Some of the lower pitches may settle down solidly at the bottom of the range, but others, just as low, may seem curiously incomplete or transitory. These and similar effects are not qualities of individual pitches, but rather of the relationships among several pitches.

These kinds of responses to pitch relationships, along with many others that we experience, can generate complex, sophisticated kinds of meaning, or fanciful, far-flung associations. In any case they are the basic stuff of music; hearing them more precisely is the goal of learning about music. But they are very easy to hear; if you have difficulty with what I write about them, the difficulty lies with the terms that I use, or with matching the terms to the experience that you have.

*A graphic analogy for movement in a tonal space*
The value of trying to hear reference pitches and tonal spaces can be appreciated through a visual analogy, as long as we recognize the limits of the analogy and do not try to push it too far. Imagine, in the graphic design of a page, a band of decoration used in the margin as a frame; the band might be narrow, bounded by straight lines and filled with complex figuration.

The possibilities are limited only by the skill and imagination of the graphic artist. Such bands are frequent in medieval art (some examples are unsurpassed in skill as well as imagination). We could focus the analogy by thinking of the antiphon *Dixit Dominus* in figure 2.2 as a header and footer on a page filled with the text of the psalm.

The effect of such a decorative band depends partly on the visual interaction between the fixed straight lines that define the space of the band and the apparently free flow of the figure that fills the space. By seeing how the figure fits into the graphic space, the eye can better appreciate the figure's free, even impulsive, movement. In just such a way, the ear can refer the melodic line of chant to the upper and lower boundaries of a *tonal* space. Here, too, the line can fill the space with intricate back-and-forth movement, circling, overlapping and interlacing, expressing endless exuberant energy, the more potent because of the restriction of the narrow frame: the melodic movement rebounds from the inner edge, reflecting back into the space.

The limits of the analogy are that in music the 'line' is not a line, and there is no graphic space. There is, instead, only a succession of differing pitches, presented to the ear for it to understand as best it can. Metaphors of space and line are only one way of grasping the music's organization.

More important, pitches come only one at a time in chant; hence, the reference pitch is only implied, not expressed in a pitch sounding continuously. The single melodic line has to express both the straight line and the freely curving decoration; hence, the straight line can be indicated only by occasional pitches in the curve. This is why identifying the reference pitch is partly a matter of a listener's judgement.

In polyphony, especially medieval polyphony from the time of the chant, reference pitches were often made explicit in the form of a drone, a pitch sounding continuously at the same time as the moving line. This phenomenon encourages us to believe that the concept of a reference pitch is appropriate to medieval music. It need not suggest that a drone should actually be added to a chant, as some modern performers do. For the Gregorian repertory, at least, such addition is inappropriate, although it might work for certain kinds of later medieval chant.

The important point of the analogy is the *relationship between* frame and decoration, no matter how these are implemented in graphics or in music. The straight edge of a band helps the eye appreciate the curves that fill the band; similarly, the reference pitch, sounding the *same* in the ear, helps it appreciate pitches that are *different*. Again, the distance between the two straight edges of a band helps the eye judge the movement of the curve by giving it a measure of difference; similarly, the distance between the boundaries of the tonal space (it is often the distance called a perfect fourth or perfect fifth) gives the ear a measure of the difference between the pitches used in the melody, making the melodic movement more meaningful.

In medieval graphic art – and modern, too – the distances used in a design are often integrated by being exact fractions or multiples of each other: this is called *modular design*. Musical design, too, is often modular, in one dimension or another, but the idea is more applicable to the kinds of chant that come historically *after* Gregorian chant. (Called *medieval chant*, these kinds will be sketched in chapter 4, and the examples on the compact disc will be discussed in the Commentary.) The only modular element in Gregorian chant is the diatonic scale itself, and this is why it is so important to our perception of chant.

## Harmony and Counterpoint

In almost all the music we hear in the modern age – the classical and popular repertories, and numerous others – we hear many pitches sounding at once. Compared with Gregorian chant, this much thicker kind of sound seems to overpower musical sensitivity with an abundance of stimulation. Classical and popular music arrive at the listening ear with an impact much greater than that of Gregorian chant: they saturate the sense of hearing with more pitch relationships than it can easily absorb.

Even just two pitches sounding at once can produce a sound that is distinctly different from either pitch sounding separately. This effect is especially noticeable when the two pitches are closely matched in timbre, for then it may not be possible to hear them separately in the combination. A good exercise is provided by automobile horns, which usually include two very closely matched sounds (often forming the kind of pitch interval called a *second* or the one called a *third*). Most people hear a single sound, the simultaneity, and it takes effort to distinguish the components. Furthermore, the individual character of the sound of a horn is due to the choice of interval as much as of timbre; the character can vary widely, for instance from the impatient, aggressive tone of a small but lively sports car to the would-be-majestic blare of a large luxury sedan.

A graphic analogy may be helpful here, too. If a single pitch is like a point, a simultaneity is like a patch, made up of points that we cannot always distinguish. If the points in a patch are homogeneous, not clearly distinguished from one another, then there is nothing to focus on save the patch as a whole.

Diatonic simultaneities of *two* pitches each have their own sound and character. With a little practice listeners can learn to identify each kind, but even without such conscious identification the sounds make their effect and contribute to the character of the music. Two-pitch simultaneities can be arranged on a continuum extending from those called *consonant*, meaning that the two pitches blend easily together, to *dissonant*, or blending less easily. These differences, too, can be learned, although they are sometimes difficult to distinguish.

Diatonic simultaneities consisting of *three or more* pitches are much more difficult to identify, and the number of possible combinations of pitches is much greater than those of only two pitches. Most classical and popular music uses simultaneities of three or more pitches most of the time, and so the unavoidable result is that the listening ear does not consciously attend to most of the pitches that it hears. These thicker sonorities are responsible for some of the most beautiful and expressive effects in music, and composers and performers devote much attention to manipulating them in order to produce these effects.

Many of the important techniques developed by European musicians over the centuries have the purpose of giving the listening ear a thread to follow through the maze of many-pitched sonorities. The most direct technique is called *melody with accompaniment*, in which a melody, usually for a singer, is accompanied by a background of simultaneities, usually played by instruments. As far as the perception of pitch relationships is concerned, the melody by itself presents no more problems than chant; the ear follows it with conscious attention, while being affected by the accompaniment only at a subconscious level.

More sophisticated solutions go under the generic name *counterpoint*, of which there are a great many varieties. In its pure archetypal state, counterpoint consists of two melodies constructed so as to fit together when sung or played at the same time. Pitches that sound at the same time in the two melodies will of course have the distinctive sound of simultaneities, and so the resultant sound will be that of polyphony, not chant. Still, the relationship between any two simultaneous pitches will be diatonic. Within either of the two melodies considered separately, any two *successive* pitches will also be diatonic, and in that respect the individual melody will sound no different from chant. In fact, a chant melody was often used as one of two or more contrapuntal lines. Usually, however, melodies in counterpoint are composed with their own distinctive kind of movement, depending on the style of the piece. In counterpoint, then, composers rely on melody to guide the listener through what may be a very dense musical texture.

In the development of polyphony from the Middle Ages on, European musicians worked out conventional simultaneities using three or four pitches that blend particularly well; these are called *harmonies*, or *chords*, and have been used for the last four centuries in a system called *harmony*. It is a very flexible system allowing a large number of ways of making music.

To guide listeners through the rich sonorities, European musicians developed many ways of using simple diatonic relationships. This was possible because the pitches making up a chord could blend so well that the chord might sound as if it were only one pitch. Sometimes when singers perform a whole song in harmonies (with no distractions of melody or counterpoint) it sounds as if they were singing in unison, just as in chant. By representing a complex chord by a single pitch, composers can use the pitch relationship between that pitch and one in the next chord to guide the ear from one complex harmony to the next. As a result, the simple diatonic relationships – the same as used in Gregorian chant – continued to function in all forms of European polyphony; they sound constantly in classical and popular music. These diatonic relationships are all around us, and we know them well.

Simultaneity in general has a powerful effect on the listening ear; and European harmonic practice has developed a very persuasive kind of musical expression. Harmony came to seem so essential to music that, in the early stages of the revival of chant around 1900, the chant was regularly accompanied by chords played on the organ – on the assumption that without harmony the chant would not be recognizable as music.

It was easy to make the mistake of thinking that no type of expression through tone was possible in Gregorian chant; and, indeed, modern technical descriptions sometimes gave the impression that the lack of harmony deprived chant of any potential for specifically musical sonority or expression. This misunderstanding was the basis for the attempt to categorize chant as something different from song – or even from music.

Our ears, however, assure us that Gregorian chant is not only beautiful melody but expressive music. We can distinguish clearly and easily between the expressive effects of European harmony and those of Gregorian chant (as well as of many other kinds of music), and we can respond to each in an appropriate way. The reason that the expressive effects of Gregorian chant are accessible to us is that, moving in the same tonal space as classical and popular music, chant makes constant use of the same diatonic pitch relationships. In Gregorian chant these pitch relationships lack the impact of simultaneity, but still participate in the overall effect of the tonal system.

# 3
# *Melodic Movement, Rhythm and Words*

The most distinctive feature of Gregorian chant is the way the melody moves through its tonal space. This space itself, as explained in chapter 2, is familiar to modern listeners, since it is defined by the same diatonic scale that has been used throughout the history of European music. It is the melodic movement, the twists and turns from one pitch to the next, that give Gregorian chant its distinctive character. If Gregorian chant sounds strange, it is because its surface detail is different from the detail of classical and popular music. Acquaintance with the way in which Gregorian chant moves will bring the melodies much closer. The paradox suggested in this book is that further acquaintance with the surface detail can reveal a deeper layer of mystery different from the indistinctness experienced from the back of the cathedral.

Melodic movement is usually regarded as only one of the elements of music. In traditional music appreciation we break music down into its elements in order to discuss it. In thinking about classical and popular music we can easily identify several separate elements, and can think about them one at a time. The most familiar elements, which are also the most important ones, are listed here.

*Melody*. In classical and popular music this is often understood in the simple sense of 'tune', and we can think about it as an easily understandable element usually sung by a solo voice or played by a solo instrument.

*Rhythm*. Much of our thinking about rhythm is in terms of *metre*, or the measuring of musical time. We can study the kinds and use of metre, and the way it is marked with a beat. In popular music there is often a rhythm section consisting of designated instruments.

*Harmony*. In classical and popular music, it tends to come in standard packages called chords that we can learn to think about separately from rhythm or timbre. Often the harmony is performed as accompaniment (see *texture*) by designated instruments.

*Figure*. This less familiar analytic term is used to identify various kinds of abstract pattern that a voice or solo instrument may perform instead of a tune.

*Timbre*, or quality of sound. We easily distinguish vocal sound from instrumental, and just as easily we recognize the sounds of different instruments. Variety of instrumental timbre is especially important in classical music.

*Texture*. This is a broad category that includes all the possible relationships among the several participating performers, whether instrumental or vocal. Some of the broadest subcategories are *melody and accompaniment*, usually involving a simple differentiation between the tune and the simple chords or rhythms in the background; and *counterpoint*, which may involve two or more melodic lines performed by different voices or instruments.

In Gregorian chant, however, none of these elements can be studied separately, for in fact they are not separate elements. There is only one element: since Gregorian chant is sung in unison, it is all vocal, all with words; there is no accompaniment, no counterpoint, no metre or measure, no marked beat. Whatever separate aspects we choose to identify simply express various aspects of one musical reality.

Rhythm, then, is simply the flow of Gregorian chant. Melody is another name for the same flow; in other words, melody cannot properly be separated from rhythm. When we think about Gregorian rhythm, we have to consider how the words fit into the movement of the pitches through the tonal space used in a particular piece of chant. And, from a musical point of view, even the words are simply the particular sonic shapes taken by the pitches in their rhythmic flow.

In this chapter we shall be concerned not so much with the referential meaning of the words, but rather with the ways in which the sound of the words contributes to the rhythm of the chant. Understanding the referential meaning of the words (and consequently their liturgical use) is difficult because the words of Gregorian chant are in Latin. None of us understands spoken Latin as a native tongue, and few can grasp the meaning completely when hearing Latin sung. As an additional obstacle, when we hear Gregorian chant sung by a choir in a properly reverberant ambient, we often cannot make out the words, so obscure is the echoey sound; indeed, that indistinctness is an important part of the mystical effect. If we are to make sense of the words, or want to see how they contribute to the music, we must study them in print, with translations. These are provided for each piece discussed in the Commentary on the compact disc.

## Rhythm and beat

When listeners feel that Gregorian chant lacks rhythm, or that they cannot hear or understand the rhythm, that is usually because they are listening for a *kind* of rhythm that is not there in chant. In much of the music we hear in the modern world we respond with a sense of its *beat*: we feel the beat, and this response is the most familiar kind of rhythm we know. Our response can be strong because we actually produce the beat inside our bodies; it goes on inside us, while the music continues to match it, confirm it, provide feedback that greatly heightens the experience. It is a form of resonance, similar to the resonance of pitches but in a temporal dimension.

The beat can be actually observed in the bodily responses of the listeners. Performers have to feel it before they start playing, and it is the conductor's chief function to cue them to the right beat. The listener, however, is cued only by the first sounds heard; and after that, the music will continue to support the inner beat as long as it conforms to the system of equal measurement called musical *metre*. Each piece of classical or popular music is usually in a specific metre, a background grid of equal durations to which the sounds of the piece are referred. The succession of equal units supports the ongoing inner beat.

The sense of beat is absent from the experience of Gregorian chant, because this kind of chant does not support a beat. Listening for a beat, attempting to match the inner beat to the sounds of Gregorian chant, is frustrated by the lack of metric regularity in the music.

Early Christian music, from its beginnings to the time of Gregorian chant, actually avoided music that would encourage a beat. As will be sketched in chapter 4, this was not because early Christians were ignorant of this kind of rhythm; on the contrary, they knew it all too well from ancient Greek and Roman music, but felt it was inappropriate – too carnal – for Christian worship. Later, after the time of Gregorian chant (from about 1100), European musicians developed a very strong system of musical measurement. It was this system that eventually provided the metre of classical and popular music, and has conditioned the modern listener to feel that rhythm in general is regular.

We are not, however, as dependent on beat as traditional music educators would lead us to believe. In much classical and popular music we hear other kinds of rhythm that do not support a beat, but instead move us in other ways. In much slow classical music, regularity is hard to hear; listeners do not respond with a beat, and often cannot detect a metre. Still, they feel the flow. Often a solo melody shows little rhythmic regularity, while regularity is being provided in some other part of the music. Especially in jazz, where the regularity is often entrusted to the drummer, the singer or other soloist is free to perform the most irregular fantasy imaginable. There are times in classical music, for instance in concerto cadenzas, where rhythm free from metre can be appreciated.

These other kinds of rhythm are difficult to teach (which is why we do not hear about them in formal instruction): there is no way of categorizing all the ways rhythm can differ from a regular beat, and there are no general

descriptions. Fortunately, modern listeners respond easily to various kinds
of free, non-metrical rhythm, without having to learn anything. It is even
questionable whether rhythm in this or any sense can be taught. There is
an archetypal anecdote of popular music in which a listener, unacquainted
with jazz, asks the performer, 'What is rhythm, *really?*' The response is
attributed to various famous performers, for instance Louis (Satchmo)
Armstrong – 'Lady, if you gotta ask, you'll never know'.

Thus the rhythm of Gregorian chant is first of all inseparable from
melody; second, being rhythm it is in itself ineluctable; third, it is free
rhythm, not to be caught in a net of systematic principles. It is no wonder
that a discussion of Gregorian rhythm from the tenth century to the twentieth can do no more than attempt to articulate how individual singers feel
the rhythm ought to be performed, or how individual observers feel the
rhythm does sound or ought to sound. All I can do here is try to describe
what seems to me to happen in chant performance in general, and to
identify the kinds of musical factors that performers can and do control in
performance. The principal factors, I believe, are *grouping* of pitches
together into small groups of several pitches each, and *lengthening* of some
of the pitches in a given piece.

## Default pulse

The unit of chant is the individual pitch, sung in a neutral duration, neither
lengthened nor shortened, but rather used as a default value. To put it
another way, many of the pitches of a piece are sung more or less the same
length; these neutral durations are not made equal by measurement, but
simply by default of any deliberate lengthening or shortening. If a singer
does nothing in particular about the length, the result is a more or less equal
succession of durations. A group of singers, say, a congregation, sings in this
way unless told to do otherwise. And this seems to have been the way most
singers have approached chant over the centuries.

By itself, such roughly regular succession provides a sense of flow but not
of momentum. It is often called a *pulse*; as a pulse it is weak and relatively
rapid, and can vary at any moment. It provides nothing to which the listener
can respond with a beat.

Gregorian chant, however, can have great momentum – as I became
acutely aware while editing my tapes for the compact disc. Most of my
experience with Gregorian chant over forty years was with singing it and
directing others to sing it; I had an inner sense of the rhythm, and hoped it
sounded good, but for better or worse I did not pay much attention to the
theoretical nature of the rhythm. In the process of cutting and splicing tape
I could not avoid listening through the interruptions temporarily intro-

duced in mid-phrase; I found myself jolted by the abrupt halt in the melodic continuity, and realized how much momentum had been accumulated in the chant up to that point.

The undifferentiated pulse acquires momentum as a result of the infinitely subtle modifications made by singers in performance. Grouping and lengthening are the kinds of modification that most affect the listener and are most easily perceived by the listener. Grouping and lengthening were used in tenth-century performance and are also used in modern performance.

## Grouping and articulation

In grouping pitches together, the singer may let a less important pitch, for instance, lead into or flow out of a more important one, so that several pitches form a coherent whole – just as, in melodious speech, several syllables are grouped around an accented syllable to form a word, and several words are grouped around a prominent word to form a well-sounding phrase.

Grouping is accomplished largely by *articulating*, or making a very slight break in the sound, so as to separate one group of pitches from the next; the break is a 'joint' in the important sense that the break both separates the second group from the first and at the same time joins the two together. *Articulation* is used as a technical term to refer to a wide variety of ways of making this kind of joint in musical performance.

Grouping in general, and articulation in particular, are the most important ways a performer has of communicating rhythm to a listener. This is true even though – by paradox – what is ultimately communicated may be a sense of absolutely continuous flow; this is an illusion as convincing as the sense of a continuous melody produced by a series of separate distinct pitches.

Long before European musicians developed a notation for metre, they had a notation that showed various kinds of grouping of the pitches used in Gregorian chant. The existence of such notation demonstrates Gregorian singers' reliance upon grouping as a means of communicating rhythm. It also gives us a very specific idea of how individual pieces of chant could have been performed rhythmically by the original singers, as will be explored in chapter 8.

### Articulation by syllables

The most basic way in which the pitches of Gregorian chant are grouped is by the Latin syllables to which they are sung. The mere sound of the Latin syllables shapes the pitches of the chant into rhythmic groups. Even though most listeners know no Latin, the sound of Latin syllables is familiar in European languages, including English, many of whose syllables are derived from Latin. Hence the sound of the syllables can communicate grouping to us just as well as to the original listeners.

A syllable is a unit of sound that includes a vowel. The vowel may be pre-ceded by a consonant (for instance, *ta-* or *ti-*). The vowel may be followed by another consonant (*cat-*), in which case the syllable is said to be *closed*. The closing consonant can also be complex, varying from a simple stop (as in *cat-*) to something more like a vowel (*cum, nil, cur-*).

Syllabic articulation is very sensitive to the quality of the sound that closes a syllable, dividing it from the next. When a closed syllable is fol-lowed by one that begins with a consonant (*et/filius*) the articulation can be made and heard very clearly, for the sound can stop on *-t* and start again on *fi-*. If on the other hand the preceding syllable ends in a 'semi-consonant' such as *-r, -l, -m*, then the sound will flow uninterrupted into the next syl-lable, as in *fil-/i-, con-/si, im-/pe-, puer/na-*. Such consonants are some-times called *liquid*, and great attention was paid to them by medieval singers of Gregorian chant (as well as by modern students of chant notation); special notes called *liquescent* may be used to mark the pitches concerned (as will be shown in chapter 8). Articulation by these consonants, when care-fully performed, has a great effect upon the rhythm of the chant.

This syllabic articulation of the pitches into groups is effective even if neither the listeners nor the singers understand Latin, and even if the singing is not very clear. In a reverberant ambient we may hear clearly only the consonants, as they begin or close a syllable; or, on the other hand, we may hear only the vowels as they change syllable by syllable. In either case, however, we hear some syllabic articulation.

Some chant uses only one pitch per syllable, with perhaps a few syllables carrying two pitches each. This happens mostly in recitation formulas, such as those used as psalm tones for singing psalms. In most Gregorian *melodies*, on the other hand, many syllables carry two, three, four or more pitches. This slows down the normal pace of syllables, and they no longer have whatever rhythm the words would have when spoken (as mentioned in chapter 1). The syllables still articulate the pitches into groups, but the rhythm of the groups becomes musical rather than verbal.

*Gregorian melodic style*

There is something very distinctive about the way pitches change in a Gregorian melody: the pitches change persistently, and their patterns change persistently. Regular patterns seem to be avoided. For instance, con-sidering motion from one pitch to the next, rarely do pitches ascend for

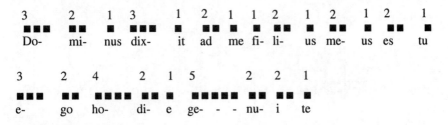

Figure 3.1 Number of pitches per syllable in *Dominus dixit*.

more that three or four in succession without some descent mixed in; usually a change of direction occurs with almost every pitch. Repetition of a pattern or figure involving *several* pitches is infrequent enough to call for special comment.

Avoidance of obvious, unvaried repetition, then, is the most basic, most characteristic feature of Gregorian melody. This feature is immediately audible in every piece; though it is heard also in other kinds of chant, its constant use in Gregorian gives that kind of chant its unique character. Furthermore, it generates the sense of mystery heard in Gregorian chant. How this avoidance of pattern operates on our musical understanding is not easily explained – in fact, it is probably not explicable at all. Hence there seems no danger of doing away with the sense of mystery by paying closer attention; and we can greatly increase our appreciation thereby.

One aspect of the avoidance of repetition is the change in the *number* of pitches per syllable. The number of pitches sung over successive syllables changes syllable by syllable, with no perceptible regularity. Figure 3.1 shows this typical irregularity in *Dominus dixit* (the chant was used in figure 2.2 of chapter 2).

In this antiphon some syllables have only one pitch, some have two or three pitches; one has four, one has five. Each syllable usually has a different number of pitches from the preceding syllable. Hence speaking the words with the default pulse would make some syllables much longer than others, and would distort the usual spoken flow of the language (as mentioned in chapter 1). Nor would this series of groups, 3–2–1–3–1–2 and the rest, mesh with any regular beat or metre in the antiphon as a whole. Gregorian rhythm is formed by whatever groups come along.

The syllabic groups with varying numbers of pitches are filled by motion in changing directions up and down. Figure 3.2 shows *Dominus dixit* again in the kind of pitch notation used in figure 2.2. (This is MIDI notation: it represents each pitch with a horizontal bar, placed higher or lower corresponding to the distance in whole steps or half steps of the diatonic scale.) In figure 3.2 each pitch has been made the same in duration, assuming a default pulse. The pitches that go with each syllable have been set off by

(phrase 1)

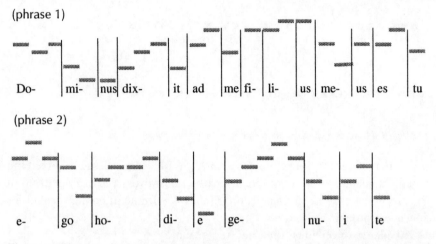

(phrase 2)

Figure 3.2 Pitches and syllables in *Dominus dixit*.

short vertical lines. The number of pitches corresponds to the numbers shown in figure 3.1.

What figure 3.2 shows is that not only the number of pitches but also the direction of motion is different over each successive syllable. For comparison, imagine instead that over each syllable the pitches – two, or three, or four, or five – descended stepwise in a short scale segment; the result would be unvaried, in spite of the fact that each syllable had a different number of pitches. In contrast, *Dominus dixit*, like every Gregorian melody, has *a different motion up or down over successive syllables*. Even when successive syllables have the same number of pitches, these pitches almost always move in different patterns, through varying distances.

Thus over *Do-* there is down-and-up motion in the first three pitches, then motion downwards for two pitches on *mi*, upwards for three on *dix-*, down again for one on *-it*, up two on *ad*, down for one on *me*. As with the number of pitches sung on each syllable, there is no regular pattern of ascent or descent. Of course, since there are only three ways for the melody to proceed (up, down, or repeating the same pitch), ascents and descents usually come in alternation. In other styles of melody it is not uncommon for such alternation to appear in a regular pattern, but in Gregorian chant the varying *number* of pitches prevents the alternating *direction* from seeming regular. If we were to take into account the varying *distances* between successive pitches (in figure 3.2 these include the diatonic intervals of whole step, half step, major and minor third), we would see how persistent is the variation of melodic detail throughout this and every piece in the Gregorian repertory.

The particular way in which this variety is carried out seems to me to be the most important fact of Gregorian style. I do not think this style can be explained, but I think it can be directly and universally appreciated. Its sense is purely musical, not verbal, or graphic, or numerical. I believe it is the source of the ultimate mystery of Gregorian chant. And it certainly makes even short melodies such as *Dominus dixit* uniquely melodious.

### Intrasyllabic melodic extension

In the Proper chants of the Mass, many syllables have more than three pitches, sometimes many more. Called *intrasyllabic melodic extension*, this is found throughout the Gregorian repertory. In any piece, however, some syllables may have only one pitch, some only two or three. Many pieces, therefore, will show a broad spread in the possible number of pitches. And, as already seen in figure 3.2, the number will vary unpredictably from syllable to syllable.

Figure 3.3 shows the beginning of the Gradual *Viderunt* (track 3 on the compact disc). The first two syllables each have a single pitch; the third syllable has two pitches, leaping up to the reference pitch (and, incidentally, sounding the pitches of a harmonic triad). The fourth syllable, *om-(nes)*, has ten pitches, winding around the reference pitch until the end of the word, on *-nes*. The next four syllables continue touching on the reference pitch along with the two pitches below, filling out a narrow band of pitches that can be regarded as the central tonal space of the piece as it continues. The syllable *ter-* has five pitches, the syllable *-rae* eight pitches.

In the longer groups of figure 3.3, those with five, eight and ten pitches per syllable, articulation *by syllables* is ineffective as a basis of rhythm. With no change of syllable, the melisma has no articulation; and without a group-

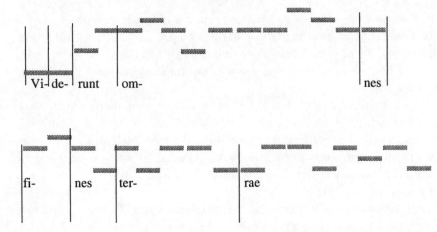

Figure 3.3 Intrasyllabic melodic extension in *Viderunt omnes* (beginning only).

ing, the default pulse runs on seemingly without shape or purpose. Rhythmic flow depends, paradoxically, on rhythmic articulation.

Hence, when the syllables are extended as in figure 3.3, the rhythm depends on other kinds of articulation. In the performance of Gregorian chant, as in all music, this is provided by the performer. The success of the performance will depend on how well, how artistically, the performer groups the pitches of the melody. How does the performer know how to do this? We could ask the performer, if he or she were still living; but the performer might be unable, or unwilling, to say. Or a performer might say that the grouping came from the composer, and we might be able to confirm that by reading whatever the composer had written down. This is a meagre trail of evidence, but in the case of Gregorian chant it is the only trail that leads back to AD 900, to the melodic notation of the earliest chant books; we shall see in chapter 8 what is involved in trying to follow it.

The principle of the early notation can be given simply here. In this type of notation, the groups of two or three pitches over single syllables are represented by special signs, a particular sign being used for a particular pattern of two or three pitches (examples can be seen in figure 8.1b). When there are more than three pitches for a syllable, the same kinds of signs (each sign indicating only two or three pitches) are used one after another even though there is no syllable change. If the singer chooses, the pitches can be grouped according to the signs just as if there were a change of syllable. In any case, the grouping indicated by the notation can give us a clue to what the grouping might have been in a performance in the tenth century.

The notations in the two earliest chant books group the ten pitches in figure 3.3 over *om-(nes)* in smaller groups of 1+3, 3, 3; on the syllable *ter-*, 3, 2; on the syllable *-rae*, 4, 4 or alternatively 2, 2, 3+1, depending on how we interpret the notation (see plates 1 and 2 and the discussion in chapter 8). Those smaller groupings are all of the kind we encounter over single syllables, and a singer can treat them accordingly. The rhythmic feeling used for the beginning of the chant can be continued right through the intrasyllabic extensions.

This wordless articulation has close analogues in modern instrumental practice, where pitches are grouped together – or separated, *as if* with syllables – by a variety of subtle techniques. We hear such articulation constantly in instrumental music; we do not notice it (at least, when it is done skilfully), but nonetheless it is the factor that more than any other gives us the sense of the rhythm.

Intrasyllabic melodic extension is applied within the Gregorian repertory in various ways to the several types of Proper chants at Mass – Introit, Gradual, Alleluia, Tract, Offertory and Communion chants (all to be described in more detail soon). It appears most in Gradual and Alleluia, less in Tract and Offertory, least in Introit and Communion. These types of chant are on a continuum in this respect, however, and the differences are not categorical.

Other, even more subtle differences of style may distinguish the types of Proper chants from each other, but these differences can be perceived only with difficulty. I would say the differences were perceptible but not identifiable; for while I can usually distinguish an Introit from a Gradual, I cannot always say exactly how I know – other than simple acquaintance with their characteristic idioms.

Furthermore, the style is not so consistent as to prevent us from perceiving the individuality of a piece. Many pieces have their own individuality; thus, a piece may be easily recognizable not just as Gregorian chant, not just as Introit, say, but as *Puer natus*, the Introit for Christmas. Recognition presupposes familiarity, of course, and the best access to Gregorian chant is through becoming very familiar with single pieces.

## Melisma

*Melisma*, mentioned in chapter 1, is a term applied by modern scholars to particular long extensions that seem to be self-contained. Scholars have never specified just how long an extension had to be before it was a melisma, or what its special qualities were. In terms of intrasyllabic melodic extension we should not think of a melisma as a distinct category of melodic event, but rather simply as a very long extension. It is useful to speak of chants such as the Gradual as being *melismatic*, in the sense of tending towards frequent and lengthy extensions; but this qualification can only be one of general impression, not categorical classification.

In addition to being expressive and sometimes brilliant melodies, melismas present the only occasion in the Gregorian repertory for exact, obvious repetition of a melodic figure or short group of pitches. Such repetition is in striking contrast to the persistent variety in the repertory as a whole. A moderate example is found in the melisma from the verse of the Gradual *Viderunt*, track 3 on the compact disc. As shown in figure 3.4, the group that is repeated is twelve pitches long; the repetition is separated from its first presentation by three other pitches that are not repeated. As in this example, there is almost always only one exact repetition; a second repetition is sometimes hinted at, but with radical change; or there may be a vague reference to the repeated figure, as in *Viderunt*; or simply a continuation in the usual, continually changing melody.

The repetition of the figure suggests if not requires that the repetition be

(from the verse of the Gradual *Viderunt omnes*)

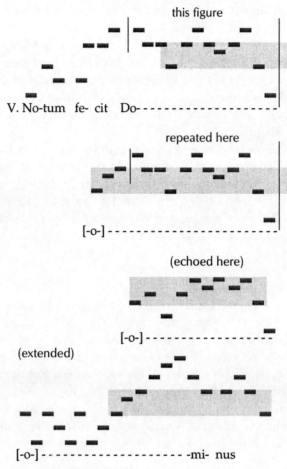

Figure 3.4 Repetition of a figure in a melisma.

set off by an articulation, and is one of the clearest indications that in melismas small groups of pitches are to be articulated just as in the rest of the chant, even though, in a melisma, there is no succession of syllables to guide the grouping.

## Lengthening of individual pitches

Besides articulation, another common technique of communicating rhythm in performance is by making some pitches longer than others; this, of course, can be easily heard – although if the performance is skilful, it communicates a general sense of rhythmic flow rather than simply calling attention to a longer pitch. In a truly rhythmic performance we scarcely notice longer or shorter pitches.

Lengthening of an individual pitch is only the most obvious alteration of the default pulse. Chant singers have always used other alterations too, such as shortening pitches or speeding up. Lengthening has been applied to groups as well as to individual pitches, and with various effects ranging from slight broadening to a full stop of the forward motion.

Such lengthenings may have been specified by the composer, or some of them may have been contributed only by the early singers. They could become part of the tradition either way. Still other lengthenings may be performed at the option of any subsequent singer. The specific effect such lengthenings have on our perception of rhythm is much discussed by music theorists and chant historians, without much agreement; still, lengthening does happen, and does communicate rhythm. Furthermore, lengthenings are clearly indicated in some of the earliest notation, although not as frequently as groupings. They were a feature of the performance of chant in the tenth century, but may have disappeared from chant later in the Middle Ages. Lengthening is used in various modern performances of chant.

Performers lengthen pitches in order to make the grouping explicit or to emphasize it; sometimes they want to emphasize a particular pitch, or some other subtle aspect of the melody. Sometimes they want to emphasize a particular word – or just want to express themselves.

In Gregorian chant, then, rhythm is produced by the singers' treatment of the default pulse. The treatment is based on grouping, beginning with syllabic articulation, and goes on to include an increasingly personal selection of subtle alterations of the default pulse. This produces a free rhythm whose only sure link with the listener is whatever degree of regularity can still be heard in the pulse; but to this is added whatever mysterious truth of human rhythm has found its way into the chant through the performer. You may or may not respond to this kind of rhythm; the performers you hear may or may not project it. It is there to be heard only if both you and the performer want it to be there. And it is there in infinite variety.

What I hear is a kind of rhythmic motion that can sweep me along without giving me the opportunity to respond with a beat. To use subjective description which may or may not match another listener's experience, I can describe the momentum as spiral rather than linear or straight on; its energy seems potential rather than actual. It is capable of a wide range of mood, yet is so specifically musical as not to allow a visual representation or an equivalent bodily gesture – even though it is capable of very eloquent expression of corporeal feeling. The same procedures can be found in many other kinds of chant, and in many other kinds of music; but Gregorian rhythm can assume specific forms not heard elsewhere.

*Idioms and formulas*

There are many conventions of melodic movement in Gregorian chant. Scholars call them *formulas*, a term that suggests some kind of system; but in reality there seems to be no system. The conventions are better called *idioms*, and thought of in the same terms as idioms of language; for, like verbal idioms, the melodic ones are used freely and in a creative way. A psalm tone, on the other hand, can well be called a formula, for it is a series of pitches that is applied automatically to each verse of the psalm.

Both formulas and idioms are fascinating to study. For the listener, however, idioms do not seem to be such an important part of the experience of hearing any one piece of chant. As we listen to a piece, there is nothing to differentiate an idiom from a non-idiom. We can recognize a fragment of melody as an idiom only if we have heard it – and remember it – from some other piece. We learn idioms by getting to know a number of pieces; in that process, we learn first and best the fragments of melody that turn up most frequently.

For listeners, this is the most realistic way to proceed: as you get to know one piece after another, you will automatically get acquainted with idioms and how they work in individual pieces. We could, of course, try to learn the Gregorian repertory systematically by beginning with the idioms and learning them all, abstractly; then, as we approached any piece, we could recognize its idioms. But this does not seem practical for listeners. And our ultimate aim is to understand *all* of a piece, not just the parts that are idiomatic.

*Mode and model melody*

*Mode*, like *tone*, is used in a confusing number of different musical meanings, related in confusing ways to the numerous non-musical applications of the term. For Gregorian chant we need to distinguish three meanings.

(1) In its simple, technical application, mode is a way of classifying Gregorian chants in eight classes *according to the ending pitch*. This classification is for the specific purpose of choosing a psalm tone compatible with an antiphon. For an antiphon classed by its ending pitch as mode 1, for instance, the singer chooses psalm tone 1; this psalm tone is selected from a set of eight psalm tones, a set that is constructed parallel to the set of eight modes.

(2) Scholars use *mode* to refer to one of eight *octave segments* associated with the ending pitches used for the eight modal classes. (See the endnotes to this chapter.) The system of octave segments, usually presented as modal scales, is a theoretical construct; its application to Gregorian chant has been overemphasized, and we need not be concerned with it here.

(3) *Mode* can refer to a group of Gregorian melodies that share enough idioms to bear a family resemblance to each other. Scholars can map out such families by comparative study of the whole repertory. Not all Gregorian chants belong to one or another family. The melodies of one family are ordinarily in the same modal class; within a given modal class, however, there may be several families.

The use of idioms in different families varies widely. In a few families all the pieces use all the same idioms, in the same order. In other words, these pieces use essentially the same melody, with slight differences to accommodate the different words in each piece. From a study of such a family we can abstract a *model melody*, also called a *typical melody* or a *melody type*. There are some relatively long, elaborate model melodies that are used for as many as ten or twenty different sets of words. One short, simple antiphon melody from the Divine Office is used for over a hundred different sets of words.

### Idioms and musical meaning

Idioms appear perhaps most frequently at endings of phrases and of pieces. In music generally, a melodic ending is often called a *cadence*, hence an ending idiom is a *cadential idiom*. Cadential idioms in Gregorian chant function much like cadential idioms in classical and popular music. They are perhaps the most useful kind of idioms to recognize, since they can mark clearly the ends of melodic phrases.

The longer melodic phrases in Gregorian chant are closely coordinated with the verbal clauses of the Latin prose: rarely does a clause come to a stop without a corresponding stop in the melody. We can hear the end of the clause by the way the singers pause (often they pause much too long); but we can also hear the close prepared by the way the melody moves. The use of a cadential idiom offers confirmation of the melodic close.

### Style, plans and procedures

The Gregorian style of melody is used to sing each of the Gregorian Propers of the Mass – the six different types called *Introit*, *Gradual*, *Alleluia*, *Tract*, *Offertory* and *Communion*. Each of these six has a different function in the worship service; their development in early Christian worship will be described in chapter 5, and their function in the Mass will be shown in chapter 6. Here we shall see the format in which each type appears.

The style of Gregorian melody used for these different types varies slightly; the most obvious difference is in the degree of intrasyllabic melodic extension. Less obvious, but ultimately more important, are the differences in format. The format is partly a result of the way the words for a specific chant have been selected and arranged for singing, partly a result of the manner in which the chant is performed on a given occasion. Performance of these six types involves several options. The principal options are the use of soloist and chorus, and the repetition of sections of the chant – singing a section twice in succession, for example, or repeating an earlier section later in the piece after some other section.

## Sentences

The basic verbal unit used in these six types is a *sentence* of Latin. Each sentence usually includes at least two grammatical clauses, and often several, making the sentence compound or complex. (A clause is a grammatical unit containing a subject and verb.) Most frequent is a pair of clauses, sometimes parallel in meaning as well as construction. Each of the six types of Mass Propers consists of a sentence and at least one other element. In the case of Offertory and Communion chant, the other element eventually dropped off, leaving only the sentence; the missing elements have recently been restored, or at least made available so that we can see what the original plan actually was.

### Gradual

A Gradual, for instance, consists of two sentences; in the Gradual *Viderunt* each sentence has two clauses (track 3 on the compact disc). In a Gradual, the first sentence is called the *respond*, the second the *verse*. Each of these terms calls for historical and liturgical explanation, to be supplied in chapter 5. For the moment we need see only what the terms mean for the manner of performance, and the use of repetition.

*respond*

| | |
|---|---|
| Viderunt omnes fines terrae | All the ends of the world |
| salutare Dei nostri: | have seen the salvation of our God: |
| iubilate Deo omnis terra. | be joyful unto God, all ye lands! |

*verse*

| | |
|---|---|
| Notum fecit Dominus | The Lord hath declared |
| salutare suum: | his salvation: |
| ante conspectum gentium | in the sight of the peoples |
| revelavit iustitiam suam. | he hath revealed his justice. |

The respond is sung by the chorus, the verse by the soloist. The respond can be repeated after the verse, and that would be one way in which the first sentence could be considered a response – in this case, a response to the verse. In practice, however, this repeat is often not made; instead, the chorus sometimes just joins in at the end of the verse (for instance, at *iustitiam suam*), thus finishing off the piece with a full choral sound while avoiding the lengthy repetition.

The term verse is used in several distinct senses in Gregorian chant (see the Glossary); here it is used to designate an episode, a section of secondary importance, following and possibly followed in turn by a principal section (in popular song it would be called a *bridge*).

Both the respond and the verse – more especially the verse – of a Gradual may have long melismas; therefore, Graduals are classed as melismatic chant. Even though the melismas in the solo verse may be more spectacular, the choral respond is still the principal section, hence this type of chant is called in general a *responsory*, and is classed as *responsorial chant*.

Two general qualifications have to be made to avoid confusion. First, in actual performance, from some time in the Middle Ages the beginning of each piece of chant to be sung by the choir is intoned by a soloist simply in order to set the pitch; this intonation is not part of the planned alternation of solo and chorus. Second, the solo part has often been performed by two to four singers rather than just one.

*Alleluia in the synaxis*
In the Gregorian Mass Proper chant called *Alleluia*, the respond consists of the exclamation 'alleluia'; it is accompanied by a sentence that functions as a verse, just as in the Gradual. In the *Alleluia* sung on track 4 the verse sentence has three clauses.

*respond*

| Alleluia. | Alleluia. |
|---|---|

*verse*

| Dies sanctificatus illuxit nobis: | A holy day hath shone upon us: |
|---|---|
| Venite gentes, et adorate | come, ye peoples, and worship the |
| Dominum: | Lord: |
| quia hodie descendit lux magna | for today hath descended a great |
| super terram. | light upon the earth. |

As with the Gradual, the respond *alleluia* can be repeated after the verse, and could then be considered a response to the verse. In addition, if the alleluia is sung first by a soloist, then immediately repeated by the chorus, then the chorus's performance can be considered a response to the soloist. Whether repeated or not, the word alleluia is followed immediately by a special melisma called the *iubilus;* if the soloist sings the word alleluia, and the chorus follows with the melisma, then that, too, can be considered a response – a choral, melismatic one.

However it is performed, the Alleluia is classed as responsorial chant along with the Gradual. Also like the Gradual, the Alleluia is classed as melismatic chant, since it can have extensions in the verse lengthy enough to be called melismas; these are distinct from the iubilus. The pitches of the iubilus, however, can also be repeated exactly as the concluding melisma of the verse, making the whole plan of repetition intricate.

### Tract

The Tract usually consists of three, four or five sentences. It differs from Gradual or Alleluia in having no repeats and no alternation of solo and chorus, being sung throughout by a soloist. As used in the earliest chant books, however, the Tract shows clearly that both repetition and use of a chorus can be options for performance rather than invariant features of the form. Certain Tracts were sometimes sung with the first sentence repeated by the chorus at the end, after the solo verses; in that case the choral repetition was a respond, and the Tract was classed as a responsory. (There is no Tract on the compact disc.)

### Offertory

Since the Middle Ages, usually only one sentence is performed for the Offertory. The earliest chant books, however, often provide two or three additional sentences. These are sung as solo verses; they are each followed by a repeat of the *last half of the first sentence*, known as a *reprise*.

Hence, when sung by itself by the chorus without a verse, the Offertory is just a sentence; when sung with solo verses, the choral reprise becomes a respond, and the chant becomes responsorial. Melismas are found both in respond and verses.

### Introit antiphon

The manner of performance described for Gradual and Alleluia is called *responsorial*, because in it a chorus responds to a soloist. There is another manner of performance called *antiphonal*; it is the simple and familiar practice of dividing the choir into two halves, called semichoirs, which sing in alternation. The development of responsorial and antiphonal singing in Christian worship will be sketched in chapter 5. Antiphonal singing, or *antiphony*, is an option in Introit and Communion, but not in Gradual, Alleluia or Tract. The labels in the chant books are 'antiphony at the Introit' (or 'antiphony at the Communion'), and it is common to speak of the *Introit antiphon* and the *Communion antiphon*.

The Introit antiphon itself consists of one sentence, often in three clauses. More sentences follow, and there exist several options for performing both the antiphon and these other sentences. There is always at least one sentence in addition to the antiphon; it is usually the first verse of a psalm. If just that one verse is sung by a soloist, it resembles the verse of a Gradual (and thus embodies the confusion between the plans of Introit and Gradual, as well as between these two meanings of 'verse'). In original practice, more verses from the same psalm could be sung, which is why the chant books label this section of the Introit as the 'Psalm'. Whether one or several verses are sung, this quotation from a psalm is followed by another sentence, a special one, the *Gloria Patri*. The following example is on track 2 of the compact disc.

*antiphon*

| | |
|---|---|
| Puer natus est nobis, | Unto us a child is born, |
| et filius datus est nobis: | unto us a Son is given: |
| cuius imperium super humerum | and the government shall be upon |
| eius: | his shoulder: |
| et vocabitur nomen eius, | and his name shall be called, |
| magni consilii Angelus. | Angel of mighty counsel. |

*psalm verse*

| | |
|---|---|
| Cantate Domino canticum novum: | O sing unto the Lord a new song: |
| quia mirabilia fecit. | for he hath done marvellous things. |

(*antiphon may be repeated here*)

| | |
|---|---|
| Gloria Patri, et Filio, et Spiritui Sancto. | Glory be to the Father and to the Son, and to the Holy Spirit: |
| Sicut erat in principio, | as it was in the beginning, is now |
| et nunc, et semper, | and ever shall be, |
| et in saecula saeculorum. Amen. | for ages of ages. Amen. |

(*antiphon is repeated here*)

In the tradition of performance that survived into the twentieth century, only a minimum of options were taken, and the plan was kept as simple as possible. The chorus sang the first sentence straight through (always with the solo intonation, as in all chants). The soloist intoned the verse of the psalm, which the chorus took up, continuing into the *Gloria Patri*, and afterwards repeated the first sentence.

In this modern practice, it was always very confusing why the first sentence should be called 'antiphon', since it was not in fact sung antiphonally. Sometimes it was thought that it was the psalm rather than the antiphon that should be sung antiphonally, since psalms were often sung antiphonally in the Divine Office; but with only one verse, antiphony does not make much sense, especially when half of that verse is intoned by the soloist. If several verses of the psalm were sung, then of course they could be sung antiphonally.

Originally the antiphon itself may have been sung antiphonally – which seems reasonable, given its name; in any case, such performance would make the use of terminology less confusing. The antiphon can easily be sung antiphonally, since the first sentence almost always consists of at least two distinct clauses, which can be sung alternately by the two semichoirs. With that option, the psalm verse, sung by the soloist, would be a verse in the same sense as in a Gradual. The Introit on the compact disc, *Puer natus*, is sung in this manner (except that the two semichoirs are represented by two solo voices, male and female).

Also in the original practice, the first sentence was repeated more often than just at the end; it followed the psalm verse, and if there was more than one psalm verse, it could follow each one. It followed the *Gloria Patri*; then sometimes yet another verse was sung solo after that, and finally one more repetition of the antiphon. The plan of the whole piece, then, was the result of applying options of solo/choral performance and of repetition, so the plan could vary from one occasion to the next.

### Communion antiphon

The Communion antiphon could be treated in the same way as the Introit, but traditional practice reduced it even further, leaving nothing but the one sentence, sung simply by the chorus. Nevertheless, the Communion is still classed with the Introit as *antiphonal chant*.

### Overall plan and detail

In itself, the plan of a Gradual, for instance, seems not very interesting or musically significant. It consists of one sentence, then another, *A B*; or, with the repeat of the first sentence, *A B A*. Since the style is melismatic, the sections are long and complex, and the repetition is not easy to hear. Thus it is difficult to perceive the significance of the plan and its relationship to the detail.

We try so hard, in listening to classical music, to teach and learn how the parts all fit together, how – in Beethoven especially – the energetic detail comes to a boil, spilling over to flood from one large section into the next. We can hear a persuasive integration of the smallest details with the huge outlines of Beethoven's symphonic movements. In Gregorian chant, by contrast, while the detail fills out the plan completely, it is not integrated with the plan.

A visual analogy would be a monumental arch from classical Rome: the large plan may have harmonious proportions, but is simple and presents only a flat surface, which is filled in with elaborate and impressive decorative designs – many designs, each occupying its own small space. The static effect of such a large flat surface was characteristic of Roman architecture, and Gregorian chant may be close to that architectural style historically as well as in spirit. Another analogy is provided by the facade of a Romanesque cathedral, covered with statuary (saints or gargoyles) that soak up the observer's attention much as does the Roman decoration.

We do not *hear* a cathedral facade, of course, nor do we *see* the plan of a piece of chant while we are listening to it. In the present case, however, the analogy with the cathedral can be pushed a little further. Starting early on (around AD 800), northern European artists and architects worked increasingly with *modular* designs; the end result was the Gothic cathedral, in which arches and other architectural elements are made to add up consistently so that exact multiples of the smallest unit produce the largest features of the surfaces, interior or exterior.

Historically, this development runs closely parallel to the development of musical style from *after* Gregorian chant through Frankish and medieval chant to medieval polyphony. The developments parallel each other most closely in the architecture and music of the cathedral of Notre Dame in Paris around 1200, but can be traced from the moment (around 850) when Gregorian chant was superseded by Frankish chant. Already in the examples of Frankish chant on the compact disc (discussed in the Commentary) we can hear an integration of detail and larger plan not apparent in Gregorian chant.

The way in which Beethoven can catapult us from detail into exhilarating flight has an artistic price, for it leaves us no time to become deeply involved in the detail. In Gregorian chant we do have time, and the detail can absorb as much of our time as we care to spend. This difference is the principal reason why Gregorian chant sounds different from Beethoven – this, rather than the sounds of the symphony orchestra, the powerful harmonies, or the driving repetitive rhythms. And if we compare Gregorian chant with the music of J. S. Bach or Palestrina, it may *not* sound so different, since in Bach or Palestrina, as in Gregorian, the large flat surfaces can be crammed full of exquisite, expressive detail.

## Gregorian chant as fantasy

The difference between looking at a facade and listening to a chant, of course, is that we can look at the visible details in any order we please, but we have to listen to the audible details in the order in which they are performed. A piece of music may have a narrative quality, as if it were an epic; or it may have a dramatic quality, sounding like the passionate confrontation of two conflicting characters. The Gregorian Mass Propers, however, are too short to give the impression of a wide-ranging narrative, and hardly ever have melodic gestures (or words) of such a nature as to suggest dramatic conflict.

In terms of broad genres, the Mass Propers can be described not as epic or dramatic, but rather as lyric. The melody presents short involuted turns of phrase that cluster around a central theme sometimes so vague as to be merely implied. The order of presentation is not significant, being arranged so as to furnish variety and avoid obvious repetition. This kind of arrangement is meditative in that it invites contemplation of various aspects of a subject without the pressure of following a closely argued discourse or of arriving at a conclusion or at a lofty vantage point – such as we experience in a Beethoven symphony.

In Gregorian chant I hear a succession of short melodic phrases (each about the length of a word or syllable); the succession itself I can only describe as *lyric fantasy*. Each phrase moves a little differently, or in a different direction; even though by itself each phrase makes a simple, easily understood melodic move, the succession from one to the next is unexpected, giving a sense of fantasy to the whole.

I find this non-narrative, non-dramatic quality throughout the repertory of Gregorian Mass Propers, exceptions being so infrequent as to be famous among chant singers. There is one instance of a long sustained ascent exceeding an octave, arriving at a climax that is foreseeable in the approach and satisfying in its completion (this is the Offertory *Iubilate Deo universa terra*). There is a descent, even longer, through an octave and a half in the Gradual *Ecce quam bonum*, although in that case the descent is so leisurely, backtracking with so many involute turns, that the overall trend may be perceptible only when the piece is complete. And in *Ecce quam bonum* the long descent accompanies words that describe the cup of fine oil that overflows and runs down the beard of Aaron – an instance of word-painting unusual in Gregorian chant.

In most melismatic pieces, however, there is no such sustained preparation for ascents or descents; usual procedures include, instead, circling around a central pitch in a complex way, or making relatively unprepared moves to the top or the bottom of the pitch set in such a way as to suggest that movement anywhere in the set is possible at any time. Melismatic chants do not conform to a simple model such as an arch; there are plenty of melodic high points, but they are not consistently located in the centre of a phrase, that is, preceded by an ascent and followed by a descent.

## Learning to listen

As we have moved from the back of the cathedral closer to where the singers are, we have lost the sense of indistinct chanting filtered through shadowed arches and clouds of incense, of incantation layered and overlapping, richly reverberating. We can experience being enveloped by the sound of a chorus;

or, in the presence of a solo voice, we can hear a clarity and feel a penetrating force. We gain a sense of pitch defined: we can begin to focus on – and respond to – individual pitches, their relationships to one another, their location in the diatonic system, the relationship of each successive pitch to those immediately preceding.

This chapter has described much more detail than we can easily notice in any one hearing of a piece of chant. Nonetheless, the type of detail described has its effect even if not noticed. And the abundance of detail that we do not notice – but still hear – seems to have something to do with music's sense of mystery.

I find that I need to learn to listen to a piece of chant just as much as I need to learn to sing it. Learning to listen, for me, is to develop a readiness to hear each pitch as it sounds. When I know what is going to happen next (although not in general, not very far in the future, and not consciously), I can more easily absorb it, when it happens, into a network of relationships that includes more of the whole piece. This kind of learning steadily increases my feeling that a chant is meaningful.

There is so much to hear – melismatic chant is so complex in its movements! The avoidance of repetition at the lowest level, from one pitch to the next, is absolutely persistent; the sense of difference is continual. After forty years I am still learning to recognize the subtle ways in which the seemingly endless twists and turns of Gregorian chant deftly define a musical shape, a musical meaning.

# 4

# Gregorian Chant, Roman Politics and European Polyphony

During the last hundred years, as people in the Western world (Europe and America) have become aware of culture in the rest of the world, music historians have drawn attention to a broad spectrum of kinds of chant. Standard historical surveys now describe Armenian chant, Coptic chant, Ethiopian chant, Georgian chant, Jerusalem chant, Byzantine chant, Old Slavonic chant, Russian chant, Syrian chant, along with Anglo-Saxon, Beneventan, Celtic, Frankish, Gallican, Iberian, and Roman chant (see figure 4.1). Ethnomusicologists have described many more kinds of chant, non-Christian and non-European, such as Buddhist chant, Jewish chant, Moslem chant, Tibetan chant, and other specific kinds from India, East Asia, South-East Asia, Africa, North, Central and South America.

Each of these kinds of chant has its own musical individuality, and its own story. There is nothing that could be said in general about them as a group. For many of them we cannot say much about them individually, for lack of examples: we know when and where they were used, but we have little or no musical notation to show how the chants went in ancient times. In fact, the written record of Gregorian melodies is the earliest preserved in comprehensive form. As a result, we know about it as a musical repertory earlier than any other repertory.

As mentioned briefly in chapter 1, Gregorian chant appears in musical notation collected into extensive chant books starting around the year 900, as a repertory of five to six hundred pieces called the *Proper chants of the Mass*; included are chants for *Introit*, *Gradual*, *Alleluia*, *Tract*, *Offertory* and *Communion*. Unlike most of the other chants in the list, the name *Gregorian* does not refer to a place or a group of people, and that difference turns out to be significant. Like the other kinds of chant, however, Gregorian chant has its own individuality and its own story.

Why do we call all these kinds by the same generic name, chant? That seems to be purely a matter of the way the word is used in two different languages, English and French. In English, the word chant has some rich and fascinating associations with incantation and enchantment; those meanings play a part in the mystical feeling from the back of the cathedral. Also in English, however, Gregorian chant is often referred to as *plainsong* or *plain-chant*, which has no mystical feeling whatsoever. In French its usual, pre-cise name is *chant grégorien*. The important work of the French Benedictine monks in the revival of Gregorian chant around 1900 naturally encouraged the use of that term in English. German uses the very interesting term *Choral*, more specifically *Gregorianischer Choral*, and that use will concern us in discussing the role of the chorus in Gregorian chant.

In French, *chant* is simply a generic term for singing, and can be used for any kind of singing, as *chant populaire*. So *chant grégorien* is 'the kind of singing called Gregorian' – and that, it seems, is the reason for using the term *chant* regularly for all the other kinds, such as Armenian chant.

As long as we take *chant* in that neutral, generic sense, there seems to be no problem. It is when we remember the experience from the back of the cathedral, when we were transported into mystic realms by the sound of 'chanting', that we have difficulty in understanding why many of these

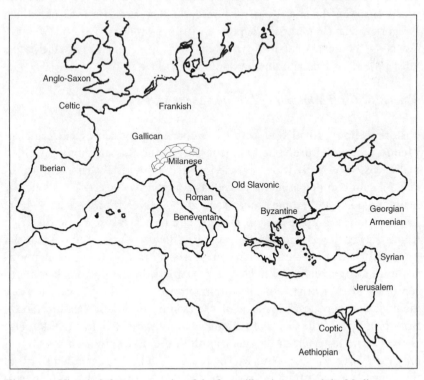

Figure 4.1 Historical chant repertories of the first millennium around the Mediterranean and in Europe.

kinds should be called chant: any one of them may *or may not* evoke the experience of 'chanting'. The problem addressed by this book is that Gregorian chant, too, may fail to evoke that experience as we get to know it close up. In chapters 2 and 3 I have tried to get past that problem to show the way to mystic realms beyond familiarity.

Historians can tell the story of how the Gregorian repertory comes down to us – when it first appeared and how it developed. Historical study can also reconstruct the environment in which the Gregorian repertory first appeared, and that may help in understanding it. There are many puzzling if not actually mysterious circumstances, however, surrounding the history of Gregorian chant before the time of its earliest written record around 900. Historians have examined data from the preceding thousand years, back to before the time of Christ; but since hardly a single complete piece of the Gregorian repertory can be found in a document from that time, reconstructing the history is necessarily a work of imagination, and must rely almost completely on evidence of the chant's environment.

The account presented here focuses on *musical* aspects of the chant's environment of origin, and attempts to sketch those musical aspects as broadly as possible. This chapter contains a brief survey of the musical practices under the later Roman Empire, the historical context from which Gregorian chant emerged. Chapter 5 will focus more closely on *liturgical* aspects – the development of Christian worship – which many feel is the most important factor in the development of chant.

## The musical environment of Mediterranean culture

Historians have provided us with two important generalities about ancient Mediterranean culture. The first generality is the Roman Empire itself. It really existed, it really was universal for several hundred years, and it provided a common denominator as well as a medium of exchange among the many linguistic and ethnic groups around the Mediterranean Sea.

The Roman Empire was formed by military pressure outwards from Rome during the second and first centuries before Christ. Subsequently it was itself under continual military pressure from the outside, until gradually but inevitably it ceased to control its borders during the fourth and fifth centuries after Christ. As an administrative unit the Roman Empire included at its greatest expansion all the land bordering the Mediterranean Sea, from Spain ('the Gates of Hercules') in the west to Syria, at least as far as the Euphrates river, in the east. South of the Mediterranean it included only the North African coast, except in Egypt, where it extended south to the upper Nile and Ethiopia. In the north the empire extended in Britain to Hadrian's Wall, roughly at the Scottish border, and on the Continent as far as the Rhine and the Danube. Control in the eastern regions was often doubtful, especially in the mountains of eastern Turkey. The empire included Palestine, but not necessarily the lands further east.

Based upon military occupation, the Roman provincial government was relatively uniform throughout and remarkably efficient. Literature, art, philosophy and religion spread easily from one end of the empire to the other: an officer of the Roman legions or a civil servant of the provincial government system might be sent anywhere, and quickly; it is said that when he got wherever he was sent he would find people who spoke the same language.

The other generality about life under the empire is more difficult and less useful. The Roman Empire is only one very strong expression of Greco-Latin culture as a whole; that culture – productive from before 800 BC to after AD 500 – has been presented mainly in the dominant image of Greek classical culture, 'the glory that was Greece'. These classic forms and values, however, come mostly from the relatively short period 550–400 BC, and are mostly identified with Athens, the Parthenon being the primary symbol. The actual achievements of Greco-Latin culture were, however, developed over more than a millennium and all around the Mediterranean, representing a very wide variety of artistic and human values. Modern appreciation has had to see past the dominant image of the Greek classics to find and admire the wealth of these other forms of art. For the most promi-nent example, the whole Hellenistic era, encompassing art, literature and science in the eastern end of the Mediterranean from 350 to 150 BC, while well known to experts, has had to be rediscovered for modern appreciation. For our purposes it is essential to look past the Greek classics and acknowl-edge the diversity of Mediterranean civilization. The universality of the Greek language, the *koiné* understood throughout the Roman Empire, was only an umbrella held over the particularism of dozens of peoples and lan-guages in a wide spectrum of cultural expression.

Even though we have only a few dozen examples of Greek music, all frag-mentary, diversity is apparent in the abundant reports of musical practice. Ancient literary and scientific accounts of Greek music occupy volumes; the literary references to Roman music, as collected by one modern scholar, number over four thousand. These provide no single picture of one kind of ancient music, but rather broad spectra of alternative ways of making music.

Greco-Latin music used a wide variety of musical instruments, and com-bined them with voices in many different ways. Instrumental music was in some ways the most important kind of music. Instruments could be used singly as solos, or many of one kind could play together (there are reports of a hundred trumpeters, or three hundred lyre players), or different kinds could play in an ensemble. Similarly voices could be used singly, as solos, or many of the same kind or different kinds could sing in chorus. Solo voices as well as chorus could be accompanied by one instrument, or by many.

Music was provided for all imaginable kinds of occasions. Music, instrumental or vocal, could be for one person meditating alone or for a small private group. A frequent and very important kind of occasion was the *symposium*, a dinner party for an intimate group with sophisticated conversation, the guests (or professional musicians) singing and playing instruments for entertainment.

Public occasions included weddings and funerals, or any kind of cultic activity. Every town had a cult of patron gods, and devotion to these in the local temple was a regular and frequent civic function. Alongside these public functions there were private, restricted ones involving initiation – the so-called mystery religions. Their music, of course, is not known to us, but for the civic cults we know at least some of the words that were sung.

The most prominent public musical performances were in connection with games, such as the Olympic games (there were also other series). Champion performers of voice or instruments, solo as well as in choral teams, competed keenly for the applause of the crowd and the prizes awarded by the judges. In Rome the tradition of such games did not continue, but there were frequent musical competitions. The emperor Nero, although he did not 'fiddle while Rome burned', practised very hard to be a virtuoso singer, and competed avidly in the performance of dramatic monologues (comparable to the modern concert performance of operatic scenes). He was obsessed with having his excellence confirmed by a fair judgement; the problem, however, was that the judges seemed inhibited by fear that if Nero lost the prize, they might lose their lives, since he had the reputation of being a tyrant.

As exemplified by Nero and many others, music was performed by amateurs as well as professionals; either could be technically sophisticated or naive; skills ranged from nil to the highest degree imaginable. Many of the better professionals were slaves, who were also the usual source of instruction for amateur freemen. Political prisoners or those taken in conquest counted as slaves, so when the Roman Empire absorbed Greece, educated Greeks became slave instructors for Romans.

While music in general rested upon a strong technological base of a variety of musical instruments, singing was prominent, with or without accompaniment. Almost by definition, the three basic literary categories of poetry – epic, lyric and dramatic – involved musical intonation in one way or another. Prose, on the other hand, was formally performed in public as oratory, for instance the speeches of lawyers in court or eulogies on state occasions. Oratory, too, was a highly developed skill, and made extensive use of intonation, but not of the kind involving fixation of single identifiable pitches, which is the distinguishing feature of musical performance. The distinction between *continuous* pitch for speech and *discrete* pitch for song was made in the fourth century BC and was taken for granted from then on.

From Greek scientific writings on music we learn of a wealth of technical resources developed over a thousand years and available for application to the various kinds of occasions just enumerated. We know that besides the diatonic scale, which was the default tonal system, there were a number of alternative scales. We know of a large number of rhythmic patterns, to be used with words or by instruments.

We can also read about a few of the ways in which an instrument could accompany a singer by playing pitches other than those of the vocal part. The information on this practice is sketchy, but when we take it together with the many possibilities of combining voices and instruments and the Greeks' detailed theoretical appreciation of the qualities of pitch relationships, we can easily imagine many additional ways in which Greek or Latin music could have combined different pitches in performance. It is improbable that any of these ways systematically duplicated the chordal conventions used by European musicians in the eighteenth and nineteenth centuries (the ways we call *functional harmony*), but there are many other possible combinations that could have been used by ancient musicians.

## Christian use of musical traditions

The traditions of musical performance accumulated in Mediterranean culture by the time of Christ presented early Christians with many more resources than they cared to use in their own worship. Much of the detailed information about music at weddings, for instance, comes from early Christian writers who, horrified by what seemed to them to be hopelessly extravagant music celebrating sexual union, gave luridly specific descriptions of such performances in the hope of warning their readers to avoid those occasions.

In tracing the development of early Christian worship in chapter 5, we shall see how important is the element of *rational selection*. While early Christians drew their worship materials, including music, from the practices they found around them, they selected only what seemed, on careful scrutiny, to be appropriate to the needs of their new religion. While they had no objection to a practice just because it was traditional, they tended to reject even venerable tradition if it did not meet with rational approval.

The use of musical instruments provides an interesting example, one of central importance. Instruments had been used prominently in the Hebrew rites of the Temple in Jerusalem; this use was described in the Old

Testament, and it would have been natural for early Christians to take that as a model. Early Christian writers, however, commented critically on those very descriptions, and urged the rejection of instruments in the new Christian music. And, at least for a while, instruments were in fact rejected in early Christian worship. More generally, early Christian music avoided all those technical aspects of music considered appropriate only for professional musicians or virtuosi.

Rational selection in early Christian worship also involved the elimination of the verbal rhythms of poetry (that is, those rhythms understood within the framework of poetic metre). This restriction, like the one on musical instruments, was merely temporary and affected only certain segments of the Christian community: together, these two restrictions most strongly affected Christian Latin worship in Rome, and were directly responsible for Gregorian chant's being unaccompanied and using only prose texts.

Verbal profusion especially could be objected to by early Christians on the basis of a saying attributed to Jesus (Matthew 6:7): 'But when ye pray, use not vain repetitions, as the heathen do: for they think that they shall be heard for their much speaking.' In the original Greek text, 'heathen' is *ethnikoi*, which in a Jewish context means Gentiles or non-Jewish people, but for Christians it meant 'pagan'. 'Vain repetitions' is the fascinating Greek term *battologia*. 'Much speaking' is the Greek word *polylogia* – even more fascinating from a musical point of view because of the similarity to the ancient Greek word *polyphonia*. Both terms can evoke images of endless repetition of praise-words by many people speaking or singing at once, possibly in an unsynchronized manner, as is frequently found in various religious contexts. This could be what is sometimes meant by 'chanting'.

What did rational selection leave for Christian use, out of the incredible wealth of musical resources available throughout the empire? It left the use of pitch, musical intonation in the diatonic scale (Christian writers specifically rejected the alternative kinds of scales). And we know from various comments by early Christian writers that they as well as their readers did not merely tolerate diatonic pitch relationships, they rejoiced in them, they celebrated these diatonic relationships as a way of making worship acceptable in God's sight. They found in the effect – or we can say, the *affect* (emotional tone) – of diatonic pitch relationships all that they wanted to save from the accumulated musical practice of the preceding millennium.

## The hymn from Oxyrhynchus

With all that information available on ancient music, it may seem strange that so little actual music has been preserved – a few dozen fragments of

po - ta - mon    rho - thi - on    pa - sai.

hym-noun - ton d'he - mon pa - te - ra ch'u - ion

ch'a - gi - on    pneu - ma pa - sai dy - na - meis

e - pi - pho- noun - ton a - men - a - men.

kra- tos ai - nos [?

] pan    ton    a - ga- thon.    a -

men    a - men.

Figure 4.2 Hymn from Oxyrhynchus. The hymn is preserved only as a fragment. Only the last half of the fragment is transcribed here, beginning in the middle of a verse. Some words are missing towards the end. This transcription gives only the pitches; interpretations of the musical rhythm vary.

Greek music, and of Roman music not a note! The reason is that in antiquity, as often in modern times, musicians did not use notation for performance. Ways of notating music did exist, and were used for special purposes, such as theoretical demonstration or analysis, or to make a visual record of a piece. None of the recorded fragments, however, gives a completely convincing impression that it represents a style or repertory of music as performed.

Perhaps out of sheer frustration with these fragments, chant historians have tended to neglect the one fragment that bears upon the history of Gregorian chant. From a famous cache of papyrus documents at Oxyrhynchus on the upper Nile in Egypt comes a third-century fragment of a Christian hymn. It is identifiable by its Trinitarian doxology ('Glory to the Father and to the Son and to the Holy Spirit'). The fragment uses standard ancient Greek letter-notation for pitch, which allows a reliable reading of the specific pitches (see figure 4.2). There are also a few indications of verbal or musical rhythm, which are interpreted variously by modern scholars; for instance, the poetic metre (anapaestic) that is used in parts of the text can suggest a musical rhythm.

The hymn from Oxyrhynchus uses a scale that is diatonic, and some turns of phrase, particularly at cadences, are very similar to what will eventually appear in certain types of Gregorian chant (specifically, canticle antiphons in mode 8). Some details, however, are alien to Gregorian style, particularly those that suggest more melodic exuberance.

Little can be shown with only one piece, and we have no other to fill the gap of five hundred years that separates this hymn from the first recorded examples of Gregorian chant. This hymn does show, nevertheless, that an expressive style of melody was available to early Christian singers whenever they wanted to use it.

## Roman chant north of the Alps?

From a survey of music under the empire, we have been able to conclude that many different kinds of music were possible, and that the kind as well as the amount of music in use varied widely from place to place. As a corollary we can conclude that there were many different kinds of Christian music, making use of existing musical practice in various ways. It is also probable, however, that many churches and monasteries made little if any use of music in worship.

Gregorian chant, as defined in this book, first appears in documents around 900; the words, as they were intended to be sung at Mass, appear before the melodies, that is, during the century 800–900, and the melodies appear at the end of that century. We do not know what forms of chant preceded the Gregorian, and we do not know – or cannot agree – when or where this Gregorian repertory was developed.

During the century 800–900, however, various kinds of information appear alongside the repertory itself. In particular there happens to be evidence that purports to tell the story of 'how they brought the chant from Rome to the north'. Both the credibility and the relevance of the story, however, are haunted by questions as well as inconsistencies. The ninth-century reports seem written to persuade: they seem obsessed with a need to convince the reader that the melodies of the Gregorian Mass Propers did indeed come from Rome. The ulterior purpose of such accounts would be to confer prestige and reliability not just on the northern versions of these melodies but also on the agencies or persons named in the reports as responsible for bringing the Roman melodies north over the Alps.

While often specific about circumstantial details, the reports are vague about the actual melodies involved. Scholars have scrutinized the reports in an effort to find positive identification for even a single *melody* of the five hundred or so eventually included in the notated chant books from around AD 900; no such identification seems forthcoming. As far as prior positive documentation is concerned, the *melodies* in the chant books could conceivably have come into existence first only around 900.

It is generally assumed, however, that the melodies *did* exist before 900. Hotly debated are the questions '*How long* before?' and '*How much* did they resemble or differ from those that were finally written down?'

Whatever its reliability, the story is a fascinating one, and reveals, indirectly, one fact of central importance. The story revolves around an ancient tension between the city of Rome and the rest of the Western world – especially the part that lay on the other side of the Alps in what is now France, the Low Countries, and the Rhineland. Romans call those people *oltremontani*, 'from beyond the mountains'; we can call them 'northerners', but we shall need to identify them more closely. For all northerners, however, the image evoked by the mere name Rome, *Roma*, was one of the most powerful of the Middle Ages, continuing as such for many people down to the present day.

The south of France, still called Provence, was regarded as the oldest and in some ways the best of the provinces of the Roman Empire. Roman aristocracy dwelt there by choice, moving in on top of the older Celtic population and producing the sophisticated culture called Gallo-Roman or Gallic. The northern part of Gaul, in contrast, came to be dominated by people called Franks from quite a different culture that had spread downwards across the Rhine from the second century on. When the Roman legions were evacuated from Britain around AD 410 and became less and less of a military presence on the Continent because of the desperate military situation throughout the empire, Frankish 'strong men' gradually established local control, replacing the Roman provincial administration as a ruling class.

Eventually Clovis (466–511), head of the Merovingian dynasty, emerged as supreme Frankish king. After Clovis, however, the Merovingian family line deteriorated and lost control. Power was effectively usurped by the Carolingian family dynasty – the 'palace gang' that actually ran the Merovingian kingdom around 700. *Their* strong man was Charles Martel ('the Hammer'); he was succeeded in due course by Pepin 'the Short' and by Charles 'the Great' – Charlemagne.

A Frankish kingdom under the Carolingian dynasty was now firmly in place, and the Carolingians were ready to raise their power structure to the next level, which was nothing less than empire. This empire was to be Christian, in other words *holy*, not pagan. But it was to be *Roman* – and not merely in a political sense, that is, to fill the power space left vacant by the now defunct western branch of the old empire (the eastern branch continued to thrive in Constantinople as the Byzantine Empire). The Carolingians had in mind to fulfil a Christian destiny for pagan Rome, and were prepared to challenge the Byzantines for that spiritual leadership. On Christmas Day in 800, in Rome at Mass (right after the singing of the Gradual *Viderunt*, track 3), Charlemagne was crowned emperor by the pope.

It was in the context of this momentous transaction that the Carolingians put out the story of bringing the chant north from Rome. It was politically advantageous for the Frankish kingdom to worship according to the liturgy used by the pope in the city of Rome. The strategy – and the deal with the pope – was that the new empire could be 'in communion' with the pope as bishop of Rome. This would bestow legitimacy, that most elusive political element, on the Carolingian power structure; and simultaneously, it would carry out the long-standing ambition of the diocese of Rome to speak at once to the city, *urbi*, and to the world, *orbi*. The phrase *urbi et orbi* thus achieved credibility, and has remained on the lips of the bishops of Rome ever since.

## Was Gregorian chant Roman?

If it was a question of Gregorian chant being Iberian, or Anglican, or Gallican, or even Italian, that might involve shades of melodic flavour that could in principle be argued about in terms of regional association (although we have almost no data to make any of those comparisons). The adjective 'Roman', however, evokes a different order of association. It refers to the place within the walls, but that is not what is summoned up by its name; rather, 'Rome the Eternal City', *Roma caput mundi* ('head of the world'), *Roma nobilis*. And not the 'holy city' or 'heavenly city', for that would be Jerusalem. What was meant was the ancient pagan city, not so old in comparison with, say, Jericho, but rather, ageless. Christians in the first and second centuries could not add to the antiquity of Rome, or to its ethos, by making it the seat of their new religion; rather, Christianity in Rome inherited the authority the ancient city already possessed, and which it shared with no other site in Christendom.

No one was more susceptible to the ethos of Rome than the Carolingian Franks. During the seventh and eighth centuries a steady stream of pilgrims returned north from Rome, giving evidence of an intense desire to worship according to Roman liturgy, and bringing back information, books and artefacts to help realize their desire. What was decisive to worshippers in the north seems to have been not the pure aesthetic or theological aspects, but instead certain details that could make worshippers feel that they were themselves virtually in Rome, worshipping on the very stones trod by St Peter and St Paul.

For instance, the earliest books containing the words of the Proper chants of the Mass also contained special indications of which church in Rome the bishop visited each Sunday on his scheduled round of visits through his diocese. In the north such indications had only the value of association: the northerners could imagine, on a given Sunday, being in the designated church in Rome, receiving the pope's visit. (See the Commentary on *Laetatus*, track 7, for a description of some of the Propers associated with such a visit.) None of this would be apparent to a northern parish congregation without much explanation; nor does it affect the melodies in any obvious way.

The fascination exercised by Rome on at least some northerners, and their desire to worship in the Roman way, provide an important sense in which the Carolingians could affirm their chant to be Roman – and this is the point implicit in their story of bringing the chant north from Rome. The Carolingian ambitions of empire were fixed on the image of Rome: they aspired not just to do things the Roman way, but to *be* Roman, not as denizens of the city, but as citizens of the empire. If they found, or made, the right kind of chant, that kind would by definition be called *cantus romanus*, just as their liturgy and their emperor would be Roman.

The desire to worship in the Roman way must have been motivated by the associations of the Roman liturgy rather than by its intrinsic nature. Considered in comparison to other liturgies eastern and western, the Roman has impressed scholars as being serious, even sombre in its action and diction, frugal and functional in its ceremonial. These qualities might recommend Roman liturgy to scholars, but did not make it attractive to worshippers. A splendid abundance of sights and sounds was much more characteristic of other rites, especially that of Byzantium. (The Roman rite and ceremonial passed on from the Middle Ages to modern Europe was substantially enhanced in these respects by the northerners themselves.) And historians of art and architecture, confronted with melismatic Gregorian chant, have been puzzled by it. What is this kind of chant (they ask) doing in Rome? For they find nothing in the designs of Roman architecture (as used by Christians) to match the musical fantasy of Gregorian style.

## If Gregorian chant is not Roman, what is?

There is another kind of chant that fits the Roman aesthetic much better; as it happens, it is called Roman chant, and located in figure 4.1 as such. It is preserved in a small set of chant books – the only ones, it turns out, from within the Roman city walls. These manuscripts are not early: they date from after 1050, that is, two centuries after the earliest notated Gregorian books. They contain the words for the Mass Propers, nearly identical to those in the earliest notated Gregorian books, and are assigned to nearly the same calendar; the melodies, however, differ in very confusing ways from the Gregorian melodies.

Some scholars have concluded that this special repertory is true Roman chant, and that Gregorian is not. This view intersects with the same older views that found it hard to believe that Gregorian chant could truly represent the Roman aesthetic. Some liturgists and even some chant historians have long looked askance at the melismatic style of Gregorian chant, questioning its propriety for Roman liturgy and regarding it as a Frankish aberration.

The melismatic style preserved in these city-of-Rome chantbooks from after 1050 is smoother, less articulated, less profiled – and for some observers much less interesting – than the Gregorian style. And some scholars argue that even this simpler style has to be stripped away to reveal what was really sung in Roman liturgy during the fifth to seventh centuries. All of that is reconstruction, completely unverifiable in any documentary way, and in any case irrelevant to the question of what the northerners heard in Roman chant. The northerners might have incorporated into their own new chant only a few elusive outlines of melodies.

## If Gregorian chant is not Roman, what kind of chant is it?

As figure 4.1 shows, there might be a number of kinds to choose from; and the possibility exists that the northern singers composed much of the repertory themselves. Once Gregorian chant does not have to be considered as Roman, it can revert to being what it appears to be – a repertory of the best melodies the northern singers could find, adapt or compose for the purpose of singing the newly imported words of the Propers of the Mass as selected and assigned to the calendar by liturgists in Rome.

As it appears in the earliest chant books, Gregorian chant has the quality of a *fait accompli*, a finished product; and indeed this repertory of chant for the Propers of the Mass was fixed from then on. The Carolingian singers had done their work well. Just as they put the Roman words into a final revision that did not change until after the Second Vatican Council (1962–5), so they gave the melodies – taken from wherever – a universal form that persisted through all the different styles of musical notation that they themselves devised in order to record and standardize the chant (described in chapter 8). The Gregorian repertory had a sheen to its melodic style, matched perhaps only by the Iberian repertory (which may have been one of its principal sources). Finally, the melodic style was distinctive, unique: it was not achieved merely by making a lowest common denominator of available materials, but achieved rather by some artistic miracle.

A paradox is involved, one that has caused modern scholars much difficulty. This completely consistent style is maintained throughout the hundreds of medieval chant books from the tenth century to the fifteenth, but
not in one absolutely identical text, rather always with slight persistent variation in musical detail. We can regard this as elegant variation: while it
clearly represents the interpretations of individual singers (those who
copied the manuscripts or on whose performance the manuscripts were
based), still the variation does not sound whimsical, or arbitrary, or merely
idiosyncratic; it does not seem to endanger the integrity of a particular piece
of chant, or the style of the repertory. This elegant musical variation is, in
fact, a basic, very distinctive part of the style. The fact that the *variation* was
a result of the musicality of the northerners suggests that so was the style
itself.

Nor can the style be described or defined by a set of rules and procedures (as has sometimes been suggested), no matter how elaborate. The
style exists only as a repertory of pieces. Knowledge of this style could
be – can be – carried only in the mind of the singer, expressed only as
singing. This would be the meaning of the statement of Bishop
Amalarius around 830: for liturgy (he said) we go to Rome, for chant to
Metz. It is true that Metz, a very important town in the Carolingian
heartland now in north-east France, was where Amalarius came from; but
his opinion is more than simple home-town loyalty. Metz was also the
cathedral town of Bishop Chrodegang, the Carolingian bishop who
worked hardest at learning about Roman liturgy and at setting up a group
of singers to perform it with appropriate melodies. In the minds of *those*
singers, says Amalarius, resides the new Gregorian style: the way *they*
sing it – that is the way it is.

Gregorian chant was the first international European musical style, but
not the last; some of the later ones showed the same success at combining –
and concealing – sundry ingredients in a new synthesis. Examples would be
Monteverdi's operas after 1600, Haydn's symphonies after 1760,
Stravinsky's ballets after 1910. None of these would be described as a
straight-line development from a single point of origin. We would not say
that Stravinsky's ballet style was nothing but the use of Russian folk motifs,
for it combined those motifs with more other elements than we can easily
specify. And if Stravinsky's friends said they heard in his music a truly
'Russian' expression, that would refer to a subtle inner quality apparent
perhaps only to them.

So with Gregorian chant: we cannot specify all the ingredients, nor judge
the importance of any one of them; and we cannot know exactly what it
meant for it to be 'Roman'. Instead we can admire the musical creativity
that produced a kind of chant at once universal and unique.

## Chants for the Divine Office

The earliest chant books contained the Mass Propers. Soon after these were codified, another repertory was written down in chant books, consisting of chants for the Divine Office – the night-and-day cycle of prayer and meditation (to be described more fully in chapter 7). Chants for the Office, much more numerous than those for the Mass, were collected and written down in their own special books.

Many of these chants for the Office were intended for use by a practised choir, as were the Mass Propers; but in this respect there were some important differences. In a monastery or convent, the congregation included all the men or women of the establishment, and since they all participated as a group in the complete daily cycle of services (several hours of worship each day), members of the congregation itself could be said to be very practised, and unlike the congregation of a cathedral, they could participate extensively in the singing.

This participation took the form of singing *complete* psalms using recitation formulas (psalm tones). In conjunction with singing psalms there was a large and growing repertory of simple melodies called *antiphons*. There were also more elaborate melodies called *responsories*, and these were sung by a choir consisting of a few of the more skilful monks or nuns, who rehearsed under the direction of a *cantor* just like a cathedral choir. And numerous segments of chant were to be sung by a soloist.

Chants for the Office, then, included a broad range from the simple chants sung by all to the complex chants sung by the choir and soloists. While the complex chants were not so melismatic as those sung at Mass, the Office included numerous chants that were much simpler than those at Mass. Even in the early chant books these were large collections, including a thousand or more antiphons and upwards of five hundred responsories; and soon the collections became much larger. Although the collection of Office chants was closed slightly later, and less firmly, than that of the Mass Propers, the melodies for antiphons and responsories of the Office in these early chant books are remarkably consistent in style; and the responsories are stylistically similar to the chants for the Mass Propers.

Chant for the Divine Office included a special form called the *metrical hymn*; this form was not included in the Gregorian canon. The form of the metrical hymn goes back to Latin poetry composed by Bishop Ambrose in the fourth century. The form contains a number of stanzas, each with exactly the same number of lines and syllables. This form is familiar in modern times from the hymns used in most European and American Christian churches; it is familiar because this kind of hymn was established as normal by the medieval northerners, and became popular already by the end of the Middle Ages. The northerners composed thousands of sets of words in metrical-hymn form, and many hundreds of melodies. At first the melodies had something of the freedom of the Gregorian style – in spite of the great regularity of the hymn metre – but gradually the hymn melodies became simple and straightforward in style, resulting in the kind of hymn tune familiar to us.

## Mass Ordinary chants

Next to the Mass Propers there appeared early on another repertory of chants to be sung at Mass, and these differed from the Propers in many important ways. As a group, these other chants are called *Ordinary chants for the Mass*. 'Ordinary', like 'Proper', is a technical term; it is easier, and more precise, to identify the chants by name – *Kyrie eleison*, *Gloria in excelsis*, *Sanctus*, *Agnus Dei* (a fifth item, *Credo*, was later grouped with these four, but for musical purposes it is separate). These items (including the *Credo*) have become merged in modern tradition and practice with the Mass Propers, and are performed in much the same manner. At an earlier stage, however, they were recorded in separate books and scrupulously distinguished from the Mass Propers. We can easily hear their stylistic differences, and can appreciate each kind for its distinctive qualities.

These Ordinary Mass chants came about in the following way. The kind of early Christian music sung at Mass by the congregation in a cathedral consisted almost entirely of short exclamations (called *acclamations*) of praise or petition, such as 'Holy, holy, holy', or 'Lord, have mercy'; these will be traced in early Christian development more closely in chapter 5. At first these were sung but not recorded in musical notation; we assume that they were sung in relatively simple style, although there is no reason why more complex melodies could not have been used occasionally.

Then, at about the time the Mass Propers appeared in collections (around the year 900), these congregational acclamations started to be recorded in collections of their own, but set to complex melodies too difficult to be sung by the congregation – even by a monastic congregation. And while these melodies were in some ways as elaborate as those of the Mass Propers, they were very different in style.

The first new *Kyries* were composed by northerners, who stabilized the form at three times *Kyrie eleison* ('Lord, have mercy'), three times *Christe eleison* ('Christ, have mercy'), three times *Kyrie eleison*. That form was provided with many different melodic settings by many different composers. A typical collection came to include a dozen or more *Kyrie* melodies, and by the end of the Middle Ages a repertory of some three hundred *Kyrie* melodies can be gathered from European chantbooks.

The new *Kyries* were sung in a special way, not used in the Gregorian repertory. Each phrase, containing either the words *Kyrie eleison* or *Christe eleison*, could be relatively long, and could be sung either with a melisma on *Kyri-e-e-e-e-e-e-e-leison* or with its own set of words sung with a pitch for each syllable. For example, the first phrase of one such piece is

Su- a- vis tu De- us, rex no- ster ve- rus es pa- ti- ens, mi- tis val- de in per- pe- tu- o
Ky- ri- e- e- e-    e- e-  e- e-  e- e-  e- e-  e- e-  e-  e- e-  e- e- e-  le- i- son

with the same melody sung either to the words *Suavis tu Deus* or melismatically just with *Kyrie eleison*. Each of the remaining eight phrases of this piece has its own set of Latin words. In one manner of performance, each of the nine phrases could be sung twice, once with words, and again without; in this case they would be sung antiphonally, alternating between semichoirs, or perhaps between soloist and choir. As another manner of performance, all phrases could be sung only with the Latin words; or as still another alternative, all phrases could be sung only melismatically with *Kyrie eleison* or *Christe eleison*. (On the compact disc, the *Kyrie eleison* is sung in its melismatic form.) The melismas of such pieces show but little similarity to the style of the Gregorian melismas.

Northern composers also set the other acclamations used at Mass, *Gloria in excelsis*, *Sanctus*, *Agnus Dei*, providing numerous individual melodies for these items. They did not use the special melismatic style of the new *Kyries*, and only moderate amounts of intrasyllabic extension. Still, the melodies sounded markedly different from the Gregorian Proper chants of the Mass, often being much more accessible, with a directness and warmth that made them popular.

In general, the Ordinary chants for Mass were not just an extension of the Gregorian repertory, but a new and different kind of music, representing a new musical mood. A few examples are on the compact disc and discussed in the Commentary for the sake of comparison with the Gregorian repertory; but a description of this new music would require a book of its own.

## Other new kinds of chant

Alongside the collections of Mass Ordinary chants there appeared other collections with still more different kinds of chant for Mass. The two most important kinds were called *tropes* and *sequences*. These were provided for many of the same occasions that had Proper chants of the Mass, such as Introits. Tropes and sequences were collected in sets arranged according to the liturgical calendar, just like the Gregorian Propers. They were usually placed in separate books, however, and the collections never became as complete or as standardized as the Gregorian Proper chants.

The melodies for sequences were in a style even more different from Gregorian. Sequences were the longest, most splendid of the new Frankish compositions. Like the *Kyries*, they could be sung either with or without their words, which were newly composed. Considered without their words, these melodies represent the extreme form of purely melodic chant produced by the northerners.

Tropes are stylistically more similar to Gregorian antiphons, and were sung antiphonally, alternating phrase by phrase with antiphons at the Introit and Communion. The words of the tropes were not taken exactly from the Book of Psalms or other parts of the Bible, but, like the words of sequences (or the words added to *Kyrie eleison*), were newly composed.

By the end of the Middle Ages the repertories of tropes and sequences, along with the Ordinary chants for Mass and the metrical hymns for the Office, had each accumulated hundreds of items, if not more. They were used in cathedral and monastic services but not always as a part of the regular order of service; they might be sung before or after a service, or as additions to items such as the Mass Propers. All represented local, variable musical practices. They continued in use for a longer or shorter time, but survived down to the present only in fragmentary form, if at all. Only a few melodies for acclamations and sequences survived in musical practice, and virtually none of the tropes. In contrast, the survival of the Mass Propers as a canon is unique in medieval music.

Many of these new kinds of chant are now being rediscovered, performed, and recorded on compact disc, often under the title Gregorian chant, in spite of being Gregorian only by association with the original Gregorian repertory. Whether they are *liturgical* depends on how liturgy is defined – which is a matter to be decided by a liturgical authority, ultimately the bishop. Whether they are 'chanting' depends on how they sound in particular circumstances. When heard with closer attention, they (like the Mass Propers) will reveal their features more clearly, along with their similarities and differences relative to the Mass Propers. Some of these kinds of chant, sequences especially, can sound very different from Gregorian chant.

Beginning with the Mass Ordinary chants, I prefer to call all these types generically *medieval chant*, and to use *Gregorian* only for the Mass Propers, because as I become more and more aware of the individuality of each of these kinds of chant I want to keep them distinct.

## European music after Gregorian chant

After about the year 1000, European music continued to develop rapidly, and since it was increasingly written down we can easily compare its new forms with those of Gregorian chant and medieval chant. In retrospect,

Gregorian chant became more and more distinctive, but more and more remote, finally receding into the dim past as some other, alien kind of music. This seems to have happened already in the late Middle Ages.

Secular song in France was collected after 1200 in large anthologies. It was different from Gregorian chant in the same ways that many of the forms of medieval chant were different. It was at this stage that the term chant became ambiguous. All kinds of Gregorian as well as medieval chant were called *cantus*, which was Latin for song. Secular song, at first with French words, was called *chant*, as the normal French term derived from *cantus*. Used in this way, chant could mean simply song.

Different from any kind of chant, sacred or secular, was a new kind of music that appeared in written collections soon after 1000. So different was this kind of music that in modern times we place it in a different musical category: we call it *polyphony* in the sense of 'more than one pitch at a time', that is, simultaneity (as discussed at the end of chapter 2).

In exploring how to make music in simultaneity instead of in unison, European musicians began to reinterpret the traditional Christian idea of 'as if with one voice' in increasingly varied and complex ways. They had always used the very clean, pure simultaneities of the perfect consonances (octave and fifth) without seriously disturbing the unified effect of *una voce* singing; now they explored how to include the rest of the diatonic intervals as simultaneities. Their problem was to do that while still singing something recognizable to their listeners as music.

The best name for the new kind of music is *discant*, a medieval term meaning essentially 'double chant'. The blending of different pitches in simultaneity now absorbed the attention of European musicians (and has continued to absorb it from that time until the present). What one voice sang, then, was only one part of the whole piece of music as performed; and we still speak of vocal polyphony as being music 'in parts', and of the various voice-parts, *soprano*, *alto*, *tenor*, *bass*.

In developing the new discant styles after 1000, and especially after 1200, composers and singers also became involved in ways of measuring musical time so that two voices could be exactly synchronized in order to maximize the effect of simultaneity. This was accomplished at first by using very regular rhythms – simple, repetitive rhythms – in all the voice parts.

The net effect was to put a very great stylistic distance between the new discant and Gregorian chant, which was now heard as lacking strong sonority and strong rhythm. It was this more than anything else that made Gregorian chant seem remote. Furthermore, as the new discant became focused and more immediate, it seemed to them and to us – for reasons we cannot fully explain – to lose the sense of mystery that was inherent in the Gregorian Mass Propers.

The new discant entered a period of intense development between 1200 and 1450, initiating a succession of musical styles that eventually produced the European traditions of classical and popular music. The medieval styles themselves, of course, disappeared, being replaced by ever new forms and styles. Completely unknown to nineteenth-century listeners, medieval polyphony has been rediscovered in the twentieth century along with medieval chant. Although at first the polyphony seemed very strange, familiarity and increasingly excellent performances (such as those on current compact discs) have revealed medieval discant to have for us a kind of immediacy, of obviousness that we do not find in Gregorian chant.

A sense of mystery returned to polyphonic music of the period 1450–1600, usually identified as Renaissance polyphony. This is not simply the effect of acoustic distance, of listening from the back of the cathedral. Rather, this sense of mystery deepens the closer we get to the music, the more exactly we hear its detail – just as is the case with the more melismatic kind of Gregorian chant. This style of Renaissance polyphony was created by Guillaume Dufay (about 1400–74), Johannes Ockeghem (about 1410–97) and Josquin Des Près (1440/50?–1521), then cultivated by an impressive number of northern composers and singers. Eventually Italian composers became expert in this style, and the music of Giovanni da Palestrina (1525–94) became accepted as suitable for use in the Roman Mass, effectively replacing medieval chant for the Ordinary items and Gregorian chant for the Mass Propers.

*Chanting 'in parts'*

At that time (1550–1600) a curious transformation took place. The kind of chanting done with psalm tones in the ancient liturgical practice by now seemed hopelessly remote, simply a relic, no longer to be considered music. Some of its functions, particularly those associated with singing psalms, were now filled by a simple kind of discant that produced the same effect as the psalm tones but used the harmonies that made Renaissance polyphony so attractive.

A new style of chanting thus came into use. It exactly matched all the characteristics of chanting described in chapter 1: the new style was repetitive in rhythm and sonority, simple, participatory, inclusive, potentially hypnotic. In one essential respect, however, it was different, for the participants now sang not just one and the same pitch, but rather the several pitches of a harmony; they sang in parts, as soprano, alto, tenor, bass.

This style became very popular, appearing in a variety of formats for different purposes. These are all new kinds of chant, and might even be added on to figure 4.1. In Italy, where it was called *falsobordone*, this kind of chant was used for psalms and other liturgical recitation, just like the old psalm tones. In England, too, it came to be used for psalms in English translation, and was regularly sung by cathedral choirs instead of the old Gregorian psalm tones; it was called Anglican chant.

In France and Switzerland it was adapted for use with the *metrical psalms*, French renderings of the psalms in verse. This use eventually intersected with the German tradition of the metrical hymn, which was called *Choral*, a term used by Germans for anything – including Gregorian chant – sung by the congregation or chorus.

For the purpose of singing metrical hymns, European musicians produced a style of hymn singing in harmonies that became standard in Protestant worship of all kinds. Churches in the English Methodist tradition, among many other denominations, still participate in the simple, repetitive harmonic patterns of hymn singing with apparently inexhaustible enthusiasm. This is participatory chant of the purest kind; the only reason it might not sound (from the back of the cathedral) like 'chanting' is that the sonorities themselves are so much the same as those we use for many other kinds of music in daily life.

*Sacred concerted music*
Meanwhile, during the period 1600–1900, music performed at Mass in Europe made increasing use of the new secular style of music developing in European concert life. These styles made regular use of instrumental accompaniment – not just the pipe organ, but also the stringed and wind instruments of symphony and chamber music, all performed by professional musicians (*concerted* refers specifically to the combined use of voices and instruments). More important, music for Mass now tended to avoid the sense of mystery immanent in the Gregorian Propers, and tried to be as familiar, as close to European middle-class urban sentiment as possible.

*Reform, Palestrina style and Gregorian chant*
In reaction to the increasing secularization of sacred music, a movement for the reform of Catholic church music took place during the period 1800–1900. The leaders of the reform turned first to the music of Palestrina as a model. Palestrina's music had long since disappeared from the development of European music; it had to be rediscovered as 'ancient'. It was understood by the reformers to be purely vocal (*a cappella*), thus avoiding the use of instruments and all the modern styles of concert music that the reformers found inappropriate to worship at Mass. These musical reforms went hand in hand with broader reforms and revivals of the traditional forms of Catholic worship, which by this time had lost meaning for many Europeans.

The Palestrina style provided music that could be heard as spiritual in the sense of being pure, distant from the noisy or seductive music of the world, but rich in spiritual mystery and complexity. These were exactly the qualities that had been realized in Gregorian chant of the eighth century. Indeed, many people have been impressed by the inner correspondence of the Palestrina style to Gregorian chant: they sound remarkably similar; more precisely, when heard indistinctly from the back of the cathedral, the Palestrina style can sound like 'chanting'. This is true even though the melodies are not really similar at all, and even though the Palestrina style is all in harmony and counterpoint, which is totally absent from Gregorian chant.

Along with the return to Palestrina as a model of Catholic music for worship came a return to Gregorian chant. Perhaps the Gregorianists were encouraged by the success of the Palestrina style in the nineteenth century; perhaps they thought Gregorian would fill the need for music at Mass even better than would Palestrina. In any case, from 1870 on a small number of scholars and singers (predominantly monastic) in France, Germany and England pushed hard for a revival of Gregorian chant, and although they encountered seemingly unsurmountable obstacles, they had remarkable success.

Under the term Gregorian chant, used loosely, were revived the following kinds of Gregorian and medieval chant:

The canon of Proper chants for the Mass, complete and intact from AD 900;
small portions of chants for the Divine Office (larger portions were revived for use within certain monasteries);
a small selection from the medieval repertories of Ordinary chants for the Mass;
a similarly small selection of metrical hymns for the Office;
a *very* small selection of medieval sequences for Mass.

There was much discussion concerning what could suitably be revived for modern use, and what could not. Since the project of revival was so closely tied to liturgy and its revival, the results were due as much to ecclesiastical politics as had been the case with the Carolingian project in liturgy and chant; and as in the eighth and ninth centuries, the terms Roman and Gregorian became slogans of allegiance.

The leaders in the revival of Gregorian chant for use at Mass were the Benedictine monks of the Abbey of St Pierre in Solesmes (France). Other monastic orders – Cistercian, Dominican, Franciscan – published and performed the repertories that they had preserved from the Middle Ages,

repertories different in particulars from the Benedictine version. Some of
the other kinds of chant located in figure 4.1 have been revived and performed, and recorded on compact disc.

*Gregorian chant and the early music revival*
Parts of the medieval repertory that have been judged unsuitable for use in
reformed liturgy have been published and performed as part of the early
music movement since 1950. Gregorian chant appealed to the growing
number of listeners in Europe and America who were fascinated by the
sounds of music from before the time of Bach. The appreciation of early
music increased slowly in the twentieth century: listeners had to learn how
to listen to early music, and performers had to learn how to perform it.
Learning to listen involved first perceiving whatever was shared with more
familiar music.

Gregorian chant had an advantage over other kinds of early European
music, especially medieval polyphony. The rich choral sound of chant,
moving in a free rhythm and in unison through a diatonic pitch set, had
strong resonance with at least some aspects of classical music. In contrast,
medieval polyphony, which did not use many triadic harmonies, confronted
the modern ear with a mixture of simple consonances (fourths and fifths)
that were thought to sound empty, and dissonances that seemed unmoti-
vated and unnecessarily dense. Compared with that sound, the *absence* of
harmony from chant made it seem not empty but merely purified.

Chant was different from other early music, then, by virtue of leaving out
certain sounds; chant did not replace these missing sounds with other very
different or alien sounds. The listener's ears are not filled with a welter of
sound demanding to be heard in an unfamiliar way. All the sounds that are
there are familiar. This was an essential factor in the renewed popularity of
chant.

Still, there remained the surface strangeness of Gregorian chant, inviting
comparison not only with other kinds of medieval music, but especially with
traditions of singing from all around the Mediterranean – indeed, from all
those kinds shown in figure 4.1, as they gradually became known to modern
listeners. Such comparisons could be very valuable in calling attention to
the way Gregorian chant presented musical possibilities outside the relatively narrow range of nineteenth-century classical music. But these same
comparisons were apt to miss the essential ways in which Gregorian chant
was European. There was, for instance, a persistent effort to make
Gregorian chant sound non-European by trying to superimpose distinctive
performance mannerisms – or what seemed like distinctive mannerisms –
from other independent traditions.

It seems to me, however, that there are conventions of pacing and vocal tone in singing that are traditional in Europe north of the Alps (although now widely diffused); these conventions seem ordinary, vernacular, not identified with specific styles, for instance of opera on the one hand or of folksong on the other. I see no reason to think that these conventions came into existence only in the nineteenth century; on the contrary, I believe they have been in place since the Middle Ages. When an idiom, a specific phrase, of European melody can be traced back to the fifteenth century (and some can), it seems historically unjustified to imagine it sung in some way very different from these ordinary northern traditions.

The fifteenth century is halfway back to Gregorian; and Gregorian idiom, too, has occasional resonances with the well-documented tradition of European song of the later Middle Ages. Whatever the farthest sources of Gregorian chant might have been, and however it might have sounded when sung in those places, we can legitimately imagine it sung by ninth-century Frankish cantors in the tone of voice that eventually became traditional in European song. That repertory of song provides the best and earliest historical evidence for imagining how Gregorian chant sounded in the early Middle Ages.

Very little description of singing from the Middle Ages has survived, and what there is seems very general. There is, however, a persistent characterization of good singing as sweet, and that is important precisely because it is subjective. Whatever may have been the objective acoustic properties of that kind of singing, we know that the sound was heard by listeners as sweet (*doux, süss*), and we know what those words mean from the continuity of language through the centuries. That would be an example of reception history, which attempts to determine the meaning of music, poetry or art from the experiences of the people who received it. And our attempts to sing chant so that it sounds sweet to modern ears need not exclude our concern to elevate or refine modern sensitivities as to what artistic sweetness involves.

Since Gregorian chant is the first European style of music, its history is coterminous with that of European music. It is there in the background of all succeeding styles, no matter how different these have become. The revival of Gregorian chant in the twentieth century makes these differences very obvious; at the same time, however, it affords an opportunity to hear the underlying similarities.

# 5
# Singing the Praises in Early Christian Worship

There must have been a tone of intense concentration in early Christian worship. Focus on inner religious experience was undistracted by the sights and sounds that characterized the various Greco-Latin rites of traditional animal sacrifice – the 'pomp' as it was called. Christian writers were sickened by the pomp, and their revulsion seemed to express a widespread Christian sentiment. At any rate, by avoiding the pomp, Christian worship developed a distinctive tone during the first two or three centuries, in spite of all the differences in local practice that could be perceived throughout the Roman Empire.

*Eucharist*

The tone of Christian worship was most apparent in the distinctive Christian service, the commemoration of the Last Supper of Jesus with his disciples. This commemoration, whose most generic name is *eucharist* or 'thanksgiving', was carried on by groups of early Christians everywhere, each group in its own way. At the same time, in any particular place early Christians would continue to observe many of the popular traditions of Greco-Latin piety and devotion that they had practised in local cults and temples. While some things about the eucharist were analogous to traditional cult, civic or domestic, in other respects – and especially in tone – the eucharist was different.

In Greco-Latin culture traditional sacrifices and the attendant celebrations could include much instrumental music and rhythmic singing and dancing, as well as personal interaction and expression (leading possibly to orgiastic demonstrations). In order to be different, the early Christian eucharist avoided instrumental music and rhythmic verse; music itself seemed inappropriate to the encounter with God, and to some Christians it seemed best to say as little as possible. One of the favourite chants used later in the Greek Orthodox Church as introduction to the eucharist began 'Let all mortal flesh keep silence' (known in an English adaptation in some Protestant hymnbooks). In the Roman eucharist the congregation made only two brief utterances, and in its fully developed form much of what the celebrant said was inaudible to the congregation. In this understanding, then, the eucharist was essentially an act, an activity; words were incidental; and music, especially as used in traditional non-Christian rites, seemed out of place.

For at least the first hundred years or so we have no complete and reliable picture of early Christian worship. One of the earliest, most famous accounts was recorded by Justin Martyr, writing in Rome around AD 150.

And on the day named for the sun there is an assembly in one place for all who live in the towns and in the country; and the memoirs of the Apostles and the writings of the Prophets are read as long as time permits. Then, when the reader has finished, he who presides speaks, giving admonishment and exhortation to imitate those noble deeds. Then we all stand together and offer prayers. And when, as we said above, we are finished with the prayers, bread is brought, and wine and water, and he who presides likewise offers prayers and thanksgiving, according to his ability, and the people give their assent by exclaiming Amen. And there takes place the distribution to each and the partaking of that over which thanksgiving has been said, and it is brought to those not present by the deacon.

Justin was addressing the growing tension between the Christian communities and the rest of society – tension that reflected the concerns not just of the imperial authorities but also of a broad class of reasonable citizens. Justin seems to be saying, 'Christian worship is not extreme, not orgiastic or demonic; nothing uncivilized happens, in fact nothing much happens at all, except in spirit. Here is what we do.'

So in Justin's account there is emphasis on *doing* the ritual acts that he lists so briefly and objectively ('... bread is brought, and wine and water ...'). No room for pomp there; only prayers, and thanks. But the simplicity of his account may be ingenuous, for it turns out that the simple actions he describes have a meaning for Christians that is ultimately inexplicable.

The Christian Gospels and other writings of the New Testament report that at the Last Supper, which was a traditional communal meal, Jesus referred to the bread and wine as his body and blood, and the meaning of that remains a central mystery in Christianity. To complicate matters further, the sacrifice of animals in traditional Greco-Roman cult (which also included a communal meal) was taken by some to be the prototype of the

Christian service. Some believed, mistakenly, that the Christians actually performed a sacrifice – possibly a human one. But a famous official report by Pliny the Younger (AD 112), a provincial governor, states very carefully, in precise Roman legal language, what the Christian service *did* contain, thereby seeming to exclude what it did *not* contain, namely a physical sacrifice. While Christians themselves, then as well as now, refer to the Sacrifice of the Mass, they emphasize that theirs is a 'spiritual' sacrifice, or a 'reasonable' (or 'verbal') sacrifice, rather than a physical, bloody one.

It is, of course, obvious to any observer that the Christian service is *not* a physical sacrifice; but it is not at all clear to an outsider exactly what it *is*. Dom Gregory Dix, a liturgical historian whose book *The Shape of the Liturgy* (1935) elicited a new wave of intense interest in liturgical scholarship, told a bizarre anecdote about his aunt, an English Methodist. She believed firmly that at the Catholic Mass the acolytes let loose a crab on the altar, and it was the duty of the celebrating priest to keep the crab from being seen by the congregation. The aunt's belief is readily understandable if we imagine her standing at the back of the church viewing the priest's gestures at the altar (with his back to the congregation), moving his arms as he prepares the bread and wine for Communion.

In the early centuries the meaning of the eucharist was defined by the bishop as spiritual leader of his congregation; the bishop was the highest human authority, reporting only to God. And while various regulatory systems and hierarchies attempted to impose controls on theological dogma and to guide bishops in all aspects of Christian religion including liturgy and music, still today the bishop is technically and practically responsible for the liturgical use of music in his diocese. So the bishop was the one to say what the eucharist meant for his congregation; and whatever way the bishop said it was, that was the way it was.

## Eucharistic prayer

The bishop made his statement at the eucharist by pronouncing the *eucharistic prayer*, a long prayer and the only prayer of the eucharist. In a sense it *is* the eucharist, for the eucharist begins when the prayer begins and is over when the prayer ends, even though it is followed by its logical sequel, Holy Communion, the 'Heavenly Banquet', at which the bread and wine are distributed to the congregation.

This prayer can be called the bishop's song, and as such was the principal form of music at the eucharist. In the early centuries the bishop composed his own eucharistic prayer – perhaps on the spot, if he was inspired. Hence the manner and form of the bishop's song, as well as its length, varied greatly according to the wishes and abilities of the individual bishop. By the fourth or fifth centuries these eucharistic prayers were written down so as to preserve the best ones as standard. Eventually bishops no longer composed their own prayers but instead used the standard ones provided by the regulated liturgies of emerging super-churches such as the Greek Orthodox or the Roman Catholic Church.

Sometimes called a 'song of victory', the eucharistic prayer had several song-like features. The bishop explained the meaning of the eucharist by recounting the story of salvation – the life, death and resurrection of the Lord Jesus. This was an epic, the Christian epic; it was accompanied by lyric descriptions of God's attributes and favours to mankind, which in turn evoked the outburst of 'Holy, holy, holy' from the congregation.

## Sanctus

The congregation's acclamation of 'Holy' was the only other kind of music within the eucharist. The cry of 'Holy' was uncomfortably close to tra-ditional Greco-Latin cult – it was, in fact, a traditional acclamation used in the worship of various deities, and (what was even worse from a Christian point of view) might conceivably be used to acclaim an emperor who had declared himself divine. To guard against such associations, the *Sanctus* was used only in a version drawn from the Hebrew Old Testament. In the vision of Isaiah (Isaiah 6:3), the prophet describes the seraphim beside Yahweh's throne crying 'Holy, holy, holy'. On this as on other occasions early Christians turned to the Hebrew Scripture as a source of texts that were dis-tanced from Greco-Latin cult. In this way, while the *Sanctus* was at first just an option in the eucharistic prayer, it became standard and universal.

## The celestial throne room

The tone of some early eucharistic prayers became high-flown, even ecstatic. In some, the bishop speaks as if he, at the head of his flock, had led them into the very presence of the Creator of the universe, into the celestial throne room, and was making a direct address to God on his throne. All the essential elements of the eucharistic prayer start to resonate in this mystical understanding. The sacrifice is that of a human, but a unique one, Jesus of Galilee, and the sacrifice was made only once at a particular time and place – Golgotha – while in metaphysical terms it was made in eternity, that is, beyond time and place. This sacrifice was made (in this understanding, *is* made) by God to God. In commemorating (the precise technical term is *re-presenting*) this sacrifice within temporal, spatial coordinates at an altar, the bishop is paradoxically bringing his flock out of time and space, through the door of eternity, to the very foot of the throne of the Almighty, in order to participate in the eternal sacrifice.

In the temporal dimension the bishop is explaining and reminding his people what happened at Golgotha; in eternity, he is bringing to mind what

God does in the eternal present – not as something God needs to be reminded of, but rather as a human affirmation of something that should be said. Under these conditions, it is easy to see why the early bishops, even if inspired, felt obliged to choose their words carefully. And while language, architecture and ceremonial found full scope for expression appropriate to this conception, the resources of music – at least in the early centuries – seemed to be excluded: only the bare elements of intonation in a recitation formula were used in chanting the eucharistic prayer. Accordingly, the *Sanctus* was sung as a simple acclamation. In later ages composers tried for more; perhaps J. S. Bach's *Sanctus* from his Mass in B minor is equal to the task.

### Hymns and hymning

The *Sanctus* is one of a relatively small number of texts that can strictly be called *hymns*. The word *hymn*, as a noun or a verb, means the same as 'laud' or 'praise'; 'we hymn thee' means the same as 'we praise thee'. A hymn, then, consists of *praise-words*, and there were not so many of these in common use in Greek or Latin (or in English). A hymn was properly addressed only to a deity, not to a human – not even a hero. Hymns were sung; or speaking more generically, *hymning* implied a kind of reiterative intonation of a praise-word that is very close to 'chanting' as discussed at the start of chapter 1.

Hymning was widespread and popular in traditional cult of all kinds, and Christian leaders were wary of using it for that reason. There was, however, a precedent in the Gospels: in fact the only Gospel reference to anything that might be called liturgical singing is a passing mention that at the end of the Last Supper the disciples, 'after hymning, went out' (Matthew 26:30: *hymnēsantes exēlthon*). On that occasion the disciples might have used the Hebrew expression *Hallelujah*; in any case Hallelujah was adopted early on as a praise-word that, coming from the Old Testament, had no Greco-Latin associations.

A single hymnic expression such as 'we hymn thee' did not make a very long piece, and required some kind of expansion for cultic use. Instead of incessant repetition, Christian practice extended praise-words with other lyric or epic expressions. Early Christians knew and used a special kind of hymn that can be called the Hymn of All Creation. This is the song of praise sung by all created things to their Creator, each making the kind of praise peculiar to its nature: the sun radiates, the storm thunders, the seas pound; each living creature cries aloud in its own way, and humans sing, with or without words; the hymn goes on unceasingly. There were many ancient poetic expressions of it, inviting humans to join in. Although the all-creation hymn is not specifically Christian, there exist several Hebraic and Christian versions. In one form used in the Latin eucharistic prayer the bishop sings,

> ... thy majesty (which) the angels praise and the dominions adore, before which the powers tremble, which the heavens and all the forces of the heavens and the blessed seraphim celebrate together in exultation. ...

This would be the form of hymn, then, sung by the countless numbers of the heavenly host arrayed before the throne of the Almighty.

### Dialogue with the people

Even though the bishop is addressing the celestial throne, in terrestrial terms he is engaged in a dialogue with his congregation; the eucharistic prayer begins, in fact, with the bishop singing 'Lift up your hearts', and his people responding 'We lift them up unto the Lord'. Then the bishop proposes, 'Let us give thanks unto our Lord God' – thanksgiving being the essence of the eucharist. To this proposal the people respond with an ancient acclamation used to confirm imperial power: 'That is right! That is the thing to do!' Then the bishop proceeds to give thanks to God. This relationship between bishop and people is the true locus of distinctively Christian worship and its music, which consists essentially of the bishop's song and his people's response to it.

More abundant forms of verbal expression, sung to other kinds of music, were used by the congregation worshipping together outside the eucharist. Some of these other kinds involved much more congregational participation, but some also involved performance by solo singers or small groups of practised singers, to whom the congregation merely listened – perhaps not even responding at the end. We shall see that Gregorian chant is mainly of the latter kind. These other kinds of worship and music were much less distinctively Christian, much more apt to resemble traditional cultic practices – and much more apt to be criticized by those Christians who wanted to pursue only pure forms of worship and had little use for music. The three early Christian services at which these other kinds appeared are the *synaxis*, the morning service, and the evening service, to be described next.

In addition, there are two more forms of religious activity that, although not strictly worship, include important musical activity. One type is called a *litany* (often in the plural, as *litanies*), a formalized series of petitions. The other is a type of group singing called *antiphony*. Either type could occur separately, or could be incorporated in certain ways into the synaxis, the morning service, or the evening service, but not into the eucharistic prayer.

## Synaxis

Synaxis is an early term for the first half of the Mass, which seems to modern Christians so firmly attached to the second half (the eucharist) that together they seem like one continuous service. But the synaxis was originally a distinct service, one that differed from the eucharist in essential ways.

The synaxis itself consisted of several different elements, not one. All these elements involved singing or saying words; they were not sacramental acts, as the eucharist was. The words were said or sung by various individuals other than the bishop. Indeed, the bishop did not have much to do during the synaxis, although he supervised its content and conduct, and specifically delegated the individuals to perform the various items.

The term synaxis suggests the term *synagogue* for a Jewish service; but, like synaxis, synagogue is also a Greek word, used among Jews outside Palestine, since they did not speak much Hebrew and used Greek *koiné* along with everyone else. The word means 'speaking (or doing) together', and simply designates group religious practice. The Jewish synagogue service was developing simultaneously with early Christian worship, first as a supplement to worship in the Temple at Jerusalem, then, after the destruction of the Temple in AD 70, as the principal form of Jewish worship service. Similarities between the Christian synaxis and the Jewish synagogue service include especially the use of readings from the Bible.

### St Paul's Corinthian synaxis
Most Christians, however, were not Jewish. The general similarity of the early Christian synaxis to the Jewish synagogue service can be understood simply as common ways people have of sharing religious experience in a group. Some of these ways were listed in an important passage in St Paul's First Epistle to the Corinthians (14:26). Paul felt that it was very important to regulate these traditional practices.

In this text Paul seems to be identifying elements in a synaxis as ordinarily conducted by the Christians in Corinth (Greece): each member of the group (Paul writes) contributes something – a song, a teaching, a revelation, an ecstatic utterance, an interpretation. These are all natural, traditional ways of expressing religious experience within the context of group worship. Each way is the expression of an individual, something that the individual brings out of his or her experience, for the sake of self-expression as well as to inspire the others. Synaxis, clearly, could be show-and-tell – possibly with unexpected results.

All the ways of participating Paul lists involve solo performance. The expression may take a musical form, and that would be a solo song; or it may take the form of a reasoned discourse, and that would be a teaching. Still another form would be a revelation, the telling of a religious insight (of 'things hidden', according to Paul's term). The last two ways Paul lists may seem strange to us, and if so, that is because they soon became so strictly regulated as to disappear from Christian worship – at least, as personal expressions within public worship.

### Ecstatic utterance

Paul's words are translated 'speaking with tongues' in the King James translation (1 Corinthians 14:6). The phenomenon, identified by scholars as *glossolalia*, is a particular form of religious ecstasy in which an individual in an inspired state speaks an unknown language. It was not uncommon in antiquity, and was similar to the unintelligible utterances of the Greek oracles (such as the one at Delphi), which had to be interpreted. Just how the interpretation was to be made was an open question, and sceptical observers in antiquity felt that the interpretations of the Delphic oracle, as well as others, were simply made up by the interpreters, even prepared ahead of time.

Paul seems willing to accept the fact that ecstatic utterances will be made, but imposes two regulations. First, the utterance must be interpreted, and by more than one other person, presumably to get some reasonable consensus that the rest of the group can understand, so that the interpretation will conform to the group's habitual religious experience. Second, Paul seems very concerned about the effect of ecstatic utterance on any outsiders who happen by – he is afraid that if all the members of the group speak in tongues at once, they will seem to an outsider to have gone crazy. Paul's fears seemed sufficiently justified for stringent controls to be imposed on the synaxis.

### Epistle

In general, the bishop soon came to designate who was to sing or speak and what they were to sing or say. It is easy to see that since one of the principal functions of the bishop was that of teacher, the teaching at the synaxis was done in the sermon or homily by the bishop himself or by someone whom he had instructed. And in the early decades the letters of instruction (the *Epistles*) of Paul and other leaders, addressed to various congregations such as the Corinthians or the Ephesians (in Ephesus, Turkey, on the eastern shore of the Aegean Sea), were used to instruct other congregations as well; these letters, or portions of them, were read aloud at the beginning of the synaxis, and found a permanent place there under the liturgical rubric of Epistle.

*Gospel*

While not included by Justin in his brief description, Gospel readings soon became part of Christian worship. The function of singing the Christian epic in the synaxis was taken over by the reading of the Gospel, which contained the story in simple prose narrative. In the early centuries there were more gospels in circulation than just the four that became canonical – the books of Matthew, Mark, Luke and John. The restriction to these four was another type of episcopal regulation of the synaxis.

The episodes selected to be read at the synaxis Sunday after Sunday told the story of Jesus' earthly mission, recounting his birth, the miracles he performed (but not so often his teaching), his passion, crucifixion, resurrection and ascension. These readings became the basis for the church year, the liturgical calendar. Together with the excerpts from the Epistles, they were analogous to the cycles of readings from the Law of Moses and from the Prophets used in the synagogue, but of course the texts were entirely different. A supplementary cycle of prophetic texts from the Old Testament was sometimes incorporated into the Christian synaxis as a local, variable practice.

*Songs and heresy*

The above account covers most of what Justin Martyr described as happening at the early Christian service; but it does not include everything that Paul had listed. In particular we are missing the solo songs and ecstatic utterances. Were they eliminated completely? Or was a place found for them?

Very few Christian songs or personal or ecstatic utterance are preserved from the early centuries; almost all that can be positively identified are those rejected by early Christian writers as unsuitable for Christian worship. In order to brand these songs as heretical and keep them from being sung, these writers had to name the songs, or even quote from them – which in some cases is the only reason we know they were there at all. Tertullian, a very creative personality and perhaps the most brilliant speaker and writer of Latin in early Christianity, devoted a whole book to exposing heretics and their songs.

The end of Tertullian's own story is ironic, and deeply revealing: he himself adopted a type of doctrine called Montanist, which was eventually judged heretical by the Catholic establishment. This happened because Tertullian's passionate concern for Christian truth was rooted in a belief in personal inspiration as a source for that truth; thus Tertullian's problem was a basic problem for early Christians (and later ones, too). In his case, the Catholic establishment was not persuaded by Tertullian's personal inspiration and conviction, and did not accept what he said as true. The logical consequence of the establishment's policy was that individuals should not be allowed to contribute in their own words to the synaxis, lest these words be not in accord with Catholic teaching.

Tertullian's own struggle with this contradiction may suggest a complicated and unexpected explanation of the musical forms used for Gregorian chant several centuries later. Tertullian was at one point involved in a confrontation with a certain Marcion, who had his own version of Christianity. Tertullian reported that a woman in his own congregation gave evidence of religious ecstasy in the form of inspired responses to prayers, lessons or psalms said and sung in the service. Tertullian challenged Marcion to produce someone who could show a comparable level of inspiration. It is clear from this that Tertullian put great faith in the evidence of ecstatic inspiration as proof of truth.

The logic of Tertullian's argument may seem unduly intricate to modern observers, but is characteristic of the early Christian concern for right thinking that produced traditional forms of Christian worship. The ecstasy to which Tertullian referred was experienced by the woman as a member of the congregation *in response to something said by someone else* during the synaxis. This response, in other words, was not a completely unsolicited contribution; hence, it could be understood as a legitimate part of the regulated synaxis. This was true whether the response was intelligible discourse, or unintelligible ecstatic utterance that required interpretation. And in *responding* to an officially enunciated truth, an individual could feel that his or her response was both truly inspired and also a personal contribution to worship.

At this point music became a crucial factor in the argument. For it was the *words* of an individual's contribution that held the danger of false doctrine, while melody, since it did not assert doctrine, was not dangerous. But Christian melody was sung (instrumental music being considered inappropriate); and singing used words. Was there a way to have melodies without words, or beyond words? There was indeed; we call it melisma. It asserted nothing, but could mean anything the singer wished, or the listener wished. What did it say? How much intuitive perception of truth is resident in melismatic chant? How much ecstasy? I can answer that question only with another: How much ecstasy did you want to hear?

Hence melisma, pure music without words, could be considered a way to make an individual response in the synaxis. No early Christian melisma is preserved in written form, simply because no early Christian music of any kind was written down. Nor did anything like the utterances of Tertullian's inspired woman survive into Catholic liturgy, at least, not into the Roman synaxis. There is, however, the coincidence that the Gregorian repertory provides melismatic music for an item which the Roman Mass Propers call

a *responsory*, the Gradual responsory. We can, if we wish, see this responsory as the last opportunity for individual expressive response to the official
readings within the synaxis.

### The psalm in the synaxis

Bishop Ambrose of Milan, writing around 380, mentions that a psalm was
sung at the synaxis. He thereby specified that it was not just any song, but
a song of David, one of the 150 Psalms from the Book of Psalms in the Old
Testament; and its performance at the synaxis was no longer by just a
member of the congregation (as Paul seems to indicate) but rather by a duly
appointed lector who sang a psalm selected by the bishop. And to this
psalm, Ambrose tells us, the congregation *responded*, singing something he
called a 'response to the psalm'. The response was specific to the psalm, and
actually used words excerpted from the psalm, so there could be no chance
that it introduced any idiosyncratic conviction or interpretation. And the
congregation responded all together.

It looks as though Ambrose, one of the most creative personalities in the
development of early Christian liturgy, was looking for a way in which the
congregation might still participate in the synaxis with a feeling of individual contribution. Ambrose's way made use of two ideas that had emerged by
the fourth century. The first was that the language of the psalms (which
could feel very personal) was in fact inspired; this was part of a much larger
programme of establishing all of the Hebrew Scriptures as inspired by God
and therefore suitable for Christian belief. This was not easy to establish,
but by the fourth century the point had been made.

The second idea attributed truth to a personal response *if it was part of
a group response*, one made by the whole congregation. There was a persistent conviction among early Christians that if a congregation responded
as if with one voice, it must have been because of an inspiration that they
all shared. Such an inspiration (so some thought) could only come from
God, and so the response was in itself evidence of God's truth. This mystical idea was articulated in a principle called *lex orandi lex credendi*, meaning roughly, 'Whatever the congregation has pronounced in traditional
public worship must be true Christian doctrine'. How complex was the
relationship of thought, words and musical performance in Christian
liturgy!

It appears that Ambrose's 'response' to the psalm was a way to guarantee
that even though an individual's response might feel like personal inspiration – or at least conviction – it could still be correct doctrine. The people
could respond with the theologically safe words of the psalms, and since
they responded as if with one voice, by the principle of *lex orandi lex credendi* it must be true.

## Alleluia in the synaxis

The mysterious expression *Alleluia* is the Hebrew acclamation *Hallelujah* rendered in Latin without the initial *h*. It turns up sporadically in the context of early Christian worship during and after the fourth century. Our lack of firm information reflects early Christian uncertainty about its meaning and value as much as it reflects varied use around the empire. The word was borrowed from the Psalter, where it was included in certain psalms. Christian writers considered it a praise-word, telling their readers that it meant 'Praise the Lord!' ('Hallelu-Jah[weh]'). As a Hebrew expression it enabled Christians to avoid the more common Greco-Latin praise-words of traditional cult, and so became not only popular but officially approved. Eventually it was used extensively in the Latin liturgy, and could even be repeated endlessly without alarming those who were sensitive to the association of such repeated expressions with non-Christian cult.

One use of *alleluia* as a praise-word was to greet the reading of the Gospel in the synaxis. In this function the word acquired two distinctive features within the Gregorian repertory, either or both of which might go back to the fourth century (or might not). One feature is a melisma on the last syllable, 'alleluia-a-a-a-a-a-a' , which has been given the name *iubilus*. The other feature was a sentence of Latin, usually a verse from a psalm, added to define the meaning of the exclamation – for not only was the Hebrew term unfamiliar, but the melisma, being pure melody without a word, could mean anything.

## The ordered synaxis

Except for melisma, then, the synaxis came in the fourth century to be performed throughout in an orderly way, as Paul had so ardently desired that it should be; but this meant that all the items he had mentioned were now either under the direct control of the bishop, or else had been discouraged. Members of the congregation were now effectively excluded from contributing individually to the synaxis by using their own words: it was no longer speaking together, sharing individual religious experiences, it was listening to what was said and sung, learning what the bishop understood Christianity to be.

## Morning and evening services

It would be difficult to identify the morning service or the evening service as specifically Christian, or Jewish, or Greek or Latin. Greeting the sun in the morning and settling down in darkness at eventide invite ritual observance more than almost any other universal human experience.

Liturgists point to hymns (that is, expanded hymnic expressions) as the primary form of sung worship, and to the morning and evening hymns as the core of the morning and evening services. We actually have what may be the Christian prototypes of morning and evening hymns, dating from perhaps the second century – and if so, they are the earliest texts sung regularly in Christian worship. They represent the quality of that worship as no other text can.

As the morning and evening services developed in the fourth century and later, the core of each service – the hymn – became increasingly difficult to see, for it was virtually covered up with a heavy layer of psalms from the Old Testament. Furthermore, in the Latin services the morning hymn was eventually shifted from the end of the morning service to the beginning of the synaxis; the synaxis followed immediately, however, so the morning hymn was not moved far, and had much the same function in the synaxis.

The morning hymn is the *Gloria in excelsis Deo* ('Glory be to God on high') and has remained familiar in its new position near the beginning of Mass. The Latin services never used the original evening hymn, the *Phos hilaron* ('Hail, joyful light'); it is used regularly only in the Greek service, but English translations and adaptations are found in European and American hymn books.

### Gloria in excelsis Deo

As a prototypical form of early Christian worship the *Gloria in excelsis Deo* includes pure praise-words, followed by the kind of language needed to give these words a specifically Christian identity. (See the Latin and English versions in the Commentary on the compact disc.)

The hymn begins with the song of praise attributed in Luke's Gospel to the angels, as heard by the shepherds in the night of Christ's birth at Bethlehem: 'Glory be to God on high, and on earth peace, good will to men' (or 'to men of good will'). The scriptural quotation identifies the hymn as Christian. Then come the praise-words, which are generic: 'we praise thee, we bless thee, we adore (worship) thee, we glorify thee'. The central expression 'to glorify' is expanded in the next sentence with the basic Hebrew-Christian idea that blessing is equivalent to giving thanks, rendered in Greek as *eucharistein* and in Latin as *gratias agere*. This is followed by divine attributes, 'O Lord God, heavenly king, God the Father almighty', and eventually by petitions and a closing doxology.

### Phos hilaron

While the archetypal evening hymn, *Phos hilaron*, never became part of the synaxis, it is another example of the way a praise-word could be expanded into a beautiful expression of religious feeling. In this case the expression was both broad enough to serve as an utterance of the whole congregation, yet focused on the particular theme of evening. While it included a theological assertion about the nature of God, the scope and tone of the rest of the poem (excluding the assertion) could appeal to anyone, Christian, Jew or non-Christian. For in the form of the Lighting of the Lamps (Latin *lucernaria*, Greek *epilyknion*) the evening service was loved and cultivated throughout the empire. The praise-word is 'we hymn ...'. It is followed immediately by one of the earliest explicit statements of the Holy Trinity, cited by Basil (around 375) in a passionate argument pleading the doctrine of the Holy Spirit as the third person of the Trinity. If Christians have sung those words in that ancient hymn (argues Basil), then it must be good doctrine. This is an early citation of *lex orandi lex credendi*.

Joyful light of holy glory
of the immortal Father,
heavenly, holy, blessed,
Jesu Christ!
Coming to the sun's setting,
seeing the evening light,
we hymn the Father and the Son,
and the Holy Spirit of God.
Thou art worthy at all times
to be hymned with blessed sounds,
Son of God, giver of life:
therefore the universe glorifies thee.

*Gloria in excelsis Deo* and *Phos hilaron* both show the characteristic transmutation of traditional forms of devotion into something peculiarly Christian. Sun-worship was widespread: early Christians were scolded on at least one occasion for pausing outside (on their way to the morning eucharist) in order to greet the rising sun as a god, thereby failing to distinguish between the sun and the true God whose light illuminated all human existence. *Gloria* is a radiation that surrounds a deity; Luke's words 'Gloria in excelsis' place this light 'on high' in the middle of the night, so this image can be used as a morning hymn while avoiding any confusion with the rising sun. The *Phos hilaron* also praises light from God, and finds it shining brightly at the very moment when the sun is disappearing. In both cases a very human act of worship is being attached to a specific theology.

No early melody is preserved for either *Gloria in excelsis* or *Phos hilaron*. We usually assume that these words were sung by the congregation to melodies appropriate to their musical experience.

The Greek hymn from Oxyrhynchus, however, discussed in chapter 4, is preserved with its own melody. Since its melody has musical notation in its third-century source, that melody is the only Christian one unequivocally documented before AD 700, since melodies of *Gloria in excelsis* and *Phos hilaron* were written down only after that time. A beautiful melody such as the one from Oxyrhynchus would be an expressive enhancement for the morning or evening hymn.

## Psalms and canticles

Just as praise-words were fleshed out with other diction to make a substantial song, so these hymns were used with other forms of worship to make the morning and evening services.

Much singing together was done at the morning and evening services. We know that by the fourth century such singing took the form of songs excerpted from the Hebrew Old Testament; these were the theologically safe Psalms of David, as contained in the Psalter, or other songs sung by individuals in the narratives of other books of the Old Testament. The first and favourite one was the Song of Moses, the victory song he sang after he led the Israelites safely through the Red Sea as the Pharaoh with his cavalry perished (Exodus 15:1–19).

Other songs were searched out and collected by liturgists; they were called *odes* or *canticles*, these being common words for song; they might be called '*spiritual* canticles'. Together with the Psalms of David they were held up to Christian worshippers as the proper alternative to what the authorities called 'personal psalms', *psalmi idiotici*, meaning songs composed by individuals (as opposed to those in the Bible, which were presumed to be inspired by God). By the fourth century the Catholic establishment's mistrust of songs contributed by individuals took the form of official-sounding injunctions. One would-be authoritative document specifically prohibited personal psalms, at least from the synaxis and eucharist.

Somewhere around this time (fourth or fifth century), the selections of psalms and canticles for the morning and evening services were standardized. We do not know if these were the original songs for those services, but they can be assumed to be at least analogues of the originals. Since they were selected deliberately, they could vary according to need and preference. They were all performed as choral odes. For the morning service as sung in Latin, some of the preferred selections were these:

Psalm 117 (118): *Confitemini Domino quoniam bonus* (O give thanks
    unto the Lord, for he is gracious)
Song of the three young men in the fiery furnace (Vulgate: Daniel 3:52)
Psalms 148, 149, 150 (as a unit)
Canticle of Zacharias (Luke 1:68): *Benedictus Dominus Deus Israel*
    (Blessed be the Lord God of Israel)

Added at the end of the morning service, this last item was taken from the beginning of Luke's Gospel, the Infancy Narrative of the birth of Jesus (Luke 1 and 2). In Luke's Gospel account it was cast as a solo song, put into the mouth of Zacharias as a greeting for his newborn son, who will become John the Baptist. Zacharias sings a blessing, a thanksgiving to God: sitting in the Temple, Zacharias meditates on the expected redemption of Israel, in which John will take a part (text and translation in the Commentary, for track 25). A congregation of Christians, having performed their morning hymn, could continue together singing Zacharias' meditation as their post-celebration song, their 'after-praise'. In the monastic Office (as we shall see in chapter 7), this service is timed to end just at daybreak ('first light', well before sunrise), so that the verse 'to bring light to them that dwell in darkness and in the shadow of death' is perfectly appropriate.

### Evening service

Similarly at the evening service, where Psalms of David precede the hymn, another canticle from the Infancy Narrative (Luke 1:46) follows the hymn. This is the *Magnificat*, the song Luke attributes to Mary the wife of Joseph, as her response to the miraculous confirmation that the baby she is carrying in her womb is unique. The song (very similar to one in the Old Testament sung by Hannah in 1 Samuel 2:1–10) also looks forward to God's saving the people of Israel. As with the Canticle of Zacharias in the morning service, worshippers could meditate on the Christian application of Mary's *Magnificat* while singing it as a post-celebration ode after the evening hymn.

In this way the morning and evening services took on specifically Christian forms and identities. These were the forms in which ordinary Christians worshipped, Christians who lived in towns and belonged to congregations led by the local bishop. The morning and evening service, along with the synaxis and eucharist, constituted what is called the *cathedral rite*, the basic rite of early Christianity. It is distinct in principle and in practice from the monastic rite, which will be described in chapter 7.

### Liturgical sentences

The morning and evening services in the cathedral included one more element, brief but essential. Just as the eucharist was facilitated by brief exchanges between the bishop and his people ('The Lord be with you', 'And with thy spirit'), so were the synaxis and the morning and evening services. Ritual worship, it seems, always made use of such short sayings to ease the liturgical intercourse between people engaged in the service; with these brief verbal exchanges they coordinated their activities and encouraged each other. This ritual rhetoric facilitated communal worship just as the rhetoric of politeness eases social intercourse in daily life.

In antiquity this ritual rhetoric was paralleled by a love of inscriptions, sayings inscribed in stone and used on grave-markers to commemorate the dead, on temple walls as witness to divine aid, on public posts for a wide variety of expressions. Such inscriptions (thousands have been collected) are often in verse (such as dactylic hexameter) or artistic prose; those in Latin draw on the natural aptitude of that language, as developed in antiquity by several generations of writers, for concise elegance in well-turned phrases. Pope Damasus, bishop of Rome in the fourth century, had a number of inscriptions made and carved in stone and displayed for all to see in prominent places around the city, usually commemorating saints and martyrs.

The distinctively Christian aspect of this widespread habit of 'one-liners' was the use of the Hebrew Old Testament, especially the Psalms of David. Christian writers of the fourth century quoted the Old Testament copiously, especially the Psalter: they knew much of it by heart, and quoted it by heart, as we can tell from the frequent slight variations in usage. They would quote a verse of Scripture to prove a point, and their knowledge of Scripture was such as to enable them to find just the verse to settle almost any question that came up. The quotations, however, might be short, and often assumed a knowledge of the context in order for the full meaning to be grasped.

To mention a few verses quoted in musical contexts, a verse from Psalm 118 (119), 'Seven times a day I have given praise to thee, for the judgments of thy justice', was quoted as a basis for including seven 'day-hours' in the Divine Office (see chapter 7). As part of an objection to music in worship, a verse was quoted from the prophet Amos (5:23): 'Take away from me the sound of your songs: to the voices of your instruments I will not listen.' A more general criticism of women making music in public quoted the prophet Isaiah (5.11–12): 'Woe unto them who drink wine to the accompaniment of cithara, aulos, tympanum and song'. A verse of Psalm 67 (68) was even shouted at the non-Christian emperor Julian the Apostate at a street demonstration: 'Let God arise: let his enemies be scattered.'

Similarly, pithy sentences from the psalms were used in worship services like audible inscriptions, or like clincher-quotes, set out for all to hear at many points during the services. They were a prominent part of the repertory of ritual rhetoric. By a remarkable intersection of desirable features, psalm quotations, if appropriately selected, could evoke profoundly human responses to the problems and opportunities of spiritual life while using a language almost distant enough to suggest to sophisticated urban Romans the ecstatic utterances of glossolalia, or at least the hoary inspired quality of the ancient Hebrew prophets. Several centuries later, by the time of the Gregorian repertory, the Latin of the Psalter was no longer everyday language; hence, by that time (if not earlier) the psalms were distanced in the same way that the King James translations used here are distanced from twentieth-century language. Finally, the theology of the psalms was sufficiently monotheistic to avoid criticism from any of the combatants in the tense Trinitarian controversies of the fourth century.

These liturgical sentences consisted of one, two or three clauses (not so often more). Their grammar was basically different from cultic, ritualistic acclamations, for those were sometimes just heaped together in a forceful, if potentially rowdy, sequence. In contrast, the sentences were always grammatically complete clauses, even when using compressed, laconic Latin word-structures, and even when the original Hebrew diction was exaggerated and metaphorical.

The sentences had been carefully selected from Scripture so as to be self-sufficient, meaningful and expressive. They expressed a wide variety of feeling, and were applied to liturgy so as to represent the deeply felt response the congregation might be expected (or encouraged) to have to aspects of religious experience evoked by the readings, odes, prayers – or by the festivity being celebrated. Here are some of the sentences assigned to the Propers for the Mass on Christmas Day, which are sung on the compact disc, tracks 2–6.

All the ends of the world have seen the salvation of our God: O be joyful
    in God, all ye lands. (Psalm 97 [98])
Thine are the heavens, and thine also is the earth:
the round world, and all that is therein hast thou founded;
justice and judgement are the habitation of thy seat.
    (Psalm 88 [89])

Sometimes the sentences were vivid characterizations of the mood of the occasion.

Unto us a child is born: unto us a Son is given:
the government shall be upon his shoulder;
and his name shall be called Angel of mighty counsel.
    (Isaiah 9:6)

Liturgical sentences were sung at the synaxis and the morning and evening services, grouped either with each other or with lessons, hymns or choral odes to make a carefully varied flow. They could be used as prefixes or introductions to odes or other parts of the service. They could return at intervals throughout an ode, like a refrain, or they could be added on to the end of another item simply as a suffix. They could even be used as an *infix*, or interlude, in some other item (this function sometimes has the name *verse*, which can be confusing because that term is used in so many other ways; see the Glossary).

Sentences could be performed in various ways to fulfil these different functions. As a suffix a sentence was often intoned by a soloist and answered by a chorus, forming a *versicle-and-response*. After a hymn, for instance, they might sing,

[*versicle*:] The Lord hath made known, alleluia [*response*:] his salvation, alleluia.

(This example is on track 24.) In the special function of *verse*, a sentence was often performed by a soloist. This often happened in combination with another sentence performed by the chorus as a response, which was then called technically a *respond*, the whole combination respond-verse-respond being a *responsory* (this example is the Gradual responsory on track 3).

[*respond*] All the ends of the earth have seen the salvation of our God: O be joyful in God, all ye lands.
[*verse*] The Lord hath declared his salvation:
In the sight of the heathen hath he openly shewed his righteousness.
[*respond repeated*]

The most complex combinations of all, however, occur in connection with a kind of performance called antiphony.

*Antiphony*

Antiphony is an important ingredient in early Christian worship. Actually it is more than an ingredient – it is itself a basic form of worship, a musical form, one whose tradition seems to go as far back in human history as we can imagine, and to be universal in use. It was used by Christians from early times, if always with some reservations.

Antiphony is produced when groups of singers echo or answer one another, singing in alternation rather than all at the same time. Singing antiphonally is *not* singing as if with one voice – and right there is the reason antiphony had such an ambiguous position in the history of early Christian worship. It has also been given confusing descriptions in modern accounts by liturgists and historians; but these are historiographical, not musical, problems. The *musical* effect of singing in alternation is simple enough to be understood by anyone, and furthermore it is all around us as an optional kind of performance in the music we hear daily.

Writing at the time when the Gregorian repertory was being completed (around 830), Amalarius of Metz gave a charming Christian interpretation of antiphony, identifying it as the love, that is, the relationship, between the two halves of the chorus; he particularly had in mind antiphony as used in group worship in a monastic community. In similar terms we can describe antiphony as an equal and reciprocal relationship between semichoirs. Antiphony is a *musical* quality, and as such cannot be defined too strictly – but we know it when we hear it.

Much of the attraction of antiphony is that it is exciting to listen to – and exciting to perform. The source of this excitement is easily identified by comparing antiphony with singing in unison. While it is true that my voice is my own and is a primary expression of myself, when singing unison with a chorus I seem to be participating in an archetypal form of worship: in unison singing my voice is joined with others' voices in one of the most beautiful close encounters humans can have. In antiphony I can have this experience of unison singing within my own semichoir, but almost at the same time have the different experience of hearing the other semichoir; and – uniquely in antiphony – they may be singing almost the same music. There is feedback, instant playback: it is not listening to someone else per- form something else. The feeling of singing a phrase and of hearing it come at once, and feel the stronger for being not exactly at once.

Of prime importance in this experience seems to be the start of each new phrase sung by each semichoir, marking the rhythm of the alternation. Each new beginning (called in musical performance an *entrance*) seems to mark a rhythmic pulse. The pulse can be slower if the phrases are long, and get faster if the phrases are shorter; but it will be just as strong whether one semichoir repeats exactly what the other sang, or whether they sing some- thing different (and both happen in antiphony). There can be a competitive quality to antiphony, which often shows up as a tendency for each semichoir to sing a little louder or faster than the other. In Christian worship the com- petition is usually friendly: we can delight in outdoing each other in love and praise. There can be eagerness, anticipation, moving us to begin phrases too soon, creating overlap with the other semichoir. Since this will be reciprocated, the two semichoirs will start to tumble over each other, with momentary confusion – but also richness – in the sonority at every exchange.

This seems a very attractive possibility for group worship; but some early Christians apparently found it too seductive. Christian prudence, alarmed at possible disorder in worship, called for control: if antiphony was to be used at all, let it be done with certain kinds of words whose phrases are long enough to restrain the buildup of momentum, and whose diction is such as to avoid the acclamations of the mob; and let there be no spontaneous change in the wording or word order.

In actual practice, early Christians probably used antiphony more frequently, and with more enthusiasm and disorder, than the authorities desired or than liturgical historians admit. It seems, however, to have been a common musical habit to resolve any disorder by adding a kind of conclusion in which the two semichoirs joined together to sing in perfect unison. An analogous procedure later became standard in European polyphonic practice, choral or orchestral.

Antiphony was used extensively for items such as hymns and choral odes. It lent itself naturally to psalms, since in Latin translation every psalm was divided up into verses, and the verses were syntactically complete; hence in *antiphonal psalmody* the change of semichoir could be made easily at every verse. Furthermore, many verses consisted of two more or less equal parts, and so the alternation could also be by half verses; but since in any given psalm some verses would not have two parts, the alternation was not straightforward and would have to be worked out ahead of time.

Psalms were sung antiphonally in monasteries, where (as we shall see) they were sung complete and in great numbers, so antiphony made the work of psalmody easier. But antiphony seems to lose its musical point after a minute or two, and when used for complete psalms does not generate its characteristic excitement.

Much more congenial to antiphony are the liturgical sentences; they provide its most characteristic application, as well as scope for artistic imagination in creating varied combinations. The Greeks, with a passion for giving everything its own name, had separate names for half a dozen different ways of performing sentences in antiphony, according to the different functions being fulfilled. The Latins, with an even greater passion for general terms denoting orderly categories, called all these different ways simply antiphon, and the only thing true of all of them was that they could involve alternation between semichoirs. The Latins sometimes exercised the option *not* to sing antiphonally: especially in later practice, longer antiphons such as those at the Introit were sung straight through by the full choir, and this is the practice that survived to the present. Since the piece is still called an 'antiphon', however, we can see that this practice has obscured the use of antiphony in early Christian worship.

Antiphony played a major role in the singing of the morning and evening services, being used most prominently for the psalms and canticles. At Mass, we shall find antiphony used before the synaxis in the entrance rite which gradually took shape as an introduction to Mass, and after the eucharist, at Holy Communion.

## Antiphony at Mass

Some early sources suggest the following scenario for the beginning of the synaxis: the people are gathered in God's holy temple waiting for the service to begin, and they occupy themselves with singing together, in antiphony, the Psalms of David, which were understood to anticipate or prefigure the coming of Christ. At some point the bishop made his appearance among them – and it seems that his entrance often coincided in a seemingly miraculous way with some especially significant verse of the psalm being sung. It was an easy step from that to providing a special sentence to prefigure the occasion of the synaxis. Similarly, after the Heavenly Banquet, singing a psalm together as after-praise would be only natural, and here, too, a significant sentence could be used in antiphony.

Especially in connection with antiphony, Christian music for worship shows itself to be a potentially complicated art form. Sometimes the complication is such as to make the distinction between antiphony and response seem to disappear. But the difference remains and is a profound one with several aspects. For instance, a response is typically made just once, while antiphonal alternation has to happen more than once to have any effect. Furthermore, the people making the response – typically the congregation – wait to hear everything they are being told, then acknowledge and confirm it. But in antiphony, the two groups may be expressing more or less the same thought, and scarcely wait for each other to finish.

An early Christian liturgist might say that response was sacred, a basic religious posture of man towards God; but that antiphony, if it involved a response at all, was the response of man to man, possibly leaving God out. In any case, antiphony has always had an ambivalent position in Christian worship, raising questions about its propriety precisely because of its popularity.

## Variation

Whether performed antiphonally or responsorially, liturgical sentences were one of the principal means of making one liturgical occasion different from another. Early Christian worship moved slowly but steadily towards a careful balance between sameness and difference – between using the same forms and same words on each occasion, and varying them for the sake of greater interest or in order to provide more opportunity for individual expression.

The synaxis was by its nature variable from one occasion to the next. The original plan of the synaxis allowed for various individuals to bring new and different experiences so that all might gain in knowledge. Furthermore, the variation in the synaxis could be specific to a particular time and place, to a 'happening'. 'Why have we come together here and today?' The contents of the synaxis would provide the answers. There is one ancient group of sentences that all begin with *Hodie* – '*Today*, let us celebrate . . .' – as a way of introducing the day's theme, the feast or saint's day. Hence even when the synaxis came to be strictly regulated as to who was to sing or read, and what words were to be sung or said, still the songs and readings were different from one occasion to the next; and it took much arranging over several centuries before all these texts were specified so that each could be said exactly the same a year later, as the annual cycle was repeated.

The generic name for all these variable sentences is *Proper*: a sentence is said to be proper to an occasion, and is called, for instance, the Proper Introit for Christmas. The variable sentences taken together are called the *Proper of the Mass*, or the *Mass Propers*. In this use the term proper can mean 'appropriate' in the sense of making specific reference to the theme of the day. It can also, however, mean simply 'appointed' or 'assigned', so that many times when we look for the specific reference in a given chant to its liturgical context we may not find an obvious answer.

For this reason it seems better to take the words of the variable sentences at their face value, to hear them articulating basic religious ideas and feelings. Regular worshippers would appreciate the fact that these verbal expressions always change from one occasion to the next: the variability has the immediate and obvious effect of producing variety in the liturgical experience, and often no other explanation seems necessary. The 150 Psalms of the Old Testament Psalter contain such a wealth of poetic expression that basic universal religious feelings can be expressed in different wordings at every one of the dozens of occasions (Sundays, feast days and saints' days) in the church year. The Gregorian repertory includes, for instance, about 150 sentences just for antiphony at the Introit; so aside from particular sentences that are memorable because of association with an important feast, many sentences will seem fresh as they appear only once a year in the annual cycle.

Singing or hearing the variable sentences is a very different experience from singing or hearing the items that do not vary, such as the *Gloria in excelsis*, the *Sanctus*, the people's responses to eucharistic prayers. Such invariable texts acquire their depth of expression from their perennial sameness: they have the tremendous momentum of tradition. Each kind of Christian liturgy sought its own balance in combining variable and invariable texts in the worship service.

# 6
# Gregorian Chant in the Roman Rite

The early Christian service of eucharist, combined with a synaxis, developed steadily during the centuries, and was elaborated in various ways in different localities around the Mediterranean and in Western Europe. At Rome, the combined synaxis and eucharist, eventually known as Mass, came to have certain features that – while not unique – were cultivated there to a distinctive degree. These features concerned liturgical sentences (described in chapter 5) and were the immediate preconditions of Gregorian chant.

By the year 700, Roman liturgists had developed a system of liturgical sentences to be sung at Mass in the synaxis. The Roman system provided sentences at the entrance rite (the Introit antiphon), after the Epistle (the Gradual responsory), before the Gospel (the Alleluia), during the collection of gifts (the Offertory), and during the distribution of Communion (the Communion antiphon). The words of these Roman sentences were taken almost exclusively from the Bible, mainly from the Book of Psalms. Following ancient civic customs of the calendar, Roman liturgists carefully assigned the sentences (along with prayers and readings) to the months and seasons. These Roman sentences were sung neither by the bishop nor by the people, but by solo singers and a trained choir. In all these respects, but especially in the reliance on soloists and a choir, the Roman system of sentences was strikingly different from the earliest practices of Christian worship.

We learn first about the Roman service of Mass with its system of sentences from a type of document called an *ordo*, which is simply an order of service. The earliest existing ordo, believed to represent Roman liturgical practice around 700, is called *Ordo Romanus I*, from its position at the head of a long series of documents that describe exactly how some part of the Roman rite (Mass, Divine Office, or some special part) was performed. (The series was published in modern times as the *Ordines Romani*.) The implication of the series as a whole is that it not only describes how the services were performed in Rome itself or according to Roman practice, but also *prescribes* how they are to be performed in the north, beyond the Alps. In other words, these orders of service implement the Carolingian project of worshipping in communion with the pope in Rome.

*Ordo Romanus I* describes *pontifical Mass*, Mass as performed by a *pontiff*, a bishop, in this case the pope as the bishop of Rome. (In the absence of the pope or some other bishop, Mass was performed by a parish priest with simpler ceremonial.) The ordo gives a detailed picture of the ceremonial performed by the pope and his liturgical assistants – what they did, where they stood and how they moved around the altar, how they handled the materials needed for Holy Communion. *Ordo Romanus I* might have been written by a church official in the city of Rome, or by an observer visiting from the north. In either case it seems to have been addressed to northern liturgists who wanted to know how Mass was performed in the Eternal City.

Description of the ceremonial of the Roman Mass has been attempted many times since *Ordo Romanus I*; detailed accounts have been published all the way down into the twentieth century. The ceremonial was already complicated when it was described in *Ordo Romanus I*, and it did not get any simpler as time went on. But no matter how full of detail a description of Mass may be, it can never account completely for how Mass *was* on any given occasion, and it can never give a definitive global concept of what Mass *is*. A reliable impression of Mass can be gained only by attending one; consequently the account in *Ordo Romanus I* cannot substitute for witnessing a Mass in the eighth century.

Furthermore, just as with the cathedral in which Mass is performed, there is too much detail in a performance of Mass to be subsumed under a single idea. An observer, even a participant, perceives only some of what goes on. For this reason Mass generates multiple impressions, varying from one observer to the next, varying also – for one observer – from one time to the next.

## Many voices at Mass

Mass generates multiple impressions for another reason, too. Mass is like a piece of musical polyphony, in which a number of distinct musical voices are combined in a way whose total resultant sense may be difficult to discern. There are a number of different voices sounding at Mass. These are not, however, actors in a drama, and it is incorrect to describe Mass as dramatic; rather, the different voices come from the various worshippers participating in the liturgical action.

First there is the voice of the bishop; then that of the congregation, which ideally speaks with one voice; then there are the deacon, the lector, the solo singer (cantor) and the choir. We can also count as voices the authors of the words that are sung, even if nothing is known for certain about them as individuals: these include whatever bishop composed the eucharistic prayer and the other prayers, the evangelist who wrote the Gospel, and Paul or who- ever wrote the Epistle. The psalms were traditionally ascribed to King David, and references to his voice are frequent in the Middle Ages; now- adays we speak of the voice of 'the Psalmist'.

The words the choir sang, then, present the Psalmist's voice. At another level the voices of the singers can be taken to represent the voices – ideally, the *one* voice – of the congregation. But whose voice is heard in the solo chants, especially in the mysterious melismas, where there are no words to identify the source? The simple answer is the voice of the singer. But who is this singer, and what role does he have at Mass? Answers to those ques- tions were not clear at the time of *Ordo Romanus I*, and have not been much clarified since. For that reason the functions of Gregorian chant at Mass are not obvious, and not stable.

## Liturgical order of events

In this chapter I describe the order of Mass – first briefly, giving the most general impression of the liturgical and musical events; then in more detail, with commentary about the meaning of the various liturgical functions and description of the chant that would have been sung in the eighth century. My account tries to give a sense of the flow of liturgical action through the several larger divisions of the whole service and an idea of the place of music within that action.

While *Ordo Romanus I* is a uniquely valuable report of early liturgy, giving us very specific information, we still have to use our imagination in reading it. Since the document gives information about ceremonial that northern liturgists might need in attempting to reproduce the performance of Mass in the Roman style, much of what it describes is of no interest to worshippers or observers; and the document makes no attempt to explore the meaning of the liturgy. While *Ordo Romanus I* is exact about the actions of the ministers around the altar, it is often casual and presumptive in its references to singers and chants. For specific information about the Gregorian chant items presumed by *Ordo Romanus I* we must go to the earliest chant books themselves, which are Carolingian.

*Ordo Romanus I* holds few surprises for readers acquainted with the Roman Mass as it was performed before Vatican II; still, a few aspects may differ. While keeping close to *Ordo Romanus I*, I have added a few essential details that in all probability reflect eighth-century practice. My commen- tary is supplemented by my reading of other liturgical information from the same period (there is not much), but more substantially by the chant as notated in the earliest chant books.

*Liturgical space*

Here I shall sketch very briefly and abstractly the kind of space in which we can imagine the rite of *Ordo Romanus I* taking place. The churches of Rome vary greatly in design (as do churches throughout the world). What is sketched here is the so-called Constantinian T-shaped basilica, referring to the type of grand structure (*basilica*) with the ground plan of a T; a number of these were built by Constantine the Great (reigned as emperor of Rome, 306–37), the first Christian emperor.

Liturgical space is the space needed to carry out the various liturgies, or actions appointed for the various participants at Mass. In the most general terms, the people congregate in the main part of the building called the *nave*, the vertical member of the T. (The crossbar of the T can be used for entrances.) The nave runs (ideally) from west to east; the congregation, standing in the nave, faces towards the east end, where just beyond the crossbar is the *sanctuary*, a smaller space appointed for the bishop and his assistants in the liturgy. The sanctuary has at its centre the *altar*, an elevated structure like that originally used for sacrifice. The actions of the first half of Mass, the synaxis, are carried out by the assistants in the space between the altar and the front of the nave, directly in front of the people. The second half of Mass, the eucharist, is performed by the bishop and his assistants standing around the altar. At Holy Communion the people come up to the dividing line between the nave and the sanctuary to receive the consecrated bread.

The choir has no specially appointed place. That is because its liturgical assignment is ambivalent. As a token chorus, the choir sings on behalf of the people, hence can stand in front of them. As appointed by the bishop (yet not ordained as clergy), the singers can also stand with the other assistants between the altar and the people, or around the altar at the eucharist.

# ENTRANCE RITE

*Antiphony at the Introit*

The choir (seven adult male singers, of which three are soloists, plus a group of boys) stand before the altar in two columns; they are between the altar and the nave, facing east, as does the congregation. They sing antiphony with a psalm, in a moderately elaborate style. This is the first item of Gregorian melody at Mass.

The bishop and his assistants (deacon, subdeacon, and acolytes carrying a processional cross, candles, censers and holy water) enter from the side and approach the altar, moving up through and past the choir. As they stand directly in front of the altar, facing east, the bishop kneels to make his private prayers. When he is ready to proceed, the choir leaves off the antiphony to sing the *Gloria Patri* (the little doxology); then resumes the antiphony briefly while the bishop and his assistants take their positions around the altar.

## Kyrie eleison, Christe eleison

At the bishop's signal, the choir begins singing the *Kyrie eleison* and all continue in congregational intonation, perhaps in antiphony, in the manner of a solemn litany.

## Gloria in excelsis Deo

Facing east, the bishop intones the morning hymn, beginning with 'Glory be to God on high', to which all respond with 'And on earth peace to men of good will', the other half of the song ascribed to the angels; then all continue in congregational intonation, perhaps in antiphony, singing praises with the greater doxology.

## Greeting and Collect of the day

After 'The Lord be with you', to which all respond 'And with thy spirit', the bishop intones the brief summary prayer appointed for the day, singing to a recitation formula. All respond 'Amen'. Then the bishop sits down on one side of the sanctuary.

# SYNAXIS

## Epistle

A lector reads the first lesson, using a simple recitation formula; the reading is usually from one of Paul's *Epistles*.

## Gradual (responsory)

A cantor ascends halfway up the steps (*gradus*) of the pulpit to sing. The choir sings the first part, the respond, in elaborate Gregorian style, and the cantor sings a verse in even more elaborate style, with at least one melisma; the choir repeats the respond. (This is the second item of Gregorian chant at Mass.)

## *Alleluia*

In preparation for the Gospel, the choir sings *alleluia*, again in elaborate Gregorian style with the iubilus melisma. Another cantor sings a verse, also melismatic, from the steps of the pulpit. (This is the third item of Gregorian chant at Mass; during the penitential season of Pre-Lent and Lent it is replaced by a Tract.)

Meanwhile, there are ceremonial preparations to read the Gospel: the deacon and assistants form a procession with candles and incense; the Gospel book is prepared and carried solemnly down towards the people.

## *Gospel*

The reading is announced, the people respond with a brief sentence (*Gloria tibi Domine*, 'Glory be to thee, O Lord'), and a section from one of the four canonical Gospels (Matthew, Mark, Luke, John) is proclaimed, sung in a relatively elaborate recitation formula; the people respond at the end.

If there is a sermon or homily, it can be given at this point. (Eventually the Nicene Creed, the *Credo*, came to be sung here by all, or by the choir; but this did not happen in Rome until much later, in the eleventh century.)

# EUCHARIST

## *Offertory*

The bishop greets the people with 'The Lord be with you', and they respond. He and his assistants collect gifts ceremonially from representatives of the congregation, and prepare the altar.

Meanwhile the choir sings a sentence (the Offertory) in elaborate Gregorian style and a cantor adds verses as needed to fill out the time. (This is the fourth item of Gregorian chant at Mass.)

## *Eucharistic prayer*

All the assistants, with candles and incense, are arrayed around the altar, behind the bishop and his deacons (information varies as to whether the bishop stands with his back to the congregation, facing east, or on the other side of the altar facing the congregation). The bishop begins the 'song of victory': he again greets the congregation (*Dominus vobiscum*, 'The Lord be with you'), then begins the introductory dialogue (*Sursum corda*, 'Lift up your hearts'), continuing with the variable part that commemorates the day (the Preface), sung to an elaborate recitation tone. It leads directly into the Angels' Hymn,

*Sanctus* ('Holy, holy, holy'), which all sing in congregational intonation. The bishop continues with the invariable part (the Canon) of the eucharistic prayer, ending with a doxology, to which the people respond 'Amen'. The bishop appends the Lord's Prayer, sung to its own recitation formula.

# HOLY COMMUNION

The bishop greets his ministers with the Kiss of Peace (and they pass it down around the congregation). Standing at the altar, the bishop and his assistants break bread (the Fraction). The bishop sits down, and the assistants regroup to distribute the bread to all present.

*Agnus Dei*

Before or during the distribution the acclamation *Agnus Dei* ('O Lamb of God') is sung, perhaps by all in congregational intonation; antiphony is an option.

*Antiphony at Communion*

During or after the distribution of bread a sentence with verses from a psalm is sung antiphonally by the choir to a style of melody comparable to that used for the Introit. (This is the fifth and last item of Gregorian chant at Mass.) The assistants clean up the altar.

*Collect after Communion*

The bishop, standing before the altar, intones a brief summary prayer (the Postcommunion Collect). All respond 'Amen'.

## Blessing and dismissal

The bishop blesses the congregation, and the deacon bids them depart: he sings *Ite, missa est* ('Go, the Mass is ended'), and they respond, *Deo gratias* ('Thanks be to God').

## The entrance

At the time Gregorian chant was being conceived there was apparently a shift in the meaning of the antiphony at the entrance. In an earlier practice, the congregation, while waiting for the arrival of the bishop, sang psalms, meditating on the way the Old Testament materials 'prefigured' or forecast the coming of Christ. At some point (not necessarily predetermined, but for best effect it could be arranged ahead of time) the bishop entered. There would be a model for this kind of entrance in Luke's Gospel (Luke 24:36). After the resurrection, Jesus made one of his several appearances (in resurrected form) to the disciples. Luke described the scene: 'And as they thus spake, Jesus himself stood in the midst of them, and saith unto them, Peace be unto you'.

In the later version of the entrance – the version that became traditional – the entrance antiphony was understood to proclaim the formal beginning of Mass in a festive manner. Some Gregorian Introit chants do indeed have a festive, proclamatory quality, for instance *Puer natus* for Christmas; but many others, especially those for ordinary Sundays, are not festive at all, but rather reflective, sombre, or even penitential. As the words come from the Old Testament, however, their use by Christians can be understood as meditative on a prefiguration, to be interrupted in a wonderful way by the feast commemorating the Christian realization of what was dimly prefigured – as Isaiah's prophecy of the birth of a saviour is fulfilled by the Nativity of Christ.

The form of the Introit antiphony presented by the earliest chant books begins with a main part, called antiphon, using words excerpted from the Bible, usually from a psalm. The antiphon can be sung antiphonally (even though this was not the later practice), alternating phrase by phrase between two parts of the choir, for instance, men and boys, or the two columns mentioned in *Ordo Romanus I*; and the antiphon can end with the whole choir singing together. Then a soloist sings a verse, usually taken from the same psalm; more verses could be used to extend the meditation, and they too could be sung in antiphony; and the antiphon itself was repeated, perhaps more than once. Track 2 on the compact disc is *Puer natus*, the Introit for Christmas Day (antiphony is rendered in that performance by alternation between male and female voices).

When psalms were sung in the monastic Divine Office (as we shall see in chapter 7), it had become standard practice early on to sing 'Glory be to the Father, and to the Son, and to the Holy Spirit' after each psalm, to ensure

Christian identity, in particular, Trinitarian identity – Catholic as opposed to Arian, which attributed less divinity to the Son. The *Gloria Patri*, being a doxology, counts as a hymn; hence, it is a formal, solemn act of worship. This doxology was used at Mass only for the antiphony at Introit and Communion.

In strict liturgical practice everything stops for this doxology; that is why *Ordo Romanus I*, in a characteristically intricate detail, has the bishop signal the leader of the choir to stop singing antiphony and sing the *Gloria Patri*, so that all may stand together in formal praise. This little doxology is distinct on the one hand from the meditative antiphony, and on the other hand from the greater doxology, the *Gloria in excelsis*, which follows as the festal morning hymn.

## Kyrie

The cry *Kyrie eleison*, Greek for 'Lord have mercy', was used extensively and traditionally in litanies sung in penitential processions that took place inside the cathedral as well as outside through the streets of the city. It is used here at the beginning of Mass as a borrowed refrain, continuing and concluding the meditative mood of the antiphony. In the practice of *Ordo Romanus I* it could have been repeated a number of times, as in a litany; and there might have been specific petitions sung by the bishop or deacon. Roman practice also included a parallel expression, *Christe eleison*, giving a Christian identity to an originally non-Christian acclamation, and specifying the *kyrie*, the lord, to be Jesus the Son of God; nonetheless, *kyrie* could also mean God the Father or the Holy Spirit in this context.

In the older Roman practice, the repetitions of *Kyrie eleison* and *Christe eleison* would have been sung in unison congregational intonation; the *una voce* sound, even when reflective rather than acclamatory, would have reverberated through the basilica as an expression of the people as a whole. But the *Kyrie* could, as an option, be sung antiphonally, the repetitions lending themselves naturally to alternation between two halves of the congregation, or between congregation and choir, or some other arrangement according to local practice. What, then, would happen to the *una voce* sound? It would still be unison singing, but the alternation, with a stereophonic effect, would introduce a different dimension. It seems, however, that it was always very desirable for all to join in for a truly unison conclusion to the series of petitions. In any case, this became a standard musical procedure in later practice.

Beginning some time after 800 the northern singers replaced congregational intonation of the *Kyrie* with much more elaborate melodies; these could be sung only by the choir, and were sometimes brilliant. But many of the new elaborate northern melodies still had a sombre, reflective cast, continuing the meditative quality of the original antiphony. At the same time that it was given elaborate melody, the litany-like open-ended succession of petitions was formalized into a closed set consisting of three times *Kyrie eleison*, three times *Christe eleison*, and again three times *Kyrie eleison*. This became the traditional arrangement, used for all Kyries at Mass from that time down to Vatican II.

### Gloria in excelsis Deo

The archetypal morning hymn appears at Mass as a festive proclamation; it is used only in festal times and seasons, not in Advent or Lent. Its Christian identity comes from the opening quotation from Luke's Infancy Narrative (Luke 2:14), telling how the angels sang to the shepherds in Bethlehem at Christ's birth; this gives the hymn a scriptural source, but does not limit it to Christmas, for it is just as appropriate to Easter. It is by nature the people's glorification of God; and here the sound of congregational unison intonation would be most prominent. But antiphony is an option, and as with the *Kyrie*, would add another dimension to the unison effect.

Also as for the *Kyrie*, northern singers soon supplied elaborate new melodies for the *Gloria in excelsis* – more elaborate than congregations could sing. Some of these new melodies were clearly festal in their musical qualities. Composition continued into the eleventh and twelfth centuries, some melodies becoming elaborate and even ecstatic. Others, even from this later time, retained some features of simple intonation, or exemplified a style that at least suggested congregational intonation, even if the congregation did not participate.

### Greeting and Collect of the day

The greeting and response *Dominus vobiscum. Et cum spiritu tuo* ('The Lord be with you. And with thy spirit') establishes the essential liturgical relationship between bishop and people, the two principals in Christian liturgy. First used here, the greeting recurs several times during the Mass. It is often followed, as here, by the bishop's *Oremus* ('Let us pray') and a prayer.

This particular prayer is a short, solemn statement of the purpose of Mass in that particular time and place – the feast or occasion of the day. It is called a *collect* because it summarizes ('collects') the thoughts that the bishop and congregation might have had individually while meditating before Mass. It is a formal address to God in Latin that is newly composed (by bishops), not taken from the Bible. Composed in a tradition of finely crafted Latin prose, Roman collects have an unusually concise and elegant diction. They are the principal element in a book called a *sacramentary*, which contains the bishop's repertory of prayers.

The function of this collect can be read in two ways – either as the conclusion of the entrance rite, or as the beginning of the synaxis. It comes as the natural conclusion of the antiphony and the *Kyrie*, and some liturgists believe that its sense is that of rounding out and completing the arrival at the altar and the preparation for Mass. On the other hand, since this marks the bishop's first greeting to the people, and his first public prayer, it seems like the proper beginning of the synaxis. In any case, the bishop, having been involved centrally in all the items of the entrance, now sits down, and the synaxis is performed by other ministers.

## Synaxis

This part of Mass can best be understood as a series of different items set out by different performers for all to hear. In the context of *Ordo Romanus I* there are two (infrequently three) readings from the Bible, each sung by a different reader to a different recitation formula. Between the readings come two different Gregorian chants, sung by the choir with various soloists, in very elaborate melismatic style. The congregation participates only in a few brief responses. The bishop has previously approved the selections of words to be sung, and also approved the selection of singers (thereby, indirectly, the melodies), but he does not participate in the performance.

### Epistle
Infrequently there is a reading from the Old Testament, called a *prophetia* (prophecy); it has a function analogous to the prefigurations of the entrance antiphony. Usually, however, the first reading is from one of the Epistles of the New Testament ascribed to Paul or to other writers. The Epistle, read from a lectern without ceremony to a simple recitation formula, is offered as straightforward moral or theological instruction.

### Gradual
In the context of *Ordo Romanus I*, the Gradual is sung by choir and soloist (singing from the steps, *gradus,* of the pulpit); nothing else is going on at the altar. This, the second item of Gregorian chant sung at Mass, is the most prominent, and is sung in the most elaborate style. As a highly developed liturgical form that already had a history of two or three centuries, it represents several accumulated layers of meaning.

The top, most recent layer of meaning, as apparent in the earliest chant books and presupposed in *Ordo Romanus I*, is that of a very sophisticated piece of music performed for whatever effect it may have on the listeners. The most general effect is that of refreshing the ear after the reading of the Epistle. The words being sung are not very audible because of the elaborate melodic style with its occasional melismas; yet the words were carefully selected, and can be understood to articulate appropriate responses in the context of Mass as celebrated on a particular occasion (this kind of meaning has to be studied case by case).

The Gradual is called a responsory because, it seems, it was once a response by the congregation to the readings – their contribution to the synaxis. As explored in chapter 5, this would be an old (but perhaps not the oldest) layer of meaning, deeply buried under two or three centuries of liturgical development. Since in the context of *Ordo Romanus I* the Gradual is sung in an elaborate Gregorian style, the congregation can participate only vicariously, by feeling the sentiment expressed by the words and the musical meaning of the singing by choir and soloist. The words are often in the first person singular (typical of many psalms); the sentiments are usually of a kind that a meditative listener could be expected to have in response to the particular occasion or feast day.

The musical form of the Gradual includes a first part for choir, called the *respond* and representing the response of the congregation; and a second part for soloist, called the *verse*. The verse acts as an episode or bridge that extends the piece and expands the meaning of the respond, which may be repeated after the verse.

## Alleluia

The *Alleluia*, sung by the choir with a solo verse (from the steps of the pulpit), also uses a melismatic style. It combines the Hebraic expression of praise with a selected psalm verse. The *Alleluia* functions as an acclamatory preparation for the reading of the Gospel, which follows immediately. For special feasts the wording of the psalm verse refers to the theme of the feast; sometimes the wording recalls an item sung previously on that day. On ordinary Sundays the wording may simply be an appropriate expression of Christian thought and feeling. Often the wording bears no specific connection to the Gospel that it introduces.

Some of the other Latin liturgies (Milanese or Gallican) occasionally provided a special chant to introduce the Gospel; this special introduction would be not a variable sentence selected from the Psalter, but rather one fixed text used to introduce the Gospel reading at every Mass.

At the same time that the northerners gave the *Kyrie* and *Gloria in excelsis* more festive music, they also provided many new *Alleluia* melodies, some of an extreme brilliance, by way of making a more festive introduction to the Gospel.

## Gospel

Whereas the Epistle, being simply instruction, was read by a lector without ceremonial, the Gospel is introduced by elaborate ceremonial, in order to solemnify the reading of an episode from the epic story of Jesus' earthly ministry. The book containing the four canonical Gospel accounts

(Matthew, Mark, Luke and John) was treasured by early Christians: it was often a deluxe edition, carefully stored and produced only for reading at Mass. When the Gradual was ended, the Gospel book was carried by the deacon to the bishop, who blessed it and the deacon; candles and incense were prepared and – accompanied by the singing of the Alleluia – carried by acolytes in procession, leading the deacon with the Gospel book down towards the congregation, perhaps into the nave. There the Gospel reading was announced, the congregation responding briefly; then the book was censed with a thurible. The deacon sang the Gospel reading in a relatively elaborate recitation formula.

At the end of the synaxis there could be a sermon or homily. Then, in the early centuries, the deacon cried 'Let the catechumens depart', meaning the inquirers who were not yet initiated; and the doorkeepers saw them out.

## The eucharist

The eucharistic prayer as a whole is the most deliberately focused part of the Mass. Its overall sense, as discussed in chapter 5, is the bishop's formal address to God, in which he states what he understands to be the rationale of the Sacrifice of the Mass, its purpose and meaning.

Before the eucharistic prayer comes the liturgical action called the Offertory. And after the eucharistic prayer comes, as the next event, the liturgical action of Holy Communion, the 'Heavenly Feast'. This is commonly included in the general notion of eucharist, but is nonetheless a distinct liturgical action as a sequel to the eucharistic prayer.

### Offertory

The bishop's greeting marks the beginning of this liturgical action. Gifts, contributions from the people, are collected from the congregation and brought to the altar; these may be money in some form, and in early centuries they were often goods, which made the collection considerably more cumbersome than the discreet collection in modern times. *Ordo Romanus I* presumes that the pontiff himself, assisted by acolytes, made the collection, at least from the most prominent citizens at the front of the congregation.

The gifts of the congregation are *an* offering, and they are presented to God at the altar by the bishop. But they are not *the* offering, which is made only by Christ as his self-sacrifice. This is what the bishop tries to make clear in the eucharistic prayer; this action is what is *re-presented*, that is, recalled and invoked, in the Sacrifice of the Mass. The language of eucharistic prayers can become intricate in attempting to include both these senses of offering while keeping them distinct.

While the collection of gifts and the subsequent preparation of the altar are going on, the choir sings the Offertory – the term is transferred from the liturgical action to the chant. The Offertory chant is the fourth item of Gregorian chant at Mass; it is in a moderately elaborate style somewhere between that of Introits and that of Graduals, but occasionally with a spectacular melisma.

The Offertory sentence is usually a psalm excerpt. While the sentence may be selected to refer specifically to the theme of one of the principal feasts, for ordinary Sundays it consists simply of words appropriate for meditation. But seldom does the sentence refer directly to the collection of gifts that is going on simultaneously, or to the liturgical Sacrifice of the Mass that is to come. *Ordo Romanus I* does not even indicate when the Offertory chant begins, but merely says that the bishop signals the choir to leave off when he is ready to proceed to the next action. The primary function of the Offertory chant, then, is to articulate thoughts and feelings appropriate to personal meditation, presenting them in a musical form that can absorb the attention of the worshippers while liturgical functions are going on.

At the time of *Ordo Romanus I* and for several centuries after, the soloist sang additional sentences as needed to fill out the time required for the collection. These additional sentences were usually selected from the same psalm, each functioning like the verse of a Gradual, expanding and developing the thoughts and images of the first sentence. There might be two or three verses, each with its own melody in a remarkably elaborate, sometimes flamboyant style, including some of the longest, most ecstatic melismas of the Gregorian repertory. After each verse the choir sang the ending part of their sentence as a reprise.

*Eucharistic prayer*
When the bishop is ready to proceed, he signals the choir to stop singing the Offertory sentence (presumably at some reasonable point in the series of verses and reprises); he greets the congregation, and initiates the brief dialogue (*Sursum corda*, 'Lift up your hearts'), engaging their participation in the giving of thanks. Then follows the bishop's victory song, the eucharistic prayer.

The bishop stands at the altar, his deacons beside or behind him. All the other ministers and acolytes stand or kneel around and behind, facing the altar, holding candles and censers. The first part (the Preface), sung to a relatively elaborate recitation formula, recounts the acts of God being celebrated on this particular liturgical occasion. From other documents originating near the time of *Ordo Romanus I* we find for this part of the prayer many alternative wordings for different occasions, but each one is relatively concise.

This Preface elicits the ultimate expression of praise and adoration,

'Holy, holy, holy', in the form attributed by Isaiah to the seraphim surrounding the throne of Yahweh (but also found elsewhere as praise of non-
Christian deities). The congregation is otherwise silent throughout the
bishop's song, but here at the *Sanctus*, as if unable to contain itself, the congregation joins in – or did before the chant sung by the choir became too
complex. *Ordo Romanus I* seems to presume congregational intonation led
by the choir. In any case, it is a solemn moment. All bow low; in one devotional practice the censers are swung in huge arcs on their three-foot long
chains, filling the sanctuary with clouds of smoke, just as Isaiah recounted.
(Very bold acolytes have been known to swing their censers in complete
circles overhead.)

Just as for the *Kyrie* and the *Gloria in excelsis*, northerners provided more
elaborate melodies to replace congregational intonation of the *Sanctus*.
Some of these later chants, sung by the choir, show a brighter glorification,
others an intensely introspective adoration. Many still use the kind of
melodic simplicity that evokes the solemnity of a congregational intonation.

After the *Sanctus*, the bishop proceeds; the Roman wording of the
eucharistic prayer was fixed from the time of *Ordo Romanus I*, but its performance has taken various forms over the centuries, and the question of
what happened in the time of *Ordo Romanus I* is the subject of intricate
research, not completely conclusive. This part of the eucharistic prayer has
the deepest sense of mystery; it was for this reason that in the Roman Mass
as performed until the time of Vatican II the prayer was said so softly as to
be inaudible to the congregation.

So although the eucharistic prayer is a unit, and can all be regarded as the
bishop's song – the victory song of Christianity – in traditional Roman practice only the first part is actually sung out loud. At the doxology that ends
the prayer, the bishop again raises his voice in the same recitation formula
used for the initial dialogue, and the people respond Amen, which, though
short, voices their essential participation in the eucharist.

The chant of the eucharist, then, includes the opening dialogue (*Sursum
corda*), the part of the prayer sung aloud by the bishop (Preface), the congregational intonation of *Sanctus*, the closing doxology, and the congregation's Amen – but no chants from the choir's Gregorian repertory.

In the Roman Mass the bishop then appends the Lord's Prayer, 'Our
Father, who art in heaven ...', so as to include Jesus' own prayer reported
in the Gospels (Matthew 6:9–13).

## Communion

From a technical point of view, the Lord's Prayer concludes the eucharist;
but the Communion service that follows is such a natural consequence that
the distinction is not very apparent to observers. In what follows, the focus

shifts to the congregation's participation in the Heavenly Feast, a traditional conclusion to a ritual sacrifice. The distinction between eucharistic prayer and Communion is important because it defines the kind of music involved.

The liturgical action of Communion is the distribution and consumption of the consecrated bread. From a liturgical or theological point of view there is nothing more to be said. On the other hand, once the bishop's formal address is ended, there is no obstacle to singing, either by the congregation or the choir. There is a tradition of Christian singing at the feast that goes back to Matthew's Gospel (Matthew 26:30), where at the end of the Last Supper the disciples went out after 'hymning' (various Bible translations give expanded, sometimes unwarranted, interpretations of this term). In broader cultural terms, singing at such a celebration would be normal, especially at a post-sacrificial feast.

## Agnus Dei

The acclamation 'O Lamb of God, that takest away the sins of the world, have mercy upon us' was not added to the Mass until close to the time of *Ordo Romanus I*. Its addition was attributed to Pope Sergius (687–701); the action of a bishop would in any case be required for such an addition. Since the *Agnus Dei* had no traditional status, however, its liturgical position was not fixed exactly for two or three centuries; *Ordo Romanus I* indicates that it was sung at the breaking of the bread.

Like the *Sanctus*, the *Agnus Dei* was in the nature of a congregational intonation, sung by all those standing around the altar with the congregation joining in, led by the choir; and the singing included antiphony. Later, northerners gave the *Agnus Dei* a more elaborate chant, to be sung by the choir.

## Antiphony at Communion

Antiphony at Communion, the fifth item of Gregorian chant at Mass, was analogous to the Introit antiphon for the entrance. Early Christians had a tradition of singing a psalm during or after Communion; sometimes it was Psalm 33 (34), including the appropriate verse 8, 'O taste and see that the Lord is good'. This would be a song of fellowship, a natural accompaniment to the communal meal. During such a song the congregation might well reflect on their shared faith and perhaps specifically on the theme of the day.

The Gregorian repertory included a Proper Communion antiphon for every feast and Sunday, in much the same format as the Introit antiphons, that is, including a verse from a psalm, and a *Gloria Patri*. The sentences provided for the Communion antiphony vary greatly (more than the other items of the Propers) in their nature and meaning: many are from the Book of Psalms, but a number are taken from the Gospels. On feasts they tend to refer to the theme of the day, and even – to a greater degree than any of the other Proper chants – recall words sung previously at the same Mass. On other occasions they may refer specifically to Communion, but more often they present merely general thoughts and feelings. The Gregorian melodies, too, vary in style: some are simple (but not so simple as to be congregational), while others approach Introit antiphons in elaborateness. A Communion antiphon may have its own individual style.

### Postcommunion Collect

When the liturgical functions associated with Communion are finished, the bishop offers a brief final prayer – again, a general summary (hence a *collect*) of private meditations.

The Postcommunion collect is nominally proper to the occasion; but many of these collects, especially for Sundays, express essentially one and the same thought, worded a little differently each time.

These Postcommunion collects, in other words, could be replaced by one standard prayer; but they are not. It seems distinctive of the Roman liturgy to provide elegantly varied wordings just for the sake of variety – or perhaps to recall the time when such prayers *would* have varied slightly because of being composed by the bishop at the moment, as inspired prayers. We can read many of the Gregorian Propers, in words as well as in melody, in the same way, understanding them to express the one constant meaning and function through endless elegant variation. This interpretation seems especially appropriate to an appreciation of the melodies, which also tend to feature elegant variation rather than literal repetition.

Mass according to *Ordo Romanus I* has neither a climax nor a big ending. Instead, after the Postcommunion collect, the bishop lets the people depart with his blessing. In later European culture Mass was sometimes read as a drama, attempting to find climax along with action, characters and plot; but those ideas are not really there. And musicians, especially in recent times, have been anxious to find an excuse for glorious music at the end of Mass. The Gregorian repertory, close to the classic form of Mass as found in *Ordo Romanus I*, provides no music after the Communion antiphony.

The northerners, however, supplied one more bit of elaborate chant for the deacon's *Ite, missa est* ('Go, the Mass is ended'), sometimes using a melisma borrowed from the opening *Kyrie eleison* – thereby using a purely musical recall for a sense of closure. In any case the congregation's response, *Deo gratias*, repeats the deacon's melody.

# 7
# *Monastic Chant in Time and Eternity*

Early Christian liturgy was an encounter with God; so was the monastic life, but by a different route. The Gospels told how Jesus went to Jerusalem – to the City – to complete his mission. And the city was where the early church was. The bishop had his cathedral in the city: there the people came together, sang together in unison, followed their bishop to the encounter with their God.

But there was another way, pursued by the many who fled the city, fled from everything and everybody in it, everything it stood for. They sought whatever they were looking for within themselves, each within himself or herself. They might call it 'God'; if they were Christians they called it 'Christ'. This was the meditative life: it was isolated, solitary, inner. For these people, group activities in general and Christian liturgy in particular, while useful for meditation, were used at the side of the inward path that led to a place known only to the traveller.

In the third and fourth centuries thousands and thousands of people fled from the cities around the Mediterranean. They came from all walks of life, all social classes, but especially from upper classes; they were well-to-do, well-educated people. They were not simply escaping from the deteriorating material conditions of the cities, some of which were very old and becoming very crowded (the population of Rome at its greatest has been estimated at close to a million). These people were experiencing all the problems of the urban environment, well known to us. But they did not flee to suburbia or to the countryside for a better domestic life, nor for better economic or social conditions. To the great alarm of established urban society – Christian as well as non-Christian – privileged members of that society went to the wilderness, to a state of nothing, or as close to nothing as they could endure. From Alexandria, one of the most brilliant, luxurious cities of the eastern Mediterranean, they fled into the Egyptian desert to live in sand-caves. Or rather, they lived inside themselves, reducing the distractions of physical existence to the absolute minimum, so as better to meditate on the ultimate realities of their existence.

Two things happened to these solitaries in the wilderness to produce the monastic life as we know it in European history. The first was of necessity, or at least expediency: as Spinoza said later about the intellectual life, 'To philosophize one first must eat'. The physical needs of existence were most expeditiously met by communal effort, and so the solitaries banded together in communities for survival.

The second element, less obligatory and always only one of several options, was social interaction and communication. In the early stages this sometimes came about through the person of the holy man – an individual famed for spiritual insight and wisdom. Crowds gathered around such individuals, and many settled down to become resident disciples. The holy man would take responsibility for their welfare, physical as well as spiritual: he would organize their material existence, and prescribe a regimen of spiritual exercises, to be done individually and together. Antony and Pachomius were two of the most famous such leaders. At first we hear only of male leaders; after some experimentation in the best way for both men and women to live the monastic life, rules emerged for separate communities for women, and eventually female leaders appeared. Radegund, in the sixth century, was one of the first to head a women's community in France.

We can think of early Christian worship on a continuum extending between the two extremes of monastic meditation in the wilderness and urban fellowship in the cathedral. Almost immediately, however, positions of moderate compromise appeared in between these two extremes. Social interaction among the solitaries in the wilderness, resulting in communal worship that included the eucharist, was one compromise; another appeared in groups who lived a separate and communal life under a rule but remained in the city – urban monastics. In still another compromise, groups of devout urban Christians within a congregation followed an intensive schedule of worship activities of a quasi-monastic type. Such groups, known in later centuries as confraternities and still later as prayer groups, might function on their own without the bishop's supervision; but to a great extent such activities were co-opted by the bishop. Taking place in the church building, these activities were controlled by the bishop just as he controlled the eucharist and the morning and evening services.

## *Benedict's* Rule

European monastic life was modelled on prominent Near-Eastern types. Europeans who visited at length in the Near East returned home to organize communities. Out of this came distinctive European types of monastic life. With the eventual institutionalization of the monastic life, the leader was titled 'abbot' (*abbas*, father), and his regimen was called in Latin a *regula*, 'rule'. The most famous European rule was that of Benedict, drawn up around the year 540. Benedict, son of a well-to-do family, retired first to the wilderness outside Subiaco (Italy), then later, as disciples gathered, to Monte Cassino. His *Rule* was very successful, becoming normative for communities that wanted to be identified as 'Benedictine', and influential as a model for other rules that governed other monastic orders.

Benedict's *Rule* was popular because it was such a skilful compromise – a civilized compromise – between the needs of physical existence and those of solitary spiritual life. His *Rule* was distinguished by its practicality and Roman urbanity. In contrast to extreme ascetic activities undertaken by some enthusiastic early monastics, Benedict's provisions for daily communal worship could be carried out without endangering personal health, yet left ample opportunity for individual spiritual development.

Still, Benedict's *Rule* perpetuates the paradox inherent in the monastic life: its very urbanity is part of what he tried to flee. A well-regulated life was not necessarily what people sought in the desert. Insofar as communal worship was regulated – no matter how well – it was not the same thing as being alone with one's inner self. The need to flee even from a regulated monastic life continued strong in Benedictine monasticism. Around the year 1000, at the very well-regulated Benedictine community of St Gall, Switzerland, the monk Hartker had himself walled up in a tower; food was passed in through a window so that he could devote himself to meditation. But even Hartker could not evade the paradox: he spent some of his time writing out one of the earliest and best complete chant books containing all the elaborate variable music for antiphons and responsories for the whole church year.

### Meditation and psalmody

This paradox in monastic life can be understood in terms of a standard technique of meditation known to us as a mantra. It involves preoccupying the lower levels of consciousness with appropriate materials of imagination while allowing the upper levels to venture wherever the spirit will. The distinctive feature of Christian monastic meditation has been the use of certain kinds of literary materials, especially the Psalms of David. Psalmody is the *singing* of psalms; from early times singing was an essential part of the use of psalms for meditation. For this purpose recitation formulas, psalm tones, seemed the proper way to sing the psalms, with most of the syllables being intoned on a reciting pitch.

The use of the 150 Psalms of David was, of course, part of the Christian turn to the Hebrew Old Testament in the fourth century. The psalms were distanced from modern city life; their Latin diction, even though well made and consistent, was not suited to urban taste. As Hebrew poetry the psalms sang of passionate or exalted feelings, existential and theological insight, history and epic. Some psalms expressed group adoration, some personal agony; and some consisted of deprecatory and self-deprecatory abuse of a particularly unattractive kind. Cathedral use of the psalms has usually been very selective, for only some psalms have seemed appropriate for public Christian worship.

No selection was made, however, for the purposes of a meditative mantra; rather, the Psalter of 150 Psalms was sung in its entirety, beginning at the beginning and continuing until the end, then starting over again. This was called the *continuous* Psalter; it was a *cursus* (course) of psalmody, called *cursive* psalmody. The only question was when to stop for rest or other physical need.

In the early days there were reports of heroic recitations of the whole Psalter in a single night. Benedict's civilized compromise was for a minimum of twelve psalms each night, and he apologized for the fact that predecessors did more. His schedule of twelve per night became standard; it was called the *ferial* Psalter ('ferial' here means daily, as opposed to 'festal', meaning for special occasions). It was arranged so that the entire book of 150 Psalms was said complete each week; hence it is also called a *weekly* Psalter. Most of the psalms – the minimum of twelve – were said at night in services called *Nocturns*, soon to be described in more detail.

What was it like singing psalms for an extended period in the middle of the night, night after night, singing by heart in a dark church by the light of a single candle (the 'light of Christ')? Only those who know can tell, and they are usually reluctant to do so. Some reports consist of the inner feelings, the mystic visions achieved during the experience. Evagrius Ponticus, one of the earliest to write extensively on the monastic life, said, '... you will be raised on high like a young eagle'. Much later the poetry of the mystic Hildegard of Bingen expressed the visions of her meditations in the musical forms of chant for the Divine Office. Other reports emphasize the outward hardship. Psalmody was known by the Benedictine term *opus Dei*, the labour for God. Eventually boys' choirs sang the Nocturns in cathedrals, and in the Middle Ages it was said that when a choir boy died young, the Requiem Mass should be said not as for a young child but rather as for a martyr. In spite of all, something sustained the nightly singing of the ferial Psalter for over a thousand years.

Not, however, without basic modifications – including the introduction of antiphony along with the melodies for liturgical sentences. Just as the Psalter itself was not a simple mantra but rather a complex, extended literary text, so the modifications brought in more and more words in increasingly varied formats. Even without considering their melodies, the new forms of words tended to be specifically poetic, and thereby to introduce new dimensions in the music of language. The new forms made extensive use of melody in the most specific musical sense, as well. Although the various modifications were all subject to rational scrutiny rather than being adopted through unconscious tradition, they seem to have entered monastic life at more or less the same time, and early on. Separately and together they brought problems, new possibilities for the monastic life, and also repercussions for cathedral practice; the eventual impact on Gregorian chant was profound. But music, while it can accommodate itself to all sorts of purposes, still has something of its own to say, and may have had its own effect on monastic life – even to the extent of changing the model for meditation.

## Eucharistic worship versus monastic meditation

Along with well-regulated modes of life, monasteries also developed elaborate services of praise and prayer. They included the services already established in the cathedral rite – synaxis and eucharist, morning and evening services – but went far beyond these to create a distinctive monastic programme that went on all day, every day.

Monastics used the cathedral worship services with the same pragmatism that they used in anything else; for in leaving the city they had left behind the bishop as well as the urban congregation. This raised problems concerning the eucharist, for the eucharist was the special function of the bishop leading his congregation. The bishop's jurisdiction was within his diocese, or provincial unit, usually a town or city; as the unit became extended, the bishop delegated priests to celebrate the eucharist at parishes in his stead; and sometimes he delegated assistant bishops to serve congregations in the countryside.

The bishop had no jurisdiction in the wilderness, however, and the solitaries were not part of any bishop's congregation, so the question arose of how to have the eucharist if they wanted it. (Down to the present, monastic congregations of women have needed a male priest to say Mass – and will as long as women are not ordained priests.) Already in early days various arrangements were made; eventually the eucharist was celebrated even more frequently in monasteries than in cathedrals; but the gap between monastery and cathedral remained, with important consequences. Monastery and cathedral were distinct administrative units within the emerging superchurch, not infrequently in an adversarial relationship, with occasional stand-offs.

The eucharist was at the centre of the monastic problem of being alone together, for it was essentially a communal worship service, hence different from the original monastic drive to be solitary. Even though communal worship, both in the eucharist and also in the other services, became basic to most monastic rules and establishments, it remained distinct from solitary meditation, and for some could be just a halfway house between the city and the wilderness. The distinction between meditation and fellowship as paths to God was to bring with it a difficult and fascinating perspective on music, especially on Gregorian chant.

## The Divine Office

The cathedral morning and evening services, on the other hand, were much closer in nature and purpose to the core of monastic meditation, which was the nightly cycle of psalm singing. By the fourth century the morning and evening services already included psalms and canticles (as described in chapter 5); in adapting these services to their own purposes the monastics added more psalms and integrated them into their extensive nightly schedule. The daylight hours were then filled out with four very short services, 'check-in' times at three-hour intervals. The four services were called *prime*, *terce*, *sext*, *none* for the first, third, sixth, ninth hour (of daylight). Finally, monastics performed the complete cycle of nocturnal psalmody, morning praise, the daylight hours, and evening praise on every day of the week, not just on Sunday.

This perpetual round of psalmody, further expanded with readings from the Bible, prayers, and liturgical sentences (to be described in more detail), is known as the *Divine Office*. The Latin term *officium* is merely a very general word for any appointed ceremony; the main reason for using it in the present context is to refer to all the parts of the daily cycle together, distinguishing them as a group from the Mass. The Divine Office was usually performed complete only in monasteries, and was also known as the monastic Office. It was such an impressive construction, however, that it came to be regarded (at least by some) as ideal worship valid for all Christians everywhere, and furthermore as a complete and perfectly unified entity. In reality, the Divine Office varied in detail from place to place, and was performed with many different degrees of accuracy and completeness; and it had been put together out of many disparate parts and materials.

In the Middle Ages, cathedrals with sufficient resources also performed the complete Office; the necessary resources, however, included a staff of resident clergy living a quasi-monastic life in the cathedral complex, the 'close' or cloister, as well as a large permanent choir. The worshippers at such a cathedral Office would be not the congregation as a whole, but small segments of it, consisting of devout urban Christians – those participating in prayer groups, for instance.

The impact of the monastic Office on the cathedral services can be seen clearly in the assignment of psalms for Sunday Vespers as contrasted with the assignment of psalms for Sunday Lauds, the morning service that would be conducted in the cathedral as part of the weekly gathering of the urban community. The psalms for this archetypal morning service had been selected because they were appropriate for the occasion – for example, Psalm 62 (63): 'O God, thou art my God; early will I seek thee'. Sunday Vespers would be the other service (besides Mass) that the urban congregation could be expected to attend. The psalms for Sunday Vespers, however, were not selected because they were appropriate to the occasion, and, indeed, are not particularly appropriate. There exist beautiful evening psalms, for instance Psalm 140 (141) with the verse 'and let the lifting up of my hands be an evening sacrifice', but these were not used for Sunday Vespers, whose psalms are 109, 110, 111, 112, 113. In the monastic Office these five psalms were assigned as part of the week-long cursus of psalmody that included the whole Psalter (Psalms 1–108 having been assigned to the Night Office at the rate of twelve a night for seven nights, the remaining Psalms 109–146 were assigned to Vespers at the rate of five a night, beginning on Sunday, as did the other elements of the Divine Office.) Their presence in a cathedral service reveals the profound impact of monastic ways of thinking on liturgy intended for urban congregations.

## Psalms, hymns and canticles of the monastic Office

The following outline of psalms, hymns and canticles in the Divine Office shows the daily cycle of monastic worship. This list shows merely the order of services throughout the twenty-four-hour cycle, and mentions the archetypal sung elements. As the Office developed during the early centuries it came to include additional elements, such as versicles-and-responses; various kinds of introductions, especially to the Night Office; a *capitulum* or 'chapter' (a sentence) with a short response for many of the hours; and prayers and devotions at the end of each hour. The hymn, known as the Office hymn, became standardized in the form of a metrical song.

### The Night Office (Matins; after midnight)

12 psalms
12 lections with responsories
3 Old Testament odes
(all alternating in various groupings
    and arranged in one, two or three Nocturns)
the psalms are taken in order from the series 1–108.

### The morning service (Lauds; by first light)
5 psalms (but some are Old Testament odes, and some are two or three
    psalms in a group)
hymn
New Testament Canticle: *Benedictus*, the Song of Zacharias (Luke 1:68)

### The day hours
*prime* (dawn)

hymn
psalm (could be a group of psalms)
*terce* (mid-morning)
hymn
psalm (sometimes sections of the very long Psalm 118 (119) were
   distributed among the day hours)
(synaxis and eucharist)
*sext* (noon)
hymn
psalm (see terce)
*none* (mid-afternoon)
hymn
psalm (see terce)

*The evening service (Vespers)*
5 psalms (taken in order from the series 109–146)
hymn
New Testament Canticle: *Magnificat*, the Song of the Blessed Virgin
   Mary (Luke 1:46)

*compline*
2 psalms
hymn
New Testament Canticle: *Nunc dimittis*, the Song of Simeon (Luke 2:29)

## Liturgical sentences

Each service in the preceding list came to be further expanded by the
addition of liturgical sentences. As described in chapter 5, liturgical sentences are short, self-sufficient one-line quotations from Scripture, used in
worship especially for singing. Coming to the monastery along with
antiphony, liturgical sentences had a decisive impact on the singing of
psalms, one which could alter the basic nature of monastic psalmody as a
platform for mystic ascent. Or perhaps the paradox of monastic worship
invited sentences and antiphony. For if the mantra did not do its job – or,
to put it positively, if the communal aspects of singing together predomi-
nated over the meditative aspects – then the meaning of the words and the
details of performance could occupy the centre of attention.

   This possibility did not go unnoticed in the early years; indeed, it elicited
a bitter complaint, reflecting a basic division in the concept of the monastic
life. According to a story told already in early centuries, Abbot Pambo, one
of the Egyptian holy men, sent a disciple to Alexandria on necessary busi-

ness; the disciple returned with glowing accounts of the beautiful *troparia* that were sung in churches in the city (troparia is a generic Greek designation for sentences). Pambo told the novice that he was risking his salvation by allowing the troparia to seduce him, and admonished him to stick to singing his psalms, accompanying them with tears of repentance. In spite of such reservations about the value of liturgical sentences, they came to be used extensively in monastic worship.

Within the fully developed monastic daily cycle of services sentences acquired a richer meaning. In the cathedral synaxis, the sentences that varied from one occasion to the next (for Sundays and feasts) could refer to some specific aspect of the occasion – mentioning the resurrection of the Lord, for instance, or his nativity. The meaning of such festal sentences was often clear: their function was to alert the urban congregation to the significance of 'today's festivity'. In any one synaxis there were not so many of these sentences (perhaps three or four); and there were not so many specific feasts that were provided with such specific references (there came to be five principal feasts). Furthermore, the sentences – festal or not – pointed directly at the synaxis in which they occurred; they did not refer to other synaxes on other occasions.

Exactly this kind of cross-reference did come to prevail in the monastic rite, through the extension of services other than the synaxis or eucharist. Sentences eventually got attached to many of the psalms sung in the daily monastic cycle – to the psalms of the Nocturns, Lauds, Vespers, and the day hours. Other sentences were added on to the canticles and the hymns; still others functioned as mini-lections called *capitula*, 'chapters', often only one or two sentences long. There were also full-length lections in the Nocturns, and each of these was followed by slightly longer sentences called *responsories*. Sentences were sung to recitation formulas or melodies, according to local practice.

In a daily cycle there might be ten or twenty sentences, offering an opportunity to repeat the same idea in the many different contexts provided by the psalms and lections. The combination of these various kinds of sentences with hymns, psalms and readings can produce a long, extremely complex series of words and melodies. There were, in effect, several simultaneous programmes or cycles of differing length – hourly, daily, weekly, yearly – with some randomizing factors thrown in. Such a series can be fully appreciated only by performing it in a monastic context.

The effect of sentences accumulated in a twenty-four hour cycle is shown here in a list of liturgical sentences for the day before Christmas. Listed here are the liturgical sentences for the part of the Divine Office said during the daylight hours. The list includes only some of the sentences, not the entire

Office. The other items – hymns, psalms, readings – are each much longer than a sentence, so they actually constitute the bulk of the performance. The two parts of the Mass, synaxis and eucharist, are listed for the times when they would occur, but the listing includes only some of the sentences appointed for Mass.

## Liturgical sentences in the Office for the day before Christmas (24 December)

(R = response; V = verse, versicle)

### at Lauds

| | |
|---|---|
| Iudaea et Ierusalem, nolite timere: cras egredemini, et Dominus erit vobiscum, alleluia. | Judea and Jerusalem, do not fear: tomorrow you will go forth, and the Lord will be with you, alleluia. |
| Hodie scietis quia veniet Dominus: | Today you will know that the Lord will come: |
| et mane videbitis gloriam eius. | and tomorrow you will see his glory. |
| Crastina die delebitur iniquitas terrae: | Tomorrow the sin of the world will be wiped out: |
| et regnabit super nos Salvator mundi. | and the Saviour of the world will reign over us. |
| Dominus veniet, occurrite illi, dicentes: Magnum principium, et regni eius non erit finis: Deus fortis, dominator, princeps pacis, alleluia, alleluia. | The Lord will come: run to meet him, saying, A great leader, and his kingdom will not end. God is strong, a ruler, prince of peace, alleluia, alleluia. |
| Crastina erit vobis salus, dicit Dominus Deus exercituum. | Tomorrow will be your salvation, saith the Lord God of hosts. |
| R. Hodie scietis quia veniet Dominus. | Today you will know that the Lord will come. |
| V. Et mane videbitis gloriam eius. | V. And tomorrow you will see his glory. |
| V. Crastina die delebitur iniquitas terrae. R. Et regnabit super nos Salvator mundi. | V. Tomorrow the sin of the earth will be wiped out. R. And the Saviour of the world will reign over us. |

| | |
|---|---|
| Orietur sicut sol Salvator mundi: | The Saviour of the world rises like the |
| et descendet in uterum Virginis sicut | sun, |
| imber super gramen, alleluia. | and descends into the virgin's womb, |
| | like the hoarfrost on the field, alleluia. |

### at the day hours

| | |
|---|---|
| Iudaea et Ierusalem, nolite timere: | Judea and Jerusalem, do not fear: |
| cras egrediemini, et Dominus erit | tomorrow you will go forth, and the |
| vobiscum, alleluia. | Lord will be with you, alleluia. |

| | |
|---|---|
| Hodie scietis quia veniet Dominus: | Today you will know that the Lord will come: |
| et mane videbitis gloriam eius. | and tomorrow you will see his glory. |

| | |
|---|---|
| V. Constantes estote. | V.Stand fast, |
| R. Videbitis auxilium Domini super | R. And you will see the Lord's help |
| vos. | come to you. |

### At Mass

| | |
|---|---|
| Hodie scietis quia veniet Dominus: | Today you will know that the Lord will come: |
| et mane videbitis gloriam eius. | and tomorrow you will see his glory. |

(Gradual)

| | |
|---|---|
| Hodie scietis quia veniet Dominus: | Today you will know that the Lord will come: |
| et mane videbitis gloriam eius. | and tomorrow you will see his glory. |

| | |
|---|---|
| Alleluia. | Alleluia. Tomorrow the sin of the |
| Crastina die delebitur iniquitas terrae: | earth will be wiped out: |
| et regnabit super nos Salvator mundi. | and the Saviour of the world will rule over us. |

| | |
|---|---|
| (Communion) | |
| Revelabitur gloria Domini: | The glory of the Lord will be revealed: |
| et videbit omnis caro salutare Dei | and all flesh will see the salvation of |
| nostri. | our God. |

### (continuing in the day hours)

| | |
|---|---|
| Crastina die delebitur iniquitas terrae: | Tomorrow the sin of the earth will be wiped out: |
| et regnabit super nos Salvator mundi. | and the Saviour of the world will reign over us. |

Crastina erit vobis salus, dicit
Dominus Deus exercituum.

Tomorrow will be your salvation, saith
the Lord God of hosts.

*at Vespers*

Rex pacificus magnificatus est, cuius
vultum desiderat universa terra.

The King of peace is magnified; all the
earth desires to see his face.

Magnificatus est rex pacificus super
omnes reges universae terrae.

The King of peace is raised up over all
the kings of the earth.

Completi sunt dies Mariae, ut pareret
filium suum primogenitum.

The days of Mary were fulfilled, that
she should bring forth her firstborn.

Scitote quia prope est regnum Dei:

amen dico vobis, quia non tardabit.

Know that the kingdom of God is at
hand:
truly I say unto you that it shall not
delay.

Levate capita vestra:
ecce approprinquabit redemptio vestra.

Raise up your heads:
behold, your redemption will draw
nigh.

R. Hodie scietis quia veniet Dominus.

Today you will know that the Lord
will come.

V. Et mane videbitis gloriam eius.

And tomorrow you will see his glory.

V. Crastina die delebitur iniquitas
terrae.
R. Et regnabit super nos Salvator
mundi.

Tomorrow the sin of the world will be
blotted out. And the Saviour of the
world will reign over us.

Cum ortus fuerit sol de caelo,
videbitis Regem regum procedentem a
Patre,
tamquam sponsum de thalamo suo.

When the sun has risen in the sky, you
will see the king of kings proceeding
from the Father, like a bridegroom out
of his chamber.

On this particular day the sentences for Mass happen to be closely cor-
related with the sentences used throughout that day for the Divine
Office; hence, the list gives us a chance to see the impact that the performance of sentences in the Office could have upon the sentences at
Mass. The correlation between Mass and Office is not usually so close;
still, it is often present in varying degrees. This is what gives a monastic
participant a perception of Mass different from that of a worshipper in a
cathedral.

The cycle of sentences listed for the day before Christmas happens to be particularly intense in its repetitions, which look forward with great eagerness to the birth of Jesus to be celebrated the next day: the cry of *Crastina*, 'Tomorrow, tomorrow, tomorrow ...', echoes throughout, in various wordings, all of which were taken or adapted from the Bible (usually the Old Testament). When read in the list, the repetitions of *Crastina* take on the insistence of a congregation's response to a litany, and even resemble the endless repetitions occasionally encountered in those popular devotions used by some early Christians – but mistrusted by others, as well as by early Christian leaders (as described in chapter 5). While characteristic of monastic worship, the repetitions in actual performance of the daily cycle would be less intense, but ultimately more effective, because they would occur in alternation with individual psalms, canticles and other material.

The monastic use of sentences in the context of the expanded daily cycle showed great art and sophistication in the pacing of repetitions, using varied wordings of the same idea, and placing it in different liturgical functions. In this way the variable sentences, those that refer to individual occasions, seem to be much more meaningful in the context of the cycle of services throughout the day than they would be if considered individually: they gain in meaning with each repetition.

Repetition of a sentence within the synaxis, however, is much less frequent than in the Office, and may even not occur at all. In the eucharist, repetitions are studiously avoided, except for the scriptural *Sanctus, sanctus, sanctus*. This reflects the avoidance at Mass of the ritualistic repetition characteristic of popular cult. Thus, a cathedral worshipper attending only Mass would hear *Hodie scietis* ('Today you will know') at the Introit simply as an exhortation appropriate to the day, then would hear those words at the Gradual as a single repetition. A monastic, on the other hand, having heard *Hodie scietis* throughout the Office for the day, would experience it at the Gradual with the impact of a familiar refrain, much more meaningful than a single statement.

The effect of sentences distributed through the daily cycle is increased by the monastic repetition of the plan of the daily Office on each day of the week: the monastic life itself is on a seven-days-a-week cycle, and in that sense different from the weekly return of the Lord's day, the *Dominica*, the day of resurrection.

In both cathedral and monastery the weekly cycle became organized into a yearly cycle. This was based on the 'Sunday of Sundays', Easter, synchronized with the Jewish feast of Passover. Cathedral worship also developed a cycle using the monthly calendar that was in effect under the empire;

this parallel cycle was partly to commemorate Christian martyrs, partly to accommodate ancient traditions of urban festivities. Within the yearly cycle certain seasons were defined, each a month or so long; the most important seasons were Advent, the four weeks before Christmas (25 December); Lent, the six weeks before Easter; and Paschaltide, the seven weeks after Easter. The seasons acquired special sets of Proper sentences, and these, too, were used in the monastery, where they tended to function more intensively than in urban practice.

Always present in monastic life, however, was a reservation about the ultimate value of these calendric arrangements, which eventually became so complex as to require the full-time attention of experts. Originally all calendric observances were extraneous to the monastic life, and along with the concept of monastic life as solitary meditation went Abbot Pambo's continuing mistrust of feasts and sentences. There is a story (perhaps only a legend, but if so, with the deeper truth of a myth) telling how people came to Benedict, who was saying his ferial Psalter in the wilderness, to bring him greetings at Easter – but he was not aware that it was Easter, so preoccupied was he with the daily cycle of psalms.

The sentences in the list for the day before Christmas can be fully appreciated only in the context of the Advent season, the month-long preparation for Christmas, in which several themes are woven into a programme that operated every day. Again, we would have to perform this as part of the monastic life: a full listing would be much too long to print here, and even when printed (as it is in a breviary), it is nowhere near the same thing as a performance.

The list of selected sentences on pages 142–3 includes the most representative themes of the Advent season; they would appear in the various functions of antiphon, short response, versicle and response, and would be sung in the interstices of psalms, canticles, readings and prayers. The most distinctive theme is 'Come, O Lord!'; some dedicated person or persons in the sixth or seventh century systematically searched the Old Testament to find the sentences that included some form of *veni* ('Come!') in order to create a collection of sentences highlighting this theme.

## Sentences, psalms and meditation

All of this was accessible and meaningful to monastics because of their daily exposure to the flow of texts. It was meaningful to them also in another dimension, one that led back towards meditation. Monastic meditation began with the Psalter, the cycle of psalms; since, in Benedict's schedule,

monastics said all the psalms each week, they came to know all 150 Psalms
by heart. So when they heard or sang a sentence excerpted from a psalm,

*Selected sentences from the season of Advent (four weeks before
Christmas)*

Aspiciens a longe, ecce video Dei
potentiam venientem, et nebulam
totam terram tegentem:
ite obviam ei, et dicite,
nuntia nobis si tu es ipse qui
regnaturus es in populo Israel.

Gazing afar off, behold! I see the
power of God drawing near,
and a cloud covering the whole earth:
run to meet him, and say,
Tell us if thou art the one who will
rule over the people of Israel.

Ecce nomen Domini venit de
longinquo:
et claritas eius replet orbem terrarum.

Behold! the name of God comes from
afar:
and its brightness fills the circle of the
lands.

Ecce Dominus veniet, et omnes sancti
eius cum eo: et erit in die illa lux
magna, alleluia.

Behold! God comes, and all his saints
with him: and there will be on that day
a great light, alleluia.

Ecce veniet Deus et homo de domo
David sedere in throno, alleluia.

Behold! God will come, and a man
from the house of David, to sit on the
throne, alleluia.

Ecce in nubibus caeli Dominus veniet,
cum potestate magna, alleluia.

Behold! God will come in the clouds of
heaven with great power, alleluia.

Ecce rex veniet Dominus terrae,
et ipse auferet jugum captivitatis
nostrae.

Behold! the King will come as Lord of
the earth, and he will take away the
yoke of our captivity.

Ecce veniet Dominus princeps regum
terrae:
beati qui parati sunt occurrere illi.

Behold! the Lord will come as first
among the kings of the earth:
blessed are those who are ready to
meet him.

Non auferetur sceptrum de Juda,
et dux de femore eius,

The sceptre shall not depart from
Judah,
nor a leader from his loins,

donec veniat qui mittendus est:
et ipse erit expectatio gentium.

until he who is sent comes:
and he will be the expectation of the
people.

Ostende nobis Domine misericordiam tuam:
et salutare tuum da nobis.

Show us thy mercy, O Lord:

and grant us thy salvation.

Veni ad liberandum nos, Domine Deus virtutum: ostende faciem tuam, et salvi erimus.

Come to free us, O Lord God of strength:
show us thy face, and we shall be saved.

Veni Domine visitare nos in pace,
ut laetemur coram te corde perfecto.

Come, O Lord, to visit us in peace,
that we may rejoice in thy presence with a pure heart.

Veni Domine et noli tardare:
relaxa facinora plebi tuae Israel.

Come, O Lord, and do not delay:
loose the sins of thy people Israel.

Canite tuba in Sion quia prope est dies Domini: ecce veniet ad salvandum nos, alleluia, alleluia.

Blow the trumpet in Sion, for the day of the Lord is at hand: behold! he will come to save us, alleluia, alleluia.

O sapientia quae ex ore Altissimi prodisti, attingens a fine usque ad finem,
fortiter suaviter disponensque omnia:

O Wisdom, which goest forth from the mouth of the Most High,
and reachest from one end to another, mightily and sweetly ordering all things:

veni ad docendum nos viam pruden-tiae.

come and teach us the way of pru-dence!

This is the first of a set of sentences called the O antiphons, all beginning with the invocation 'O' addressed to some aspect of the deity; this first one is to *sapientia*, Wisdom, 'Sophia'. The second letter of this sentence is *s*, which together with six others forms an anagram, *sarcore*, which spells backwards *ero cras*, 'I will be tomorrow'; these seven sentences are said one a day beginning eight days before Christmas. Here is the last one.

O Emmanuel, rex et legifer noster, exspectatio gentium, et Salvator earum:
veni ad salvandum nos Domine Deus noster.

O Emmanuel! king and lawgiver! the desire of nations, and their salvation:

come and save us, O Lord our God.

they could easily be aware of the rest of that psalm: it would form an alternative context for the sentence, parallel to but different from the context in which the sentence was being performed.

On Christmas Day, for instance, Psalm 2 is sung with the antiphon, 'The Lord said unto me, thou art my son, this day have I begotten thee' (as on the compact disc, track 20). This is verse 7 of the psalm, understood to prefigure the birth of Christ. Verse 1 of the psalm, 'Why do the heathen so furiously rage together?' is taken to refer to the crucifixion of Christ, commemorated in the calendar in Holy Week just before Easter. So while verse 7 inflects the psalm towards Christmas, verse 1 and the psalm as a whole have strong associations with Good Friday.

For someone who knows the psalms, this kind of cross-reference occurs over and over again for all the sentences that are taken from psalms. Sentences from other books of the Bible will elicit similar associations, if not so strong. The Psalter is the principal medium through which the connections travel: the whole yearly cycle (as it was eventually worked out) is open to simultaneous contemplation, to global access, every detail potentially resonating with every other.

In principle, this mechanism of global association should offer the monastic a timeless contemplation of the events of Christian religion. In practice, the way sentences are used as antiphons, and especially the kind of melodies they have, give them a prominence that can defeat the sense of timeless contemplation. After singing an antiphon, then encountering that same sentence in the psalm, I notice it with an indescribable mixture of confirmation and surprise: I have just been reminded of the words of the antiphon in the context of the feast; but I am surprised to rediscover them in the psalm. What sticks in my mind, then, is the sentence and its festal referent, not the rest of the psalm.

The sentence is highlighted in the psalm: that verse, not the others, is the focus of attention. Hence, the apparatus of sentences fixes my attention in the temporal dimension. The end result may be that the annual cycle of feasts is experienced by the monastic in the same way as it is perceived by an urban cathedral worshipper – as a narrative of the life of Christ, with all the associated events of the life of the church in the world. The experience becomes a pilgrimage, a progress locked into a succession of events.

*Monastic antiphony*

There are still more complications that can enmesh the monastic in the temporal flow of singing the Office. Antiphony came to be widely used in the monastic Office, and monastics employed it in various ways ranging from simple and systematic to very complex.

Antiphony, as described in chapter 5, was used in the cathedral for singing hymns, odes and canticles, as well as the acclamations at Mass. Monastics applied antiphony enthusiastically in all those functions, and, in addition, since they knew the psalms by heart, they found antiphony especially useful for singing the entire Psalter of 150 psalms every week throughout the year in the monastic Office. This way of singing psalms was called *antiphonal psalmody*, and while in Benedict's *Rule* it was always only one option among several, it was practised so often that for some observers it has appeared to be the only or original form of antiphony.

The purpose of antiphony was to introduce variety and interest into musical performance. Already complicated when first used by Christians, techniques of antiphonal singing continued so in monastic practice. This complexity was normal, in spite of the fact that in a monastery the hymns, psalms, odes and canticles were sung by the whole monastic congregation, not just by a select choir.

As a relatively simple procedure that combined a psalm with a short sentence, the two semichoirs (that is, the two halves of the monastic congregation) could alternate verse by verse throughout a psalm, each semichoir including the short sentence at the end of their verses; or the two semichoirs could join in singing the sentence after each verse. One of the more complex ways combined antiphony with solo psalmody (an early monastic solution to the problem of singing psalms); in this case the semichoir sang the short sentence after each verse. The two semichoirs (call them I and II) each had a leader:

> leader I sang a psalm verse, and
> choir I responded with the short sentence; then
> leader II sang the next verse, and
> choir II responded with the *same* sentence.

This procedure combined solo-choral response with semichoir antiphony.

### The monastic choir
This is an architectural term – an important application of a musical term to an architectural design. In very large monastic churches constructed in northern Europe from about the year 1000, a long space was inserted between the nave and the sanctuary (see the brief description of the T-shaped Constantinian basilica in chapter 6). The structure of the nave was simply continued on past the crossbar of the T, just as wide and just as high. This new space between the nave and the sanctuary was called the (architectural) choir. Into it were built long rows of seats, running lengthwise in the now greatly elongated building; there were usually two or three rows, called stalls, on each side of the choir, facing each other across the building,

*not* facing the altar. There could be enough seats to accommodate even the two or three hundred monks of a large monastery.

Besides its great length, the distinctive feature of the architectural choir was the way in which it was set off from the nave; in many buildings a huge screen was set up all across the entrance to the choir. The screen started at the step that marked the east edge of the nave and rose much of the way to the roof. It often carried a large crucifix, and since that was called in Anglo-Saxon a 'rood', the screen was called in England a *rood screen*. It could be elaborately carved or decorated, and was usually not solid but perforated, so that those standing in the nave could at least glimpse the altar. In really large buildings, such as Westminster Abbey, the screen as a whole was so large that a pipe organ could be mounted on its second storey, being played from a console on high.

The monastic community sat 'in choir', in the stalls; this automatically divided them into two semichoirs that could sing any psalm or canticle in alternation verse by verse. Over the centuries standard procedures of antiphony were developed, governing which side should begin, and under what circumstances both sides should sing together. In this way the practice of antiphony became closely linked to the architectural plan, and almost dependent upon it.

The purpose of the rood screen was the same as that of the cloister as a whole – to separate monastics from the world. The rood screen was used particularly in England, where, by accidents of history, monasteries were often closely associated with cathedrals; there would be a congregation in the nave, from which the monastics in the performance of their Office should be shielded.

## Chant and meditation

Cloistering of monastics was a necessity for the original purpose of meditation, which was to free the mind of the individual from the world and its temporal flow. But what about the expressive sentences and complicated antiphonal ways of singing them, procedures that became fixed in stone in the massive structures of the architectural choir? Did not that musical complexity engage the mind in the flow of performance, in the warp of time? How was the mind to free itself, to gain the unconnected insight into reality? These elaborate procedures of the monastic Office seem to lay themselves open to Pambo's ancient charge, that they are death to the spirit.

There are, certainly, monastic positions more moderate than Pambo's that try to accommodate meditation on the ultimate human condition with contemplation of beautiful words and music. What interests me, however, is not how things beautiful can be included in the life of the spirit, but rather how that life can be understood as analogous to the encounter with the beautiful, and vice versa. If meditation is an adventure of the mind, cannot music be one too? Or, to read the analogy the other way, could the fantasy of melismatic chant be a model for the process of letting the spirit soar in unforeseeable ways through hidden stages of experience?

Literal contemplation of the sentences, working *through* the words, seems not to escape from their meaning, while monastic meditation, using the Psalter as a mantra, rises above the words. Parallel to that difference there is another. Intonation (as in a reciting pitch) is a sonic platform for the words with their referential meaning, while a melody can rise above the literal, referential meaning of the words into a realm of pitch relationships.

Monastic music, monastic life, finds various ways through the midst of these distinctions. Measured up against the rigour of Pambo, or the young eagle's ascent of Evagrius, it is anomalous that monastics should love fancy Gregorian chant. Measured up against the early historical development, it is anomalous that we should identify Gregorian chant as monastic, since the setting of liturgical sentences to elaborate melody seems not to serve meditative purposes. Still, the revival of Gregorian chant in our time has been due largely to the fact that Benedictine monastics have regarded fancy Gregorian chant as their most treasured occupation. Its great value for them seems to reflect the ultimate impact of music on the monastic life.

Perhaps contemplation of the sentences operates like a mantra after all: perhaps the mind, in responding to the manifold associations and cross-references of the sentences and led through the profusion of the Psalter in unexpected directions to hidden places, can actually be borne up 'on eagle wings' to mystic heights. In any case, that seems to me very much like responding to the manifold relationships that form among the pitches in melismatic chant, where I find my mind being similarly lifted up in ways and to places that I am at a loss to describe.

# 8

## *Gregorian Chant in Notation and in the Mind*

Perhaps the most important thing we can learn about the development of chant notation is that it was developed *after* the chant itself: first the singers conceived the chant; later they wrote it down. Gregorian chant was in the first instance not only sung without notation, it was also composed without notation. Acknowledging this – that a piece of chant could exist in completed form in the singer's mind without any notation – is the most important step in understanding early notation, and in understanding the chant as well. One of the greatest problems modern scholars have faced in trying to understand Gregorian chant and its notation has been in grasping how the original singers could *know* chant, how they could perceive it, learn it, and remember it without notation. A principal solution to this problem is the realization that not only was it *possible* for chant singers to learn and know what they sang without notation, it was and is the basic way we learn any kind of music.

Knowing music, for a singer, is the ability to reproduce very long intricate sequences of vocal actions with a high degree of precision and reliability – such reliability that the singer can allow the actions to be controlled by those mysterious intuitive impulses that spring from deep within and make the performance musical. This is the meaning of the common expression, 'know by heart'.

When musicians in the past used notation, they left written records that we can study; when they did *not* use notation, we have no way of knowing exactly what music they did make. Some argue that if Gregorian singers thought about music the way we do, they would have written it down the way we write it down; the argument goes on to conclude that since they did *not* write it down, they must have thought about music differently. That conclusion, however, is completely unwarranted. It is much better to assume that they could have known music in the same way that we know it *when we do not use notation*. And by observing carefully how we do use notation, we can gain insight into the role notation plays in knowing music.

When we try to imagine Gregorian singers singing without notation, we can depend on the diatonic scale to give us a precise sense of the tonal space in which they sang. As the default scale of antiquity, the diatonic scale was used regularly by early Christians, and continued in use without interruption into the European tradition. Thus we can imagine, even without notation, the sound of all the kinds of melodic movement the Gregorian singers sang; what we lack is a knowledge of which specific melodic movement they used for a given set of words.

We also know the words the early Gregorian singers sang. In fact, they wrote down the words about a century before they wrote down the melodies. Since the words came from the Bible, they had of course been written down long before; but the assignment of psalm quotations as Proper chants for the Mass was first recorded in books in the ninth century. So during that century we can imagine them singing the words that we know in a tonal space that we know. It is easy for a modern singer to learn a Gregorian melody by heart, or even make up a melody for a given set of words, then observe his own inner experience of singing it. I see no reason to think this experience would differ substantially from the experience of the ninth-century singer.

## *Verbal utterance and vocality*

Gregorian chant used Latin words, but by the time the Gregorian repertory developed – the seventh to ninth centuries – Latin was no longer the singers' native tongue; the singers who were involved in the original development of the Gregorian repertory spoke early forms of Italian, Spanish, French, German and English. In that respect these singers' use of Latin was much like ours: they did not learn Latin as a language but only as sets of words used for singing chants in the Gregorian repertory.

More important, the original singers' experience of verbal utterance, or even more generally of vocality, is directly accessible to us: we know what it is like to speak, and also to sing. We all breathe and speak with the same mechanism, the same lungs, diaphragm, vocal cords, pharyngeal wall, palate, tongue, lips and teeth. As humans we all have the anatomical capacity to make the same sounds. An infant can be heard to try out all these sounds during the first year after birth. The entire spectrum of human vocables is there, ready to be selected for use in a given linguistic environment. The selection happens quickly – during a year or two – and is drastic: only a few of the possible sounds are selected and combined into the native tongue. But the capability of making all the sounds remains; sounds other than those of the native tongue can be learned later, if needed.

Latent awareness of this capability can provide a substratum of shared vocal experience. Asian or African singers from various cultures can and do learn to produce the vocal sounds appropriate to European musical styles; and there seems to be no obstacle to their doing it as well as if not better than Europeans. Meanwhile, Euro-American students of singing in India, Japan and Indonesia have demonstrated expert ability that sounds authentic – to everyone except those most committed to the idea that only natives can sound like natives.

Early Christians made the music in the world around them acceptable for Christian worship by stripping off elements whose physical associations were too strong or too specific, thus maintaining Christian ideas of purely spiritual music-making. Early Christian writers urged elimination of the luxuriant timbres of instrumental accompaniment, with its vibrant intoxicating rhythms; and also of the colourful poetry with its verbal rhythms, which the many surviving examples show can be seductive. When physical movement – dancing or playing instruments, plucking strings, blowing pipes or banging on resonant objects – was eliminated, only sheer vocality remained; but, ironically, vocality was the most physical of all musical activities, the one perceived most intimately by the human body.

The experience of singing was not the same for a solo performer as it was for one singing in a chorus, especially a member of the congregation. It is true that when the congregation sang in unison, each individual would experience music as physical vocality, just as would a soloist. But the point of *una voce* singing, the reason it was emphasized so by Christian writers, was that in unison singing the experience of individual vocality was submerged in the music of all – ideally, of all Creation. Singing in unison could be felt as spiritual rather than physical.

## Learning and remembering

In connection with the Gregorian repertory of Mass Propers (some five hundred complex items) people often ask, How did they remember it all? Considering that five hundred songs may not be too large a repertory for a modern folksong singer, or that ten roles in full-length operas is a reasonable repertory for an opera singer, or ten concertos for a piano soloist, there does not seem to be a problem with the human capacity for memorizing music in the case of the Gregorian repertory. What people mean, I think, is, How did they *learn it without looking at it in written form*? The answer is, from their teachers. And there are modern opera singers (including a very famous one) who do not read notation; they learn their roles from hearing someone sing them over and over.

## Recitation and improvisation

To compare learning music with learning language may be helpful, in spite of the fact that we do not know how people learn language either; but we observe that they do it, and without formal instruction. Without trying to say *how* people learn to speak a language, we can observe some of the results.

Knowledge of language enables the speaker to use it in a variety of daily situations without having prearranged or practised exactly what to say, often speaking without thinking even at the moment. In music this is called improvisation and singers as well as instrumentalists can learn to do it; again, some can do it without formal instruction. As with language, musical improvisation presupposes that the singer already knows much music, since the process of improvisation, like verbal conversation, involves accommodating known elements to new situations.

Sometimes, on the other hand, we learn a speech or a poem exactly as it was composed, and we recite it; we do the same with songs. *How* we learn for recitation we can know only through introspection, and so we each have our own idea of the inner process. The test of the process is not *how* it is done, but rather the fact that it *is* done: people really do reproduce exactly poems and songs that have been prearranged in a particular form.

In antiquity people learned and recited much poetry. In general, memory was a very important part of intellectual life in the Greco-Latin world. Memory was personified in Mnemosyne, the mother of the Muses; she was considered a Titan, that is, one of a very old generation of gods that pre-dated the new Olympian gods headed by Zeus. In addition to Homer's *Iliad*, which was a basic part of a young person's education, choruses of the tragedies were learned by amateur civic groups to be performed at the annual festivals.

Cicero, reputed to be the greatest Latin orator in antiquity, laid great stress on memory as an indispensable part of a courtroom lawyer's equipment. He himself published many of his own orations (after their delivery). What he wrote down and what he actually said on the occasion may have been somewhat different, but there is no reason to doubt that he could have memorized the written form. All of the many theatrical performances that went on in Rome and elsewhere during the early Christian centuries would have involved memorized routines, even when combined with improvised performance.

Most important, recitation and improvisation were *both* used, in language as in musical practice. The mix is indeterminate: we cannot say in general that one precedes the other or that one or the other predominates. The use varies from case to case and person to person; and the two alternatives lie on a continuum that includes all possible intermediate stages.

Singing in chorus is necessarily more like recitation. Since unison singing
– so prized by Christians – was achieved by everyone singing exactly the same
pitches at the same time, the members of the congregation would have to
follow exactly the melody they knew by heart. If they did not know the melody
very well, they had to follow as closely as they could the singing they heard
around them. So as far as the development of new music was concerned, congregational singing tended by nature to be conservative: the requirements of
singing together discouraged inspiration and spontaneous change.

The experience of the solo singer, on the other hand, encourages improvisation. Inspired, spontaneous change can happen easily, the more so as the
singer knows a melody very well. Singing a beautiful melody by heart, the
singer can be moved to extend the fantasy, to move freely through melodic
motions that go beyond those just sung.

## Variation

It has long been recognized that solo performers tend to change the
melodies they have learned even in the midst of performance; indeed, this
is a characteristic and basic musical activity for them. Such change can
happen with musical instruments just as well, and in fact is more familiar to
us in that form. It is most easily understood by observers as *variation*, as
when a performer varies a familiar melody by decorating it with faster notes,
leaving the original outline intact and plainly audible. That is easy to do,
and easy to understand in listening; there are clear traces of it in the
Gregorian repertory, especially in connection with the formulas of recitation, where decoration is easily perceptible.

On the other hand, in the case of chant that is already decorative, as
melismatic chant, a singer's changes may better be described not as variation but rather as extension. Such extension, which can be thought of as
improvisation, is a also basic kind of music-making that we can assume goes
on anywhere, any time. It would be the primary mechanism by which the
chant repertory was developed over time. When an improvised extension is
learned so that it can be reproduced in performance, and refined so as to
present an integrated and polished appearance, the result can be called a
musical composition. Learning melodies already composed, varying and
extending them in performance and learning the results can all go on simultaneously in a musical repertory that is in current use.

## Development of musical notation for chant

Within the historical period in which Gregorian chant emerged, forms of
verbal notation and also musical notation were in common use, and had

been in use for well over a millennium. Christian culture from the second century on became firmly tied to books: all the words said or sung at Mass and in the Divine Office eventually came to be learned from books and – even if learned by heart – still performed from books. It was an eventual liturgical requirement that the Missal, which contained all the words to be said at Mass, should be open on the altar. This requirement applied in particular to the canon of the Roman Mass, the part of the eucharistic prayer that, once it had been developed into a standard wording, was to be said exactly as written.

Systems of musical notation were available: we have the one hymn from Oxyrhynchus, a third-century papyrus, with the pitches of the melody written in Greek alphabetic symbols referring to the diatonic system. In this kind of notation we know exactly what pitches were intended. From this and other fragments of ancient music we know that musical notation was available to the early singers of Latin chant.

European singers, however, did not make consistent use of notation before 900, apparently because of certain widespread convictions and prejudices about the proper place of music in Christian worship. Specifically, there was a long-standing tradition that professional music-making with instruments should be avoided, and this would include the kinds of notation that referred precisely to traditional pitch configurations.

It was for this reason, apparently, that when European singers *did* start to use musical notation, they developed a new kind of notation that had no exact antecedents even in the richly varied musical practice of antiquity. Sometime in the ninth century, Gregorian singers developed a musical notation that did not show exact pitches, but did show other aspects of melody – aspects not necessarily shown in previous systems of notation.

## New notation north of the Alps

Learning the Gregorian repertory without notation had not been a problem as long as it was a matter of local tradition, carried on and even developed by a small face-to-face group of singers. It became a problem, however, in connection with the diffusion of this repertory throughout the Carolingian Empire, especially since the music was disseminated by urgent order of the emperor. The Carolingian authorities wanted the repertory to be sung uniformly throughout the empire, so some means of standardization became necessary.

Starting after the year 750, the singers north of the Alps had to learn the new sets of words that came with the Roman liturgy (it was the assignment of liturgical *sentences* to Sundays and feasts that was new, for the words themselves were mostly excerpted from the Book of Psalms). Roman singers

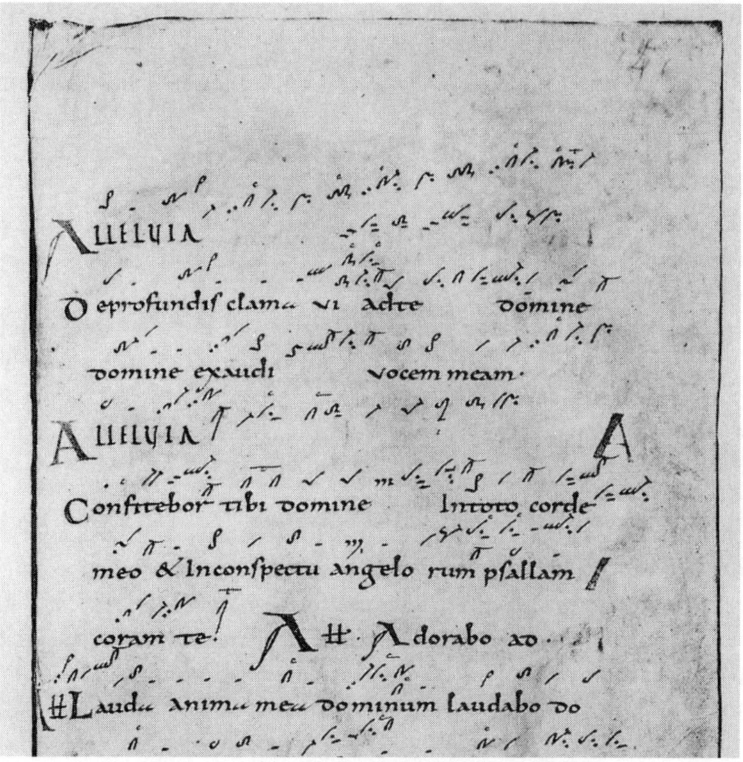

Plate 1 Staffless musical notation in St Gall
Codex 359, p. 151

were asked to come to teach the northerners – but not many came, and they did not stay long. It has been pointed out that northern reports document only a few Roman teachers, who remained in the north usually not more than a year; but it took ten years (the northerners said) for a cantor to learn his business. The Romans, it is said, also sent north a book with all the sentences written down; but no such book survives, and the only books we have are chant books made somewhere in the north. It is conceivable that the Roman singers themselves did not use books for this purpose. In any case, it seems certain that they did not write the melodies down in musical notation.

At first, the northern singers wrote down only the words of the sentences in the liturgical order in which they would be used. This amounts to a chant book without musical notation, and we have a number of them from the ninth century. The singer would use this kind of book to remind him of the words (which he had already learned) to be sung at Mass, and he would sing them by heart. But then, in order to expedite the uniform performance of Gregorian chant throughout the empire, the Frankish cantors developed their new kind of musical notation. By 900 the kind of book that had

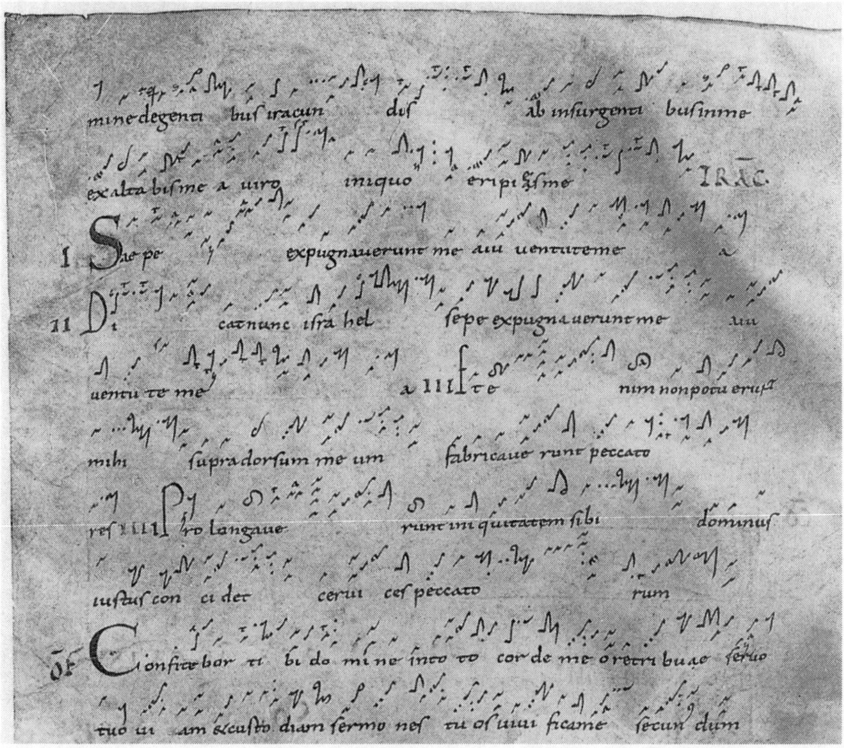

Plate 2 Staffless musical notation in Laon MS 239, p. 39

contained only the words came to be provided completely with this musical notation, in order to remind the singer of the melodies as well as the words.

## Inventing Gregorian notation

Having experimented with musical notation throughout the ninth century, northern cantors in different localities had developed several slightly different workable systems of notation. Some of the notational systems look as though they had been designed to record, by means of dictation, what a singer sang (some of the notational signs resemble modern Gregg shorthand; see plates 1 and 2). In any case, what the notation represents is the way the melodies were sung by the cantor, or by the scribe himself.

Some scholars feel that this development of musical notation is a watershed in the history of music, especially in its performance, and that the use of musical notation gave performers quite a different way to know music. Consequently (it is argued) we should imagine that after the introduction of notation the chant sounded different – perhaps very different – from the way it had sounded before. Of course, we do not know how it did sound

Plate 3  Musical notation on a four-line staff in the Sarum
Graduale, p. 31

before, since it was not written down; so a more prudent conclusion is that while a given piece might have sounded different before it was written down, it could just as well have sounded the same before as after. In any case we cannot determine anything definite about the preceding development of musical style from this notation, or from its creation or use.

Even after the new chant notation came into use, chant singers did not perform at Mass or in the Office by reading from a chant book. They continued to learn from a teacher, using a chant book primarily to check their memories; and they performed by heart. We can easily understand this, since it is the way much music is made today; and we can relate it to various kinds of medieval evidence, of which the most practical is that early chant books are small and, although often written very clearly, are sometimes barely legible even in good light; they were certainly not legible in candlelight in a dim cathedral. Not until after 1300 do chant books become large enough to be read by a small group of singers standing around the bookstand, singing from a book, as shown in pictures from the late Middle Ages.

## Notation without pitch

The earliest Gregorian notation did not show the exact distance up and down from one pitch to the next – a fact that concerns us in several different contexts. (See plates 1 and 2.) First, this lack makes it obvious that a singer had to know the melody in order to read the notation. But since the singers had previously known and sung the whole repertory without any notation at all, the new notation's lack of specific distance between pitches would not have been a problem.

This lack of pitch information is more of a problem for modern scholars: we would not be able to read the melodies if it were not for the subsequent development of notation. After AD 1000 some notational systems gradually came to show exact distance between pitches, and the melodies could be read directly out of the newer manuscripts (see plate 3). As it turns out, the Gregorian melodies in this later notation are similar enough to the earlier notation to make us certain that we are dealing with the same melodies. Therefore, once we have learned Gregorian melodies out of the later chant books, we are in the same situation as the tenth-century singer: we know how the melody goes, so we can read it when we find it in one of the earliest chant books, even though its notation there does not show what the pitches are.

In spite of using notational techniques that varied from place to place, the northern chant books for the Proper of the Mass produced over the next several centuries show a uniformity of detail unique in European music. This uniformity indicates that singers throughout Europe all knew the same basic versions of the melodies (and this is what makes it possible for us to use the later manuscripts to read the earlier ones). The uniformity is easily explained by the Carolingian political programme of installing one system of liturgy – the Roman liturgy – with one set of melodies throughout the empire. This diffusion of one set of melodies was accomplished by teachers going out from (or singers coming to) a central school such as the one at Metz in France; notated chant books would be prepared to provide individual localities with a permanent record of what their singers had learned.

## Notation and performance

The early chant books' lack of pitch information has been most puzzling for modern observers. Perhaps it is because reading is so basic to us: if we cannot read a piece of music, we conclude that we cannot know it – hence neither could they. But that is very dubious logic. Part of our problem is in failing to see that musical notation does not tell us what a piece of music *is*. The notation, which is addressed only to the performer, merely tells him certain aspects of how to perform. Reading the notation and knowing the piece are two different activities. A singer who knows a song can proceed to sing it; if he does not know the song, he has to learn it from someone who does. If no one is available, then the singer might have to read it in a book, but that is a poor alternative.

It is essential to distinguish reading music from knowing it, and we can become aware of the distinction by observing how modern musicians perform with and without notation. In general, we should imagine early Gregorian singers singing as an opera singer does, without reading or even glancing at any form of musical notation. It is true that some singers may be able to see and read notes in their head as if the notes were printed on a page, just as they may be able to imagine the words they are singing as if those were printed; but that would only be if they had learned the notes as graphic images, or had a special kind of ability known as 'eidetic imagery'. Most singers either cannot do that, or are not interested in relying on it for performance. As an alternative, singers may be able to *hear* internally, phrase by phrase, how the melody is going to sound; but then they have to keep thinking ahead, singing one phrase while hearing the next internally.

Often it seems that a singer sings without any conscious projection of the melody in any form inside his head; he just sings it, and visualization (in any of the many forms it can take) may simply go along with the performance. The singer may register what the melody is doing as if he were listening to someone else sing it. But the singer is not really *following* the visualization; the performance is being guided by something not in the singer's inner field of vision. An intermediate technique that works for me is to remind myself consciously what the next phrase is going to be, then let the unconscious mechanism produce it – much as in delivering a memorized speech I can simply announce to myself what the next paragraph is about and perhaps start the first few words, letting the rest come to mind without my conscious effort.

## Staffless notation

The most obvious difference between early chant notation, such as that in plates 1 and 2, and modern notation is the absence from early notation of the musical staff, the rows of horizontal lines on which the notes are placed. Simply the appearance of a musical staff can indicate the presence of musical notation, even to a modern observer who knows nothing about how musical notation works. The staff locates each note in the diatonic scale; performers who have the diatonic scale in mind can read the exact distance up and down between pitches. In spite of the lack of a staff, the early note shapes give in other respects a clear, simple representation of the pitches to

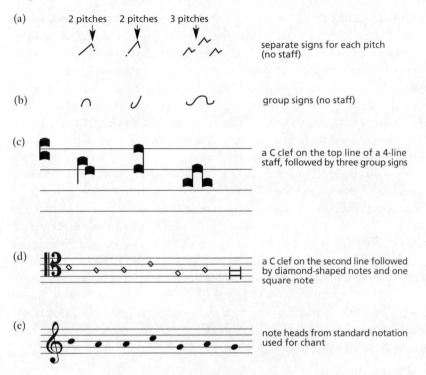

Figure 8.1 Development of European pitch notation: (a), (b) early chant notation (about AD 900) (c) later chant notation (about AD 1300) (d) later polyphonic notation (about AD 1500) (e) modern chant notation (about AD 1950).

be sung. Some of these, in particular the notes that represent single pitches, are easily identified; examples of signs for single pitches in one early style of notation are shown in figure 8.1a. Other signs, however, represent *groups* of two or three pitches together; examples are shown in figure 8.1b. It is these group signs that strike the modern eye as unusual. (Modern notation, too, has its own group signs, equally unusual to a non-musician.) And even though the staffless notation does not show the exact distance from one pitch to the next, for instance whether the interval is a whole step or half step, it does often show up-and-down *direction* in melodic movement, for instance that the second of two pitches is higher or lower than the first, as in figure 8.1a.

Chant notation was transformed rapidly during the Middle Ages. In addition to the development of the staff (which by 1200 assumed the form in which we still use it), the note shapes themselves changed, eventually producing after 1600 the modern note shapes familiar to us; some of the steps in that development are shown in figures 8.1c, d and e.

The first step involved thickening the early group signs to emphasize individual pitches; this changed a group sign from a thin smooth curve to a series of squares connected by thin lines, as in figure 8.1c and plate 3. Then the group signs were abandoned, and the squares were mostly replaced by diamond-shaped signs, and these eventually by ovals which we still use. The ovals have gradually acquired other signs, very familiar to the modern eye but too complicated to explain or even describe in this book (stems, flags, beams, dots, and so on), all associated with rhythm and metre. When we want to represent chant in modern notation, we use only the note heads, showing pitch without the rhythmic-metric superstructure, as in figure 8.1e; we also place the note heads on a staff to represent diatonic distance up or down between pitches.

Readers familiar with staff notation may need to be reminded that the staff by itself does not identify the notes with the diatonic scale exactly; that identification has to be provided by a special code, or key, for which the French word *clef* is still used. Medieval chant notation used the 'C clef' to show which line indicated the note called C; this C clef can be seen in figure 8.1c, and in later graphic form in Fig. 8.1d. Modern notation uses two more clefs: called 'treble' and 'bass' clefs, they represent G or F – but that is not clear just from looking at them. Treble clef is used for transcription of chant into modern notation, as in figure 8.1e.

## Notation for groups of pitches

Gregorian melody, especially the melismatic kind, moves in very distinctive ways, and a sequence of single signs and group signs in early notation indicates a specific melody just like a thumb print; but, as with thumb prints, identification depends on finding a match with a print that has already been recorded.

In Gregorian chant the curves of the melody often fit together with the syllables in very intimate ways; but, paradoxically, the fit can take many dif-

An intonation:

| pitches in the mind: | words in the book: | group signs in the book: | as sung: |
|---|---|---|---|

Notum fecit   No-tum fe- cit

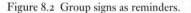

Figure 8.2 Group signs as reminders.

ferent forms. If I see only the words, and have only a vague outline of the melody in mind (as at the beginning of figure 8.2), I may not anticipate exactly how the steps and leaps up and down are aligned with each syllable, and consequently I will fumble and not be able to start singing the phrase. In figure 8.2 there are only one or two pitches for each syllable, but the pitches could be allotted to the syllables in different ways, each stylistically appropriate. A glance at the group signs in figure 8.2c shows me exactly which way they are aligned with the syllables, and once the correct sequence of ups and downs is initiated, the melody becomes locked on to its track with a special sense of rightness unique to the Gregorian style. Given the words and the pitch outline, the group signs seem to be an excellent representation of the melody.

Grouping pitches is important in all kinds of music: any listener can hear a difference between a performance in which the pitches are grouped in some way, and one in which the singer or player just offers one pitch after another without grouping them. The singer has to let the melody flow smoothly ahead, connecting several tones together, then articulating slightly so as to close one group and start another. Less important pitches must lead into or flow out of more important ones so that several pitches form a coherent whole – just as, in melodious speech, several syllables are grouped around an accented syllable to form a word, and several words are grouped around a prominent word to form a well-sounding phrase.

What the group signs in the early chant books record is the way some singer habitually sang the melody, his personal style of doing it; because it was a very successful way, or for some other reason (for instance, because the singer had a great reputation), other singers wanted to be reminded of exactly how the performance went, in case they did not have sufficient opportunity to learn it well. The signs record a *tradition* of singing, a way of singing handed down in the first instance by live performance from teacher to pupil. A number of traditions were maintained by different singers in different places.

## Adjunct letters

In a few of the earliest chant books, the group signs are supplemented by even more specific directions about grouping, inflection and accent. These directions come in the form of alphabetic codes added to the group signs; they are notated differently in different books (and appear in relatively few books); they produce varying results. Figure 8.3 shows an unusually dense application of these *adjunct letters* to the beginning of an Alleluia chant. In this manuscript (Laon 239), the letters seem to have these meanings:

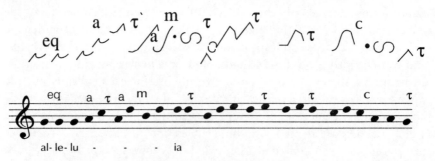

Figure 8.3 Adjunct letters. The beginning of *Alleluia Pascha nostrum*, as notated in Laon MS 239 with adjunct letters showing rhythmic nuance.

**a**     broaden (Latin *augete*, comparable with modern Italian *allargando*)
**t**     hold (Latin *tenete*, comparable to modern Italian *tenuto*)
**m**    moderately (Latin *mediocriter*, comparable with modern Italian *mezzo*)
**c**     quickly (Latin *celeriter*)
**eq**   (Latin *equaliter*) indicates that the next pitch should be the same as the preceding)

These adjunct signs sometimes call for the emphasis of a grouping; but sometimes, on the contrary, they diminish or even eliminate the effect of a grouping. In this example the letters *a* and *t* both call for a lengthening of the pitch signs; the *t* seems to stop the forward motion briefly, while the *a* merely broadens it. The *c*, on the other hand, cautions against a lengthening at the end of that particular group. Sometimes their use seems personal, as when the *m* for *mediocriter* says 'not too much' relative to the preceding *a*. (The sign *eq* is used occasionally to remind the singer that two successive pitches are the same.)

Here, as elsewhere, the letters need to be taken in the context of the overall sense of a passage. They represent individual ways of singing the melodies: they show one specific interpretation of a melody, one way a live singer knew of singing it. This gives *us* more to know than what we can learn from the pitches alone: it can give us examples of the musical sensitivity of the original singers, examples of their knowledge of the melodies.

The adjunct signs appear in only a few of the earliest manuscripts, and soon disappear completely from chant books. It is generally assumed that later medieval chant notation gives no indication of rhythmic inflection of any kind; in this respect the later notation corresponds to late medieval chant performance in which every pitch had about the same length. This in turn corresponds to the late medieval designation *cantus planus*, plainchant.

## Changes in the medieval singer's perception

Around the year 800, Gregorian chant was at the centre of the northern chant singer's experience; it replaced previous kinds of melody which were no longer in use (and, since they had not been written down, they are lost to us). The Gregorian repertory, in spite of being written down, also disappeared gradually from the inner field of vision of the northern singers. This happened when they developed their own new repertories, each with its own distinctive style.

By the year 1000, melismatic Gregorian chant was rapidly being overtaken by new kinds of chant for the Mass – *Kyrie*, *Gloria in excelsis*, *Sanctus*, *Agnus Dei*, along with sequences and tropes. These gave the singers melodic models different from those of the Gregorian repertory. Later, by 1200, various kinds of discant 'with more than one voice' gave singers something quite different to hold in their minds – a kind of singing that used two different pitches sounding at the same time.

## Measured rhythm

Another change affected the way singers perceived rhythm. During the medieval development of discant, music teachers and musicians constructed a temporal continuum called *metre*, within which rhythm could be imagined to move. Metre was like a framework, a grid of equally spaced markers in time. It was located primarily inside the singer, but was soon graphed in musical notation in increasingly precise and elaborate ways.

This medieval development was the origin of the concepts of metre and rhythm in the classical repertory. These concepts feel very familiar to us – so familiar that modern observers may have difficulty in imagining any other framework for rhythm, or in imagining that rhythm could ever have been any other way. But within the European tradition these concepts of metre were new and different from concepts in Gregorian chant, where there was no metre and consequently no single rigid framework within which rhythm could be understood. The new system of metre was very useful for conceiving and performing music that happened to have regular rhythms, rhythms made of equal durations and equal patterns of duration. These coincided with the equal markers of the metric grid, so were easy to teach and to learn.

The rhythms of chant, on the other hand, did not coincide with the metric grid, and so metre was not used for chant performance and was not reflected in chant notation. To put it another, more important way, singers trained in the use of the metric grid had difficulty with the irregular rhythms of chant, and that contributed to the gradual but steady disuse of chant. The rhythmic elements of Gregorian chant actually disappeared from European singers' musical experience in a way that the melodic elements never did.

## A singer's perception of chant in the modern revival

In the revival of Gregorian chant towards 1900 (mentioned in chapter 4) the tension between chant notation and the singer's mental image became acute. This was because of the loss of tradition: a singer in 1900 had little opportunity to learn chant from a teacher, or to sing along with a group that had sung in a certain way for a long time. The Gregorian tradition had been eroding since the Middle Ages; but probably the greatest loss occurred between 1700 and 1900.

To be sure, the tradition was never broken completely. Of the various kinds of Gregorian chant, the simple congregational responses and recitation formulas survived in cathedrals, and the psalm tones in monasteries. In the absence of the more elaborate chants, this simple chanting was known, if at all, as a sad caricature of a forgotten glory. And yet many European cathedrals and monasteries still had chant books, and sang some items for special occasions. Some monasteries maintained the tradition of singing the whole Divine Office, and a few seem to have sung it well. In general, however, the loss of tradition meant the loss of an artistic way – a musical way – of singing the pitches recorded in the chant books.

By 1900, then, all that survived was a notation of pitches, and a musically neutral way of intoning them – 'chanting' them – in a way that to a musical person seemed categorically different from music. The miracle of the chant revival was that people began hearing these neutral sounds in a new way, the way described at the beginning of chapter 1. Or better, people were ready to hear something new in the neutral sounds. All of that belongs to the story of the listener's experience. The singer's problem was how to perform chant so as to evoke these new associations. In practical terms, singers had to develop an image of chant that would enable them to perform chant musically and convincingly; but they had to do this with no audible model, basing their conception completely on the pitches notated in the books.

### New chant books

Since the neutral way of singing those pitches produced inadequate results, singers and scholars felt at first that there must be something wrong with the books. They believed that the melodies had become corrupted, that in the course of a thousand years the melodies had changed from their original beauty, and that a beautiful performance could only be achieved by restoring the melodies to the way they were in the Middle Ages. Singers and scholars generally agreed about the importance of finding out exactly how the melodies went in the oldest manuscript sources.

Around 1900, various scholars proposed re-editing the Gregorian chant

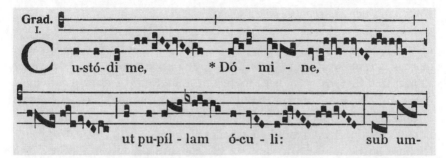

Plate 4 'Square' musical notation in the Vatican edition of the Graduale (1908), p. 295

books to bring them into better accord with the earliest manuscripts. Not everyone agreed that philological recovery of the chant was possible; but with the help of the programme of chant reform pursued vigorously by the Benedictine monks of Solesmes (France), there was enough agreement to produce in 1908 a new edition of the Gregorian repertory of Proper chants for the Mass. This edition is usually referred to as the 'Vatican edition' of the *Graduale*. It was accepted, for the time being, as the way the melodies went, that is to say, how they went originally, and how they ought to go now. The musical notation used in this edition appeared as in plate 4.

The notation, called *square notation*, resembles the kind of group notation used around 1200 (see plate 3), which still shows some of the grouping of the earliest notation. Square notation was read by singers and scholars around 1900 as 'plain', without rhythmic artifice, each pitch about the same length regardless of the note's shape.

## Controversy about rhythm

The Vatican edition was indeed closer than the immediately preceding chant books to the pitch configurations of the Gregorian melodies in the Middle Ages, but that did not solve the problem of making the melodies sound beautiful, or of making them evoke the experiences people expected and hoped for from chant. It was clear that singers needed much more information about pace, tone, timbre, inflection and phrasing. Such factors, lumped together under the heading *rhythm*, immediately occasioned a profound disagreement, in sharp contrast to the widespread agreement concerning the *pitch* configurations of the melodies. The disagreement about rhythm became polarized around the beliefs of the two principal figures in the chant revival, Dom André Mocquereau (1849–1930), monk of Solesmes, and Professor Peter Wagner (1865–1931), historian in Fribourg, Switzerland.

## Dom Mocquereau and Professor Wagner

Dom Mocquereau, at the Abbey of St Pierre in Solesmes, came out of a fifteen-hundred-year tradition of Benedictine monasticism, and also a much shorter tradition that went back to the mid-nineteenth century at Solesmes, to the work of Dom Guéranger and Dom Pothier, and to the way the monks of Solesmes sang chant. Dom Mocquereau himself had a burning conviction of how the chant should go, a belief of unique vividness and intensity. His idea of the appropriate rhythm was the most prominent aspect of this belief. In order to communicate this rhythm, he worked out a system of explaining it, as well as a method of teaching it and using it in performance. He devised a simple system of signs to be added to the square notation of chant, so that anyone could learn to sing the Gregorian melodies in his kind of rhythm.

Dom Mocquereau's rhythmic system is complex, and his published explanation of it (in *Le nombre musical*, 1908–27) has been difficult for many to understand; but his rhythmic signs are few and simple. The three types are shown in figure 8.4, and can be seen in plate 5. They include the dot, placed after a note; the *episema*, a short horizontal stroke placed over or under a note; and the *ictus*, a short vertical stroke placed over or under a note. The dot doubles the duration of a pitch, the episema lengthens it by a variable amount; the ictus indicates where to count 'one' while counting pitches in groups of twos or threes. The intended rhythm cannot be read simply from these signs: as with the earliest group notation, the singer has to know what rhythm is intended (in this case, Dom Mocquereau's rhythm). The signs merely remind singers of the rhythm they already know for a particular passage.

Dom Mocquereau had pushed hard for the new Vatican edition, along with Professor Peter Wagner and other scholars, and was committed to the version of the melodies published in it. He was very clear in his own mind, nonetheless, about the rhythm of the chant, and he felt it essential for the Vatican edition to include his rhythmic signs.

Professor Wagner objected strenuously to Dom Mocquereau's proposals for adding rhythmic signs to the Vatican edition. As a philologically trained historian, Wagner, along with many other scholars, felt that Dom Mocquereau's reading of the notation was far too subjective and was based

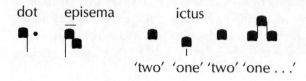

dot   episema        ictus

'two' 'one' 'two' 'one . . .'

Figure 8.4 Dom Mocquereau's rhythmic marks.

Plate 5 'Square' musical notation in the Solesmes edition of the Graduale (1945), p. 345

completely on modern rhythm. In accordance with philological method as understood around 1900, he believed that a true understanding of chant, as of any historical work of art or literature, could be reached only through a sophisticated analysis of the objective data supplied by documentary sources.

The disagreement between Dom Mocquereau and Professor Wagner was expressed not by direct confrontation, but rather indirectly through scholarly publications and eventually editorial committee work by others; furthermore, discussion took place in an environment dominated by religious beliefs, which encouraged a kind of verbal expression that was indirect, allusive and presumptive. The sense of the disagreement can be grasped from the following purely imaginary dialogue (as far as I know, they never met, and if they had, they would not have spoken in this manner).

*M.* Here is how I sing Gregorian chant. You can tell that it is the right way by reading it in the manuscripts.
*W.* I am following along in the manuscripts, and I do not see anything that looks like what you are singing.
*M.* That is because you are not reading with my system of rhythm in mind. You have to understand the system, and know that it is the same system used by the original singers.
*W.* I know of no documentary evidence for that. Your system is completely a product of modern thinking, and therefore inappropriate to the original chant.

However it was expressed, the disagreement was complete, the stand-off was absolute, and given the scholarly tradition that Professor Wagner represented, the result was clear and final. The editorial committee supervising the Vatican edition did not include any rhythmic signs.

## Dom Mocquereau and the monastery at Solesmes

Alternative systems of Gregorian rhythm were proposed during the first half
of the century; Wagner himself had one, and there were others. None, however, was developed to the point where it won general scholarly approval or
adoption by enough singers to generate a tradition. Meanwhile, Dom
Mocquereau's way of singing turned out to be spectacularly successful in
performance. His rhythmic signs were included in chant books published by
the monks of Solesmes: these publications included a *Graduale*, with
melodic versions scrupulously the same as the Vatican edition but with
rhythmic signs added (see plate 5 and compare it with plate 4); and also the
*Liber Usualis*, which became the most widely used chant book ever. During
the 1930s the monks of Solesmes made sound recordings of their performances of Gregorian chant as models of how it could sound when sung according to Dom Mocquereau's method of rhythm. Dom Mocquereau himself
published books and articles describing his method and – most important –
taught and demonstrated in person how he thought the chant should go.

Thousands of people learned this way of singing chant, and while it was
possible for an imaginative person to learn it out of Dom Mocquereau's book,
it was much more reliably learned from a teacher. I learned Dom
Mocquereau's method from someone who had studied with someone who had
studied at Solesmes and had heard how they did it there. While I listened carefully to the phonograph recordings, they simply confirmed what I got from my
teachers. The musical idea communicated by a live teacher – always a mysterious process – seemed to be central to learning the chant, just as it had been in
the ninth century, before the use of notation. And Dom Mocquereau's way
could be transmitted with great reliability: I have had the experience of singing
chant with a stranger, as if from the other end of the earth, and, both singing in
Solesmes style, we were perfectly together the first time through the first piece.

## Performance of 'nuanced' chant notation

Successful as it was, Dom Mocquereau's system of rhythm never persuaded
everyone that it was the *original* way of singing Gregorian chant. In addition
to the rhythmic system, the Solesmes style imposed an aesthetic system
whose sense of musical beauty and expressiveness was clearly a product of
its own time, and more appropriate to the nineteenth century than to the
ninth. The Solesmes style sounded so good to us only because it had much
in common with music from our own time that we thought sounded good.
Some scholars and singers had the persistent idea that chant in the ninth
century must have sounded different, that it would be valuable to know how
it was sung then, and that we ought to be able to find that out. But how?

Plate 6 The *Graduale Triplex* (1979) with 'square' musical notation on the staff and staffless notation from Laon MS 239 (above the staff) and St Gall Codex 359 (below the staff)

While pondering the apparent inaccessibility of ninth-century perform-ance, some scholars and singers became increasingly aware of a serious contradiction among the medieval manuscript sources for Gregorian chant – not in the sources themselves, actually, but rather in the standard philological way of thinking about them. According to literary philology, the best source of a text would be the one closest to the author; that usually meant the earliest source. And according to mid-twentieth-century music theory, the most essential part of a piece of music was its pitch configura-tion, as created by its composer (its 'author').

These two axioms, however, could not be applied simultaneously to chant manuscripts, because these first gave consistent indication of specific pitches only around the year 1200. Manuscripts before that time gave less specific indication of pitch; the earliest notated chant books from around 900 gave almost no indication. And in the period in which the chant is usually thought to have been created, singers did not use pitch notation at all. So it seemed that either the earliest sources were *not* the closest to the original (and therefore the standard philological method of establishing the original would not work) or the pitch configurations were *not* the basic element of the music (and therefore the standard way of analysing and eval-uating the melodies was irrelevant).

During the first half of the twentieth century, chant scholars tried not to think too hard about these implications; they tended to accept these contra-dictions regarding the behaviour of the sources as one of many peculiar things about ancient music. They continued to use the later chant books (from around 1200) in spite of their distance from the original chant, which was perhaps as much as 600 years. Since mid-century, however, scholars have gradually come to the idea that if philological method had any validity for chant, then that would suggest that the earliest sources did in fact record what was most important for the original performance – not pitch, but instead something else. That something else would be the manner of singing, which would include what modern singers and scholars have called rhythm.

The irony was that chant specialists had always known that some kind of rhythmic indications were to be found in at least some of the earliest manuscripts. The Benedictines of Solesmes had taken these indications seriously, and Dom Mocquereau employed them in his rhythmic system. Dom Mocquereau, however, did not use them rigorously: he did not derive his system completely from the indications in the manuscripts, but rather from his own inner vision, using these early manuscript indications only to support his inner vision.

At first Dom Mocquereau was criticized by philologically-minded scholars for making any use at all of these early manuscript indications of rhythm. Their meaning seemed too obscure to be accurately understood; even if a meaning *could* be determined, it seemed too individualistic to be understood as part of a standardized form of the melody. In any case, Dom Mocquereau's use of the meanings seemed to some to be purely arbitrary.

## Dom Cardine and 'nuanced' notation

After mid-century, Dom Mocquereau's work was criticized for quite a different reason, and from an unexpected source. In 1970 Dom Eugène Cardine, monk of Solesmes and in a sense the successor to Dom Mocquereau as the chant scholar representing the Solesmes tradition, called for a renewed effort at studying and understanding the musical notation of the earliest manuscripts, especially their rhythmic indications. He thought that the meaning of the signs could be determined, and would show how the chant was originally performed. In other words, he proposed to do for rhythm what philological method had done for pitch, that is, establish a standard version as close to a presumed original form as possible. To do that, Dom Cardine insisted on treating the use of the rhythmic signs in ancient manuscripts rigorously, consistently and objectively – which is what Dom Mocquereau clearly had not done.

Dom Cardine called this study of signs 'semiology' (the word refers to 'signs', but others have applied 'semiology' to quite different aspects of musical research). He understood that the signs would produce nuances, subtle variations in rhythmic inflection. Dom Cardine called for a detailed systematic study comparing how the signs were used in early manuscripts. In coordination with Dom Cardine's programme, Rupert Fischer, a chant scholar, made exact copies (by hand, not photography) of the notation of the two earliest notated chant books, Laon 239 and St Gall 359, both from around 900; Fischer meticulously entered these signs over and under the square notation as used in the Solesmes publications (that is, the Vatican edition versions of the melodies but including Dom Mocquereau's rhythmic marks; see plate 6 and compare with plates 1, 2, 4 and 5). This was published in 1979 as the *Graduale Triplex*, and it is the most valuable chant book for the modern chant singer.

While the emphasis that Dom Cardine placed on the signs and their possible meanings has been decisive in new studies of the early chant notation of rhythm, something about his method and purpose prevented the results from becoming generally useful. Dom Cardine wanted to recover a single original rhythm for each chant, just as the goal of traditional text criticism was to recover the single original 'authorial' text. But, as a matter of principle, scholars in the last half of the century have been less and less interested in a presumed original; in fact, they have been willing to consider that a single original version may never have existed. Scholars now seem more interested in the particular, singular ways that melodies were sung at particular times and places, by particular individuals. Precisely that is what is recorded by manuscripts such as Laon 239 or St Gall 359.

Hence, study of the signs of rhythmic nuance can result in a more exact understanding of some one style of tenth-century performance, but not of a single original or authentic style. Furthermore, Dom Cardine studiously avoided making specific aesthetic presumptions or conclusions about the chant, apparently imagining that the signs of nuance, once they were determined objectively, would produce a correct musical effect.

While it seems true that the signs of nuance are indeed a product of a tenth-century musical sensitivity, it seems equally true that their effect on performance must depend upon the sensitivity of the singer reading them. The effects of the group signs and adjunct letters are sometimes extremely subtle, barely perceptible to the listener and difficult for the performer to determine. Finding them depends on a delicate interaction between reading the early notation of a chant and building a personal conception of it, and that is a process as mysterious in Gregorian chant as in any other kind of music.

What works best for me is to begin with whatever way I sing a given chant melody; this is usually a mixture of how I first learned it and how I have sung it over a period of years. I compare my performance with one of the early notations in the *Graduale Triplex* as I sing, noticing whether the rhythmic signs there indicate anything different from the way I sing. If there is a discrepancy in a group or a phrase, I have to try to imagine other ways of singing until I find a way that matches the notation better. So far a better way has always presented itself, even if I have to try many different ways before finding a better one. Sometimes solutions, evolving step by step, lead me far from what I once felt was right.

The interesting – to me compelling – part of this process concerns the musical value of what I learn. The nuanced notation results in a better way to sing the melody; and this happens more frequently the better I get to know the repertory. In almost every case where a phrasing in one of the two earliest books (Laon and St Gall) was different from what I first expected, I have come to feel that the different way was an improvement. This gives me the very strong conviction that when I learn the pitches that tenth-century singers knew, and read the notation that tenth-century singers looked at, my inner experience produces a performance similar to what they sang.

This is not to assert that the way indicated in the earliest chant books is the best way, nor that one or the other of these books contains the original version. Since the grouping of pitches is decided by the individual performer, and since there was more than one performer, there was no one original way. And we have no reason to think that the best performance was necessarily made by the earliest performer, or by the one who came from a particular place, such as Rome – or even from Metz, which is where Bishop Amalarius said (in 830) that the best chant was sung. That was only what *he* thought. The best version is the one *we* think is best. And to say that a version is authentic turns out to mean the same as saying that it is best. The transcendent value of the earliest books is that they can suggest ways that we might not otherwise find in our inner experience right away, or ever.

# Commentary to the Chants on the Compact Disc
## Gregorian Chants for the Proper of the Mass, the Ordinary of the Mass, and the Divine Office

This book includes a compact disc with recordings of my performances of a selection of Gregorian Proper chants for the Mass, along with samples of chant for the Ordinary of the Mass and for the Divine Office. Listening to this or some other recording should be considered the primary way of becoming familiar with, and understanding, Gregorian chant. The chapters in this book provide an introduction to various contexts for the chant; the Commentary includes materials to guide the hearing of each individual item on the compact disc.

The contents of the compact disc are as follows:

1. *Haec dies* (Gradual)
2. *Puer natus* (Introit antiphon)
3. *Viderunt omnes* (Gradual)
4. *Alleluia Dies sanctificatus*
5. *Tui sunt caeli* (Offertory)
   verse *Magnus et metuendus,*
   verse *Tu humiliasti*
6. *Viderunt omnes* (Communion antiphon)
7. *Laetatus sum* (Gradual)
8. *Adiutor in opportunitatibus* (Gradual)
9. *Custodi me* (Gradual)
10. *Alleluia Dominus dixit*
11. *Alleluia Excita Domine*
12. *Super flumina* (Offertory)
13. *Exaltabo te* (Offertory)
14. *Psallite Domino* (Communion antiphon)
15. *Qui meditabitur* (Communion antiphon)
16. *Kyrie eleison* ('Conditor kyrie')
17. *Gloria in excelsis Deo*

18. *Sanctus*
19. *Agnus Dei*
20. Psalm 2, *Quare fremuerunt gentes* and *Dominus dixit* (antiphon)
21. *Magnum mysterium* (responsory)
22. *Parvulus filius* (antiphon) and Psalm 150, *Laudate Dominum*
23. *Multifarium* (chapter) and *Verbum caro* (responsory)
24. *A solis ortus cardine* (Office hymn)
25. *Gloria in excelsis* (antiphon) and Canticle *Benedictus*
26. *Salve Regina* (antiphon)

These items are taken up in this chapter according to the order of the tracks on the disc. For each item there is first a general characterization of the melody, sometimes including a note on its position in the repertory, or my own personal evaluation of its musical qualities. This is followed by a brief guide to identifying the tonal space in which the chant moves, along with the reference pitch, if one is easily audible. Then the Latin words of the piece are supplied in full, with English translation. Comments, shorter or longer as needed, are provided concerning the liturgical use of the item. Finally, a very short technical note locates the piece on the diatonic scale with pitch letters, for the benefit of those readers who want to refer to them (see the endnotes). Pitch letters are used according to the following system, in common use for chant in the Middle Ages:

$A\ B\ C\ D\ E\ F\ G\ a\ b\ c$ (= middle $c$) $d\ e\ f\ g\ a$.

The identification of tonal space and reference pitch applies the principles described in chapter 2. Where possible, the comments point out ways in which the melodic movement is analogous to modern major and minor scales in order to help the reader compare Gregorian melody with the more familiar melodic styles of classical and popular music.

The assignment of mode is indicated at the start of each piece, and the reasons for the assignment are mentioned in the technical note. As discussed in chapter 3, the reasons for the assignment include the note in the diatonic scale on which the piece ends, and the range above and below the ending pitch occupied by the piece. The combination of these two factors results in assignment to one of the eight modes (see the endnotes to chapter 3).

The Latin words provide a map of the piece, and can be used to locate details of the pitch plan just as a musician uses a score. The paragraph headed 'tonal space' uses the Latin words to identify the boundary pitches of the central tonal space. If there is a reference pitch, it is identified by the syllables on which it is easily audible. Once the ear can locate these pitches, it can follow the movement of the melody around the reference pitch, or inside and outside the central tonal space.

The pieces of chant vary greatly in the arrangement of tonal spaces, and also in the degree of reliance on reference pitches. For example, *Adiutor* (track 8) presents a central tonal space marked out clearly in the very first pitches and maintained with a strong reference pitch at the upper boundary throughout; but the melody refuses to be limited by that space, venturing above and below with apparently no interest in defining any other space. *Alleluia Excita Domine* (track 11), on the other hand, seems content to remain almost completely within a clear tonal space, with concentrated motion. Each melody has to be considered individually.

For the three pieces *Puer natus* (track 2), *Super flumina Babylonis* (track 12) and *Sanctus* (track 18), diagrams of the entire piece are provided which illustrate different arrangements of tonal spaces. The diagrams focus attention on the more easily audible markers of the movement by indicating the approximate motion of the melody over each word; melodic movement within the tonal space can be followed while listening to the piece. Sometimes the diagrams become complex, but that is because the melodic movement of that particular piece is complex.

The pieces recorded on the compact disc were selected primarily to represent various melodic styles of the Gregorian Proper chants for Mass. Track 1 has the Proper Gradual for Easter. Tracks 2–6 include all the Proper chants for the Mass for Christmas Day (Third Mass of the Nativity), in the order in which they appear in that Mass. These are perhaps the most familiar chants in the Gregorian repertory. The verses for the Offertory, however, are not often performed; since they are very long, only two of the three available verses have been included. Such Offertory verses are among the most elaborate and remarkable of the repertory.

Tracks 7–9 were selected from the very rich collection of over a hundred Gregorian Gradual chants to give a sampling of the variety and depth of expression of this genre of Gregorian melody. Similarly, tracks 10 and 11 give examples of Alleluia chants, tracks 12 and 13 of Offertory chants, tracks 14 and 15 of Communion chants. These two Alleluia melodies, together with the *Alleluia Dies sanctificatus* (track 4), are the three most frequently used model melodies for the Alleluia, and are presumably the oldest.

The better I come to know the repertory, the more difficult I find it to select chants that are representative, simply because each piece is different. In some cases the selections have to be understood merely as personal preferences. An adequate idea of Gregorian chant can be gained only by listening to the entire repertory; given strength and time, I hope to provide the means of doing that in another format.

Tracks 16–19 represent the Ordinary chants for Mass; these selections were chosen from sets of a dozen or so of each type found in twentieth-century chant books, and for each type the medieval repertories may contain two hundred or more.

Tracks 20 and 21 show the two principal types of chant for the Divine Office – antiphons with psalms, and responsories. The medieval repertories of these types are very large; no accurate count has ever been made. Tracks 22–25 are a sequence of items taken out of the Office of Christmas Lauds, according to the Benedictine use as set out in standard form in the *Liber Usualis*. These tracks are intended to give the listener an idea of the continuity of varied genres as found throughout the Divine Office. Track 26 contains one of the most well-known antiphons in honour of the Blessed Virgin Mary.

## Chants for the Proper of the Mass

### 1. *Haec dies* (Gradual, mode 2)

While serene, perhaps subdued, this melody has a way of rising with great expression, as in the melismas at the end of the respond and in the first part of the verse, at '*quo-(niam bonus)*'. The second-mode melody used for this Easter Gradual is one of the best-known of the Gregorian model melodies; this version, *Haec dies*, is prominent because assigned to the Easter Mass. Its words are a prototypical liturgical sentence (see Words and liturgical use).

*Tonal space*
The melody flows through a relatively restricted central tonal space: its upper reference pitch appears immediately on '*di-(es)*', settling in on '*fe-cit Do-mi-nus*'. A lower reference pitch is, however, much less prominent; while easily audible on '*(di-)es*', and eventually as the ending pitch of respond as well as verse, it merely suggests that the central tonal space does not extend far down.

The most expressive parts of the melody rise up above the reference pitch – far above, on '*quoniam bonus*' in the verse, where it reaches a pitch seldom used in the other versions of this model melody. In such exalted moments the melody seems to have none of the sombre quality of the minor scale suggested by its ending.

## Words and liturgical use

*respond*

| | |
|---|---|
| Haec dies, quam fecit Dominus: | This is the day which the Lord made: |
| Exsultemus, et laetemur in ea. | let us rejoice and be glad in it. |

*verse*

| | |
|---|---|
| Confitemini Domino, quoniam bonus: | Let us trust in the Lord because (he is) good: |
| quoniam in saeculum misericordia eius. | because for ever (is) his mercy |

Assigned to Easter Sunday, and repeated (with different verses) on each day of the following week.

'This is the day ...' comes from Psalm 117:24 (118:24), the victory song of a king, presumed to be David. Christians adopted it early on as the resurrection song of the risen Christ. The Gradual consists of two clauses ('*Haec* ...', '*exultemus* ...'). The Gradual verse uses the beginning – the first verse – of the psalm; or, on the weekdays, some other verse of the psalm.

The words of the respond may be one of the earliest sentences excerpted from the Psalter for Christian liturgical use. As the liturgical sentence for Easter, this is the most prominent among the two dozen versions of the model melody; and at the same time this Easter version is one of the least typical melodically, with some distinctive features.

### Technical note

This melody (in all its two dozen versions) is usually written ending on *a*; this has occasioned much analytic comment, since the systemic ending pitch for Gregorian melodies in mode 2, like those in mode 1, is *D*. One reason for placing the ending on *a* is that this particular melody makes use at one point of a pitch a semitone above the lower reference pitch (which will become the ending pitch). If this ending is placed on *D*, the special pitch a semitone higher is *E* flat, and as a matter of notational convenience Gregorian chant is notated so as to avoid accidentals other than *b* flat. When notated on *a*, the semitone is *b* flat.

Another reason is that this melody makes much use of the pitch a minor sixth above the ending pitch; writing the melody with the ending on *a* places this minor sixth on *f*, which avoids having to write even the *b* flat that would be required if the ending were on *D*.

With the ending on *a*, the upper reference pitch is *c*, and the central tonal space is the minor third *a b c*. The *F* a major third below the ending pitch is yet another reason for notating the melody on *a*, since if it were notated on *D* this required major third below would be on low *B* flat, and that note was not present in some medieval notational systems.

Figure 9.1 *Puer natus* (antiphon at the Introit). Motion within and above the central tonal space.

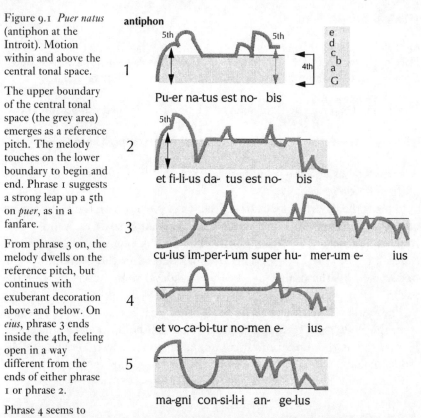

**antiphon**

1 — Pu-er na-tus est no- bis

2 — et fi-li-us da- tus est no- bis

3 — cu-ius im-per-i-um super hu- mer-um e- ius

4 — et vo-ca-bi-tur no-men e- ius

5 — ma-gni con-si-li-i an- ge-lus

The upper boundary of the central tonal space (the grey area) emerges as a reference pitch. The melody touches on the lower boundary to begin and end. Phrase 1 suggests a strong leap up a 5th on *puer*, as in a fanfare.

From phrase 3 on, the melody dwells on the reference pitch, but continues with exuberant decoration above and below. On *eius*, phrase 3 ends inside the 4th, feeling open in a way different from the ends of either phrase 1 or phrase 2.

Phrase 4 seems to repeat and expand phrase 3, and even ends as if rhyming melodically with phrase 3 – on the same word *eius*, and with the same pitch pattern.

Phrase 5 wraps up the antiphon by leaping through most of the pitch set, returning with emphasis to the top of the 4th, then descending rhetorically to the ending.

### Psalm tone for verse and *Gloria Patri*

Here the melody changes to a recitation formula. This is a relatively ornate kind of formula chosen according to the mode of the antiphon from a set of formulas used especially for the verse at the Introit.

The formula recites on the 5th above the ending, that is, on the first high pitch of the antiphon (as on *Puer*). It has a pause at mid–point (*novum*), which hangs suspended above

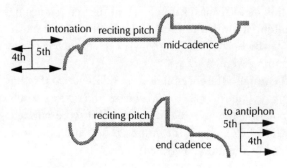

the reciting pitch. Then at the end it descends to the lower pitch of the 5th. The same formula is used for the *Gloria Patri*.

At its beginning and ending the formula touches on the two pitches that form the interval of the 4th used as the central tonal space of the antiphon.

## 2. *Puer natus* (Introit antiphon, mode 7)

This is a festive antiphon of celebration, pitched high as an acclamation; it has short phrases with clear shapes. The mood is bright: the melody moves in a tonal space that has the familiar quality of a major scale. While feeling stable and firmly rooted, however, the melody still has the open-ended quality of all Gregorian melody.

This entrance song for Christmas Day seems unusually accessible in its simple phrase shapes and uncomplicated melodic movement. Perhaps the melody reflects the straightforward verbal expression; or perhaps the melody is intended to be appropriate to the more appealing aspects of a popular public festival – the Nativity scene in the manger – avoiding abstruse theological aspects of the Incarnation of the Son of God.

### Tonal space

After beginning with a strong leap upward, *Puer natus* settles into a central tonal space with a strong reference pitch emerging at the upper boundary (see figure 9.1). This reference pitch can easily be heard towards the end of phrase 2: at the second *nobis*, *no-* circles close around the reference pitch at the upper boundary of the central space, and *-bis* drops down to the lower boundary. The reference pitch continues to sound throughout the antiphon, especially towards the end, where the lower boundary comes to feels like another reference pitch, framing the central tonal space. The reciting pitch of the psalm tone, however, is higher than the reference pitch.

### Words and liturgical use

*antiphon*

| | |
|---|---|
| Puer natus est nobis, | Unto us a child is born, |
| et filius datus est nobis: | unto us a Son is given: |
| cuius imperium super humerum eius: | and the government shall be upon his shoulder: |
| et vocabitur nomen eius, | and his name shall be called, |
| magni consilii Angelus. | Angel of mighty counsel. |

*psalm verse*

| | |
|---|---|
| Cantate Domino canticum novum: | O sing unto the Lord a new song: |
| quia mirabilia fecit. | for he hath done marvellous things. |
| (*antiphon may be repeated here*) | |
| Gloria Patri, et Filio, et Spiritui Sancto. | Glory be to the Father and to the Son, and to the Holy Spirit: |
| Sicut erat in principio, | as it was in the beginning, is now |
| et nunc, et semper, | and ever shall be, |
| et in saecula saeculorum. Amen. | for ages of ages. Amen. |
| (*antiphon is repeated here*) | |

Assigned to the principal Mass (the Third Mass) of the Nativity (25 December).

The words are taken from the book of the prophet Isaiah (Isaiah 9:6). Among his many lengthy prophecies, Isaiah predicted the coming of an anointed one who would save Israel; in this excerpt he imagined the words of acclamation with which the birth of Israel's saviour would be greeted. As Christian liturgy developed, these words were selected to celebrate the birth of Jesus. The psalm verse is from Psalm 97 (98); it contains the solo singer's exhortation to general rejoicing.

The words of the antiphon have been arranged from the biblical text into five short phrases. In medieval practice the antiphon may be sung again after the verse, then again a third time after the *Gloria Patri*; and in some performances there could be another verse followed by yet another repetition of the antiphon. In traditional performance since the Middle Ages, the Introit antiphon – in spite of its name – is sung straight through by the full choir. But in *Puer natus*, words and melody both lend themselves beautifully to singing in alternation, with the two semichoirs joining together for the emphatic last phrase, *magni consilii Angelus*. Many other Introit antiphons can be sung antiphonally in a similar way.

*Technical note*

The ending is on *G*, and the motion is mostly above that, so the antiphon is classed as mode 7. Accordingly, psalm tone 7 is selected for the verse. Psalm tone 7 recites on *d* a fifth above the ending of the antiphon.

3. *Viderunt omnes* (Gradual, mode 5)

Moderately melismatic, *Viderunt omnes* is a confident, expansive melody. It has a proclamatory quality, sometimes insisting on a few patterns in the middle of the pitch range, then surging up to the top. There is a long melisma in the verse that is expressive without being spectacular.

The bright character of the melody is due largely to the use of a pitch set very close to the major scale (see the technical note), which gives the piece a stable, firmly rooted feeling. Strong insistence on the middle part of the pitch set is combined with rapturous ascents to the top of the set, as well as reflective exploration in the lower part and a leisurely descent to an ending that seems fully expected.

The melody of *Viderunt* seems to me to be beautifully suited to the celebration of the simple event of the Nativity. Like *Puer natus*, the Introit antiphon for Christmas, this Gradual avoids abstruse theological issues such as those referred to by the Offertory. *Viderunt omnes* makes its musical point with three well-placed ascents, which stand free, casting their glow over the whole scene. We can be reminded of the star, rather than of the things that Jesus' mother Mary kept hidden in her heart.

*Tonal space*

On the word *Viderunt* there are leaps that mark out the central tonal space. The upper boundary of the space is the reference pitch. The lower boundary, touched upon as the first pitch, is then not heard for a while, but towards the end of the respond it becomes another reference pitch framing the central tonal space from below. Both the respond and the verse end on this lower reference pitch.

*Words and liturgical use*

*respond*

| | |
|---|---|
| Viderunt omnes fines terrae | All the ends of the world |
| salutare Dei nostri: | have seen the salvation of our God: |
| iubilate Deo omnis terra. | be joyful unto God, all ye lands! |

*verse*

| | |
|---|---|
| Notum fecit Dominus | The Lord hath declared |
| salutare suum: | his salvation: |
| ante conspectum gentium | in the sight of the peoples |
| revelavit iustitiam suam. | he hath revealed his justice. |

Assigned to the principal Mass (the Third Mass) of the Nativity (25 December).

The words are excerpted from Psalm 97 (98), the same psalm used for the psalm verse in the Introit *Puer natus*. In Psalm 97 these words exhort the people to praise the wonderful works of the Lord, including the extension of salvation to the whole world.

The Christian liturgical use of these words understands them to be a response by the people to the birth of the Saviour – 'Praise the Lord, for we are all saved'. In its Gregorian setting, of course, this response is sung by the choir on behalf of the people. The verse can be understood as the soloist's elaboration on the theme of the respond.

As the Christmas liturgy developed in the fourth century it included several different themes and addressed several issues, including the universality of the Christian faith and the manifestation of salvation by God in the person of his Son. While this particular Gradual is a simple popular acclamation, it could perhaps be read as an affirmation that Christian faith is not limited to one group of Christians. The theological status of Jesus as Son of God, however, could be understood in this Gradual only as an obscure extension of the meaning.

In terms of its more obvious surface meanings, the theme of this Gradual forms the culmination of a long series of sentences that extends throughout the four-week season of Advent, announcing the coming of the Lord. The Advent season featured scriptural texts analogous to those used to proclaim the coming of the Roman emperor (literally his *adventus*, 'advent') to one or another city as he moved around the empire on a perpetual circuit of administration. Part of the traditional rhetoric that greeted the emperor entering a city referred to his fame throughout the known world. Hence, 'All the ends of the earth have seen . . .'.

As with all Graduals, the words are arranged in two sentences, one for the respond, one for the verse. In *Viderunt* each sentence has two clauses, punctuated with a colon. The intrasyllabic melodic extension (see chapter 3) makes some of these clauses very long, and difficult to hear as melodic units. They tend to break down into shorter melodic phrases, as shown in the arrangement of the lines here. In *Viderunt* the colons are not provided with distinctive cadential idioms.

The family of Graduals in mode 5 is large, including about half of all the Gregorian Graduals, far more than those in any other mode. The fifth-mode Graduals share a well-defined set of idioms, and often resemble each other closely. The Gradual *Viderunt*, however, does not use so many of these idioms, and does not closely resemble other Graduals of the group. Even though it is assigned to one of the most important feasts of the year, it tends to use a simpler selection of idioms, and – except for the long melisma on *Dominus* – not much melismatic extension.

*Technical note*
The ending is *F*, the pitch set extends upwards one octave to *f*; hence, the melody is assigned to mode 5. The reference pitch is on *c*. Both *b* natural and *b* flat are used, each in different contexts.

## 4. *Alleluia Dies sanctificatus* (mode 2)

Clear and basically serene, this Alleluia matches the clarity of the verse's proclamation and invitation to celebrate the glorious coming ('advent') of the Lord. The melody moves with broad and simple motion through a limited pitch set. The Alleluia itself has a relatively short melisma (called the iubilus); the verse, although long in words, lacks a long melisma.

The melody for the Alleluia with iubilus uses well-defined but uncomplicated gestures. The melody for the verse alternates between some brief recitation and more complex, ornate melismatic phrases, usually heard here at the beginning and end of phrases. In the middle of the phrases are short passages of recitation, which is unusual in Proper chants for Mass. There is melodic repetition in the ornamental passages, which highlights the plan of phrases, suggesting balance and formality. This carries out the overall formality of the plan of performance (*alleluia*, verse, *alleluia*) with the repetitions of the acclamation *alleluia* before and after the verse. The Alleluia may be sung once or twice before the verse, and once after – the practice varies.

In its breadth and simplicity, the *alleluia* with iubilus would be appropriate to a congregational intonation and may represent the survival of such a simple melody from the time before the Gregorian repertory replaced congregational singing with a select choir. The melody ends in a more sombre place, and the verse as a whole dwells there, with a tone of serious solemnity. This particular melody, while beautifully decorative, does not seem to suggest a personal response to the words or to the occasion.

## Tonal space

For the most part, the pitch set of the piece is limited to a scale segment of just six pitches; a seventh pitch lies below this scale, and is heard only once (in the verse on *venite*), with special effect. The ear can easily follow the melody as it moves through simple relationships to nearby places.

The tonal plan, however, has an ambiguity: on the one hand it allows for a reference pitch, most audible in the melisma on allelu-*ia*, and moves around that pitch in a manner suggesting a major scale. On the other hand, the verse moves in a central tonal space marked out on *Dies*, and this sounds more like a minor scale. The iubilus ends on the lower boundary of this space.

## Words and liturgical use

*respond*

| | |
|---|---|
| Alleluia. | Alleluia. |

*verse*

| | |
|---|---|
| Dies sanctificatus illuxit nobis: | A holy day hath shone upon us: |
| Venite gentes, et adorate Dominum: | come, ye peoples, and worship the Lord: |
| quia hodie descendit lux magna super terram. | for today hath descended a great light upon the earth. |

Assigned to the principal Mass (the Third Mass) of the Nativity (25 December).

Not taken from the Psalter or from anywhere else in the Bible, these words are apparently common rhetorical idioms used in antiquity for public festal occasions, perhaps specifically the advent of the emperor. The words include the direct reference to 'today's' festivity, and also the image of light or *gloria* that was perceived to surround manifestation of divinity.

The melody is one of the model melodies, used for several different sets of words throughout the liturgical year, with only very slight changes in pitch configuration; it is one of three model melodies used for the Alleluia at Mass. This model melody is one of several melodic families in mode 2; it does not share many idioms with the other families.

### Technical note

The ending is on *D*; the lowest pitch is on *A* a 4th below *D*, and the highest one only a 5th above on *a*; hence, the chant is classed as mode 2. The reference pitch is *F*, which is supported by the *C* below, forming with *F* the interval of a fourth and strengthening the impression of a major scale.

The melody's ambiguity arises from the interplay between the segment of the major scale, *C–D–E–F–G–a*, and the segment of a minor scale established in the verse, *D–E–F–G–a*, which encompasses a firm 5th anchored on *D*.

## 5. *Tui sunt caeli* (Offertory, mode 4)

This long, intricate melody moves in a relatively restricted set of pitches with great concentration to produce a remarkably reflective mood; it gives opportunity for the theological issues raised by the words to receive attention.

The melody moves in a sombre way; this is most evident at the ends of certain phrases and at the end of the piece. The use of a restricted set of pitches makes it possible for the ear to be aware of the qualities of each pitch by itself. The pitch selected for the ending seems to be the least likely – or, at any rate, the least conclusive.

In the body of the piece, tonal relationships are established firmly, permitting strong melodic assertions at places other than the ending. The melody moves twice to pitches outside its usual set: once it touches on an inconspicuous pitch below; and once it rises above the set to a very conspicuous pitch, clearly placed there to accentuate the word *tu* ('thou').

I hear this as a meditative piece; and as I follow the detail of the melodic movement closely, becoming aware of the position of individual pitches or groups of two or three pitches in the relatively small pitch set, I can feel the expressive quality of individual pitches or small groups as an inner intensity shining through a cloudy exterior.

There are solo verses that can be sung as options to fill out the liturgical action. The melodies for these verses are strikingly different from the Offertory sentence itself: they move through much more extended pitch sets at much greater length, with expressive and occasionally flamboyant melodic curves. In what follows, I shall first describe the Offertory sentence and then the verses.

## Tonal space

During the first half of *Tui sunt caeli* there is a strong reference pitch, heard as the first pitch on *Tu-*. This reference pitch is the upper boundary of a very narrow central tonal space, which includes only the two pitches immediately below the reference pitch; these are all heard on the word *Tui*. The leap up on *tu* (*fundasti*) is 'way over the top' of this central space.

In the second half of the piece, from *iustitia* on, the same reference pitch is surrounded above and below by a wider tonal space, which is marked out clearly at *praeparatio*, and sounds like a minor scale. The ending, however, seems inconclusive because it does not end on the bottom of this scale nor on the reference pitch, but on the pitch in between – which seems to be the least likely place to end this piece. This quality of ending is frequent in the Gregorian repertory, and often takes this specific form in chants classed as mode 3 or mode 4.

## Words and liturgical use

| | |
|---|---|
| Tui sunt caeli, et tua est terra: | Thine are the heavens, and thine is the earth: |
| orbem terrarum, et plenitudinem eius | the circle of the lands, and the fulness |
| tu fundasti: | thereof, thou hast founded: |
| iustitia et iudicium praeparatio sedis | justice and judgement are the foun- |
| tuae. | dation of thy seat. |

Assigned to the principal Mass (the Third Mass) of the Nativity (25 December).

The words are selected from Psalm 88 (89), verses 12 and 15. The theme is evidently God the Creator of the universe, who is simultaneously the source of justice. It is not immediately apparent how these words apply to the birth of Jesus. That God the Creator was also the Father of the Lord Jesus became clear only after the Christian controversies of the second and third centuries had been settled by the great ecumenical councils of the fourth century. Therefore, the relevance of the creation of the universe to the baby Jesus lying in the manger was for Christians a matter of hard-won theological position; in any case, it could inspire reflection on the part of the faithful. The singing of these words along with other verses from the same psalm provided an opportunity for meditation during the collection of gifts at the Offertory.

The Offertory sentence is cast in three phrases; the third, lengthened by some moderate melismas, falls into two sub-phrases. Each of the three is an independent clause, and the third, beginning *iustitia*, is used as a refrain after each of the three verses.

*The solo verses*

For many Offertory sentences, one, two or three solo verses are provided in the earliest manuscripts. These were used during the early Middle Ages, but eventually went out of use. The words of the verses for *Tui sunt caeli* are excerpted from Psalm 88, the source of the Offertory sentence itself. The verses are long: each has its own melody, composed in an elaborate style with occasional melismas and including interesting patterns of melodic repetition. In performance, each verse is followed by the return of the latter part of the Offertory sentence.

*verse*

| | |
|---|---|
| Magnus et metuendus super omnes qui in circuitu eius sunt: tu dominaris potestati maris, motum autem fluctuum eius tu mitigas. *reprise* Iustitia et iudicium praeparatio sedis tuae. | Great, and much to be feared by all in the path: thou rulest the raging of the sea, and the rising of the waves thou stillest. Justice and judgement are the foundation of thy seat. |

The melody for this verse is placed higher than the Offertory; it begins forcefully at the top of its pitch set, and maintains a reference pitch at the top, with descents for the ends of phrases. The melodic motion is intense, with much ornamental twisting and turning in the upper subset. The melodic phrases are very long and are marked with only brief cadence idioms, at *eius sunt*, *maris*, and *mitigas*; the last one is an open ending that leads necessarily to the return of *iustitia*, the second part of the Offertory sentence.

*verse*

| | |
|---|---|
| Tu humiliasti sicut vulneratum superbum: et in virtute brachii tui dispersisti inimicos tuos: firmetur manus tua et exaltetur dextera tua, Domine. *reprise* Iustitia et iudicium praeparatio sedis tuae. | Thou hast humbled the proud as if wounding them: with the strength of thy arm hast thou scattered thine enemies: strong is thy hand, and high is thy right hand, O Lord. Justice and judgement are the foundation of thy seat. |

This verse also is placed high in the range, but is continually active throughout the whole range. Phrases end at *superbum*, *tuos*, and *Domine*, the last being another open ending. The melody seems rhetorical throughout, especially in the second phrase, *et in virtute*. The last melisma circles around a pitch in the middle of the range several times, with vigorous movement by leaps as well as by steps, above and below.

### Technical note

The Offertory sentence itself is classed as mode 4, since it ends on $E$ and its range is restricted from the $C$ below $E$ to $a$ above it (except for the high $c$ on *Tu*). Hence the pitch set is almost that of a major scale, firmly based on the low $C$; but the melody does not end on $C$, nor does the set sound like a major scale.

The verses are effectively in mode 3, with the same ending ($E$) as the sentence; the high $c$ is prominent, and the verse melody moves within a frame $G-c$, mostly above the pitch set of the sentence. The verses sometimes use $b$ flat, sometimes $b$ natural.

## 6. *Viderunt omnes* (Communion antiphon, mode 1)

This is a sprightly, lyrical melody. Although it ends with the tonal colour of a minor scale, the mood is on the bright side. Compressing intense, animated movement into a short space, the melody seems so compact as to resist critical analysis. It gives the impression of intimate lyric individuality, and it is finely crafted and balanced.

### Tonal space

This melody flows up and down throughout its pitch set. A reference pitch, implied rather than expressed, can be heard in the middle of the set; it is the opening pitch. The set as a whole, similar to a major scale, can be heard as divided into an upper space above the reference pitch, and a lower one below.

On the last three syllables of the antiphon the motion settles into a narrower space (from *-i nostri*). The same reference pitch is still implied at the centre of this space, but the ending makes it sound like a minor scale.

The psalm tone recites on a pitch higher than the implied reference pitch, and the tone as a whole occupies the space above; but it falls rapidly to end where the antiphon ends.

*Words and liturgical use*

*antiphon*

Viderunt omnes fines terrae salutare         All the ends of the earth have seen the
Dei nostri.                                  salvation of our God.

*psalm verse*

Cantate Domino canticum novum:               Sing unto the Lord a new song:
quia mirabilia fecit.                        for he hath done marvellous things.
(*antiphon can be repeated*)

Gloria Patri, et Filio, et Spiritui          Glory be to the Father and to the Son
Sancto.                                      and to the Holy Spirit:
Sicut erat in principio, et nunc, et         as it was in the beginning, is now and
semper,                                      ever shall be,
et in saecula saeculorum. Amen.              for ages of ages. Amen.

*antiphon repeated*

Assigned to the principal Mass (the Third Mass) of the Nativity (25 December).

The antiphon from Psalm 97 (98) recalls the Gradual sung earlier, in the synaxis of this Mass, thus providing an opportunity for meditation on that theme after Communion. As at the Introit, one or more verses from the psalm could be sung, and since the psalm is the same one that provided the verse at the Introit, cross-referencing takes place; this in turn suggests connections to the theme of the Introit antiphon, which was from another place in the Bible.

Having only one clause, this sentence is not clearly divided into units that can be sung antiphonally. Still, there are purely musical articulations after *terrae* and in the middle of *De-i* that can be used for alternation between semichoirs.

*Technical note*

With an ending on *D* and range up to *c*, this melody is classed as mode 1. The implied reference pitch is *F*; the space above it is *F– c*. The melody uses neither *b* natural nor *b* flat, making the scale *gapped*. The lower space is *C D E F*, so the whole pitch set extends through the octave *C– c*.

## 7. *Laetatus sum* (Gradual, mode 7)

Shortly after beginning, *Laetatus* sounds a peal of joy. The mood seems bright, even excited; the excitement comes from the abrupt leaps up and down. *Laetatus* seems to me to be an excellent use of melodic resources in a frankly expressive piece. The leaps, unmistakable as expressions of joy, seem to burst out of the neutral introductory phrase; afterwards, the melody resumes a more controlled course, eventually moving through the lower pitches that undergird the high leaps, giving them context and musical meaning. The melodic movement through the reiterated ascents and final descent in the verse seems beautifully paced.

## Tonal space

A reference pitch emerges out of the intonation of the first two words *Laetatus sum*; it is the pitch from which the melody leaps upwards. At *in domum* the respond moves down into the central tonal space, which lies *below* the reference pitch, between it and the ending pitch; the space is marked by (*Domi-*)*ni i-*(*bimus*).

The verse alternates several times between the space of the high leaps and the central tonal space; the latter is marked out in the verse by *et abundan-* and *in turri-*(*bus*).

## Words and liturgical use

*respond*

| | |
|---|---|
| Laetatus sum in his quae dicta sunt mihi: | I was glad at what was said to me: into the house of the Lord let us go. |
| in domum Domini ibimus. | |

*verse*

| | |
|---|---|
| Fiat pax in virtute tua: | Let there be peace in thy walls: |
| et abundantia in turribus tuis. | and plenteousness in thy towers. |

Assigned to the Fourth Sunday in Lent.

The words of *Laetatus* are excerpted from Psalm 121 (122), the Psalmist's joyful cry at the prospect of entering the Temple at Jerusalem. In spite of the first person singular, 'I was glad ...', the Gregorian setting puts the respond into the mouths of the congregation (but sung by the choir). And in spite of the meaning of the words ('into the house of the Lord let us go'), they are used for the Gradual rather than for the Introit (but they do appear also as a clincher quote for the verse of the Introit). In the Gradual, the solo verse expands the congregation's joyful response with a blessing taken from verse 7 of the same Psalm.

On the Fourth Sunday of Lent the schedule of *stations*, the bishop's visits to the churches of Rome, specified the church called Holy Cross in Jerusalem; the name of this church in Rome refers to an actual church in Jerusalem dedicated to the Holy Cross. Thus, the congregation in Rome could imagine themselves in Jerusalem, and the words for the Proper chants for this occasion seem to have been selected (in the sixth or seventh century) to express a theme appropriate to the occasion. We can imagine the members of this particular congregation recognizing with appreciation the inclusion in the Gradual (and also in the other Propers for this Mass) of the scriptural mention of Jerusalem, or some reference to it, through the medium of Psalm 121. This reference would have the effect of making this Mass proper to the place, like a station on a pilgrimage to holy places.

Because of the rejoicing in the psalm, apparent in its first word *Laetatus* ('I was glad ...'), the occasion of this Fourth Sunday in Lent became joyful, and in order to explain such a joyful occasion in the middle of the otherwise penitential season of Lent, this Sunday came to be considered a relief from the rigours of fasting and repentance, a temporary respite before the next two weeks, which, as Passiontide, commemorated the suffering and crucifixion of the Lord. This was an instance of a specific set of words influencing the general character of a liturgical occasion.

### Technical note

The melody is classed as mode 7 with an ending on *G*. The upward leaps are from *d* to *g* (an octave above the ending pitch), which is not so frequent in mode 7, and there is an *a* above that, which is unusual.

## 8. *Adiutor in opportunitatibus* (Gradual, mode 3)

This is a restless, passionate melody that explores far from a small, well-defined centre to search out dark places. It makes extravagant use of a pitch set whose extremities are not well defined.

*Adiutor* has a strange, inconclusive ending, which it shares with other chants classed as mode 3 (see the technical note). This kind of ending is one of the main features of Gregorian chant that makes it sound different from classical music. The strangeness, however, concerns only the ending; before their endings, the respond and the verse use a familiar segment of the diatonic scale as their central tonal space. The ending, the last thing we hear, makes us remember the rest of what we have just heard from a peculiar angle.

The passionate character of *Adiutor* is most perceptible in the explorations made by the melody into regions higher or lower than the central space. The pitches relatively far below or far above seem to have no clearly defined relationship to the central pitches. And the ending pitch has the least well-defined relationship to the central space.

### Tonal space

The central tonal space has a reference pitch at its upper boundary marked out by the first word, *Adiutor*. This central space, along with the reference pitch, persists throughout respond and verse, and is strongly confirmed at the end by *exsurge, Domine*. There are frequent distractions, however, in the form of beginnings of phrases that surge upwards through an octave or more (*quoniam, in finem, patientia*), and phrase endings that wind their way downwards into ill-defined regions (*noverunt te, quoniam non, pauperis*). Respond and verse both end below the central tonal space.

## Words and liturgical use

*respond*

| | |
|---|---|
| Adiutor in opportunitatibus, in tribulatione: | O Helper in good times and in tribulation: |
| sperent in te, qui noverunt te: | they hope in thee, that have known thee: |
| quoniam non derelinquis quaerentes te, Domine. | for thou dost not abandon those seeking thee, O Lord. |

*verse*

| | |
|---|---|
| Quoniam non in finem oblivio erit pauperis: | For the poor one will not be forgotten forever: |
| patientia pauperum non peribit in aeternum: | the suffering of the poor will not perish for ever: |
| exsurge, Domine, non praevaleat homo. | Arise, O Lord, let not man prevail. |

Assigned to Septuagesima Sunday.

The words are excerpted from Psalm 9, verses 10–11 and 19–20. Psalm 9 begins as a psalm of thanksgiving: it might have been a king's song, giving thanks for victory after tribulation; or it might have given thanks on behalf of the oppressed people.

In the respond of *Adiutor*, words of generalized supplication are placed in the mouth of the congregation. In the verse the soloist makes the petition more specific. The conclusion, 'Arise, O Lord, let not man prevail', seems to be used as a specifically Christian adaptation of the Hebrew text.

These verses from Psalm 9 are assigned to the beginning of pre-Lent, the three weeks before the beginning of Lent, added as penitential preparation. Many of the chant Propers during the pre-Lenten and Lenten season are supplications for protection; then, as the shadows of Lent deepen into Passiontide, the supplications become ever more clearly the agonized cries of the suffering Christ.

Graduals in mode 3 are heard only in the pre-Lenten and Lenten season; they form a small group of closely related melodies.

## Technical note

With an ending on *E*, and moving mostly in the octave above, this chant is classed as mode 3. The reference pitch is *c*, which forms with the *G* below a clear central tonal space. Both *b* natural and *b* flat are used. It is the ending on *E* that makes this and other chants in mode 3 sound 'modal'.

## 9. *Custodi me* (Gradual, mode 1)

The melody is sombre and serious, but illuminated from within by a brighter intensity, sometimes exalted. The mood seems ambiguous owing to a pitch set that moves through many clear, bright intervals, but also alludes to and eventually ends in a way that sounds to us like a minor key.

The illuminated seriousness of this melody is characteristic of Graduals and other types of Gregorian chant in mode 1; it is directly traceable to the structure of the pitch set (see the technical note). Graduals in mode 1 are by no means the most frequent or prominent in the Gregorian repertory, but their mood has become the one most usually taken as typically Gregorian. They remind us of classical melodies in the minor scale.

### Tonal space

As is frequent in chants classed as mode 1, the tonal structure is complex. In addition to the principal reference pitch, first heard on *me*, there is a higher one in the verse, first heard on (*de vu-*)*ul-*(*tu*). More than one tonal space is established.

On account of a restricted range of motion, especially in the low-lying introductory part of the respond, not much sense of tonal space appears near the beginning. A narrow space can be found, however, between the reference pitch on *me* and the first pitch, *Cus-to-*(*di*). In *sub umbra alarum tuarum* appears a broader, higher tonal space with the reference pitch as its lower boundary; it has a major sound. Simultaneously, an adjoining space is suggested *below* the reference pitch. From *protege* to the end of the respond, an alternative tonal space with the reference pitch at its centre is established as the ending space; it has a minor sound. The verse ends in the same tonal space as the respond.

### Words and liturgical use

*respond*

| | |
|---|---|
| Custodi me, Domine, ut pupillam oculi: | Keep me, O Lord, as the apple of an eye: |
| sub umbra alarum tuarum protege me. | under the shadow of thy wings protect me. |

*verse*

| | |
|---|---|
| De vultu tuo iudicium meum prodeat: | Let my judgement come forth from thy presence: |
| oculi tui videant aequitatem. | and let thine eyes look upon what is equitable. |

Included in the pool of Graduals used after Pentecost (usually on the Tenth Sunday).

The words for this Gradual, excerpted from Psalm 16 (17) are a selection that has remained popular and almost proverbial ('the apple of an eye'). As a plea for protection, this verse 8 functions in Psalm 16 as a clincher metaphor. Although expressed in the first person singular, the words are placed in the mouth of the individual worshipper as a member of the congregation, then in Gregorian chant sung by the choir. The solo verse presents a related thought from earlier in the psalm.

As a general sentiment, this Gradual it is not proper to a feast or season; it is merely appropriate to Sunday worship, hence classed as *dominical*.

*Technical note*

The ending on *D*, with motion up to *d*, places this chant in mode 1; both *b* natural and *b* flat are used. The reference pitch is *F* for the respond, which along with *C* below expresses the bright side of this melody. In the verse *a* seems to be the reference pitch, eventually supported by the *D* ending, which expresses the dark side.

10. *Alleluia Dominus dixit* (Alleluia, mode 8)

This Alleluia has a richly festive character. The words are given a formal but ornate presentation – including two broadly conceived melismas in the verse. The melody is bright without being exuberant: it moves out from a central pitch to neighbouring locations in a way that seems to explore all reasonable possibilities. This is accomplished by a relatively elaborate tonal plan. The bright overall tone of a major scale is maintained throughout the melody; there are, however, vagaries that give it a distinctive, sometimes oddly expressive quality (see the technical note).

I find *Alleluia Dominus dixit* to be a radiant melody, full of twists and turns that absorb my attention. The melody seems completely engaged in beautiful movement within each short phrase, and not much concerned with long-range direction. Yet it balances the clarity of its tonal centre with temporary digressions very successfully.

*Tonal plan*

There is a strong reference pitch throughout the Alleluia, heard right away on *-lu-*. It forms the upper boundary of the central tonal space. The lower boundary is clear at the end of the iubilus.

The first pitch of the word *alleluia* returns just often enough to remind the ear that it is there. In the verse, on *hodie* the melody descends to that pitch with such conviction as to establish it as a real foundation, the bottom of what seems like a central tonal space. That effect, however, occurs merely in passing, even though already hinted at on the word *tu*, and twice more on the last word, *te*. The ending of the verse returns to the bottom of the central tonal space marked out at the end of the iubilus.

*Words and liturgical use*

respond
Alleluia.                                                    Alleluia.
verse
Dominus dixit ad me:                        The Lord said unto me:
Filius meus es tu,                                Thou art my son,
ego hodie genui te.                            this day have I begotten thee.

Assigned to the First Mass of the Nativity ('Midnight Mass', 25 December).

The verse, from Psalm 2, is used also as the antiphon for that psalm when it is sung in the Night Office (track 20 on the compact disc), and elsewhere on the Christmas feast as a clincher quote. The quotation was used to identify Jesus as the Son of God, although there has been discussion over the centuries as to exactly how it does that.

The psalm quotation, sung by the solo singer, gives festal definition to the acclamation of the people. The Alleluia may be sung once or twice before the verse, and once after – the practice varies.

The specific melody of *Alleluia Dominus dixit* is used in almost the same form on a number of other liturgical occasions, so it is classed as a model melody; but its resemblance to other families in mode 8 that do not use this model melody is limited to a few closing idioms.

*Technical note*

The ending is on *G*, and since the melody spends some time below *G* it is classed as mode 8. The reference pitch is *c* a fourth above, so while a descent to *G* can sound momentarily like the bottom of a *G*-major scale, the emphasis on *c* ultimately prevents the *G* from sounding like a tonic. That is characteristic of all chants in mode 8.

The starting pitch is *F*. At various places *b* flat is used, and that, together with the strong descents to the 5th below the reference pitch *c*, can make *F* sound temporarily like the lower boundary of a tonal space.

11. *Alleluia Excita Domine* (Alleluia, mode 4)

The melody flows through a small pitch set easily and gracefully with an intricate recircling motion; certain figures are repeated, but not exactly. The tonal movement is ambiguous, suggesting a central tonal space but avoiding its boundary pitches at endings.

The central tonal space, marked out in the first few pitches, has the sombre sound of a minor scale. The melody sometimes moves through the space clearly, but then pauses or stops in ways that make it seem incomplete. The ending, too, sounds incomplete: it shares in the inconclusive quality of all melodies with this ending, that is, in modes 3 or 4.

Several of the idioms of this melody are distinctive, not shared with other melodies in mode 4. But this Alleluia melody as a whole is used in this exact form for a number of other occasions at Mass, adapting the verse melody to different sets of words. It is, therefore, classed as a model melody, one of the most frequently used. It has the special musical feature, found in many other Alleluias but not in other types of Gregorian chant, that the iubilus is repeated exactly on a different word, *nos*, at the end of the verse. This is followed by yet another repetition of the melisma when the opening *alleluia* is sung again.

The melody seems to me wistful, restless, inconclusive; it explores the possibility of a kind of lyric expression that seems more tuneful than usual for Gregorian. Tunefulness, however, can involve artistic risks, and sensitive to that danger, the melody seems to avoid full commitment in its melodic motion.

*Tonal space*

The melody remains almost completely within the tonal space marked out by the initial rise through *Allelu-*. The top boundary is a reference pitch (there is only one more pitch above it). The lower boundary (on the second pitch of *Al-*) also feels like a reference pitch; these two pitches frame the tonal space, but both the iubilus and the verse end on the pitch just above the lower boundary.

*Words and liturgical use*

*respond*

| | |
|---|---|
| Alleluia. | Alleluia. |

*verse*

| | |
|---|---|
| Excita, Domine, potentiam tuam, et veni, ut salvos facias nos. | Stir up, O Lord, thy strength, and come to make us safe. |

Assigned to the Third Sunday in Advent.

The verse is an excerpt from verse 3 of Psalm 79 (80); it is a lament for God's anger at Israel, and a plea for renewed assistance. The words could be understood as two roughly equal phrases, but are set as three melodic phrases because of the melisma on *veni* ('come').

As a petition for God's mercy, this verse along with others from Psalm 79 was used at several points in the Advent cycle of liturgical sentences; these verses express the penitential tone of the season. It is one of the minor mysteries of Christian worship that such a text can be used together with the praise-word *alleluia*.

As a melody type, with other words for the verse, this Alleluia is used throughout the liturgical year in various contexts. It is one of three Alleluia melody types used in this way (the other two are *Alleluia Dominus dixit* and *Alleluia Dies sanctificatus*).

*Technical note*
The ending is *E*, and the range extends only up to *b* flat, so the melody is classed as mode 4. The reference pitch is *a*. The central tonal space is the 5th from *a* down to *D*. While in many pieces in mode 4 *b* flat is a frequent option, in this melody it seems to be required; at any rate, it is always there, in spite of the diminished fifth it forms with the ending *E*.

The nuanced rhythm in the iubilus in the early notations of the *Graduale Triplex* does not agree with Dom Mocquereau's application of the ictus.

## 12. *Super flumina Babylonis* (Offertory, mode 1)

This melody has much mobility for one that is relatively short: it moves up and down through its pitch set with a remarkable fluidity and great expressiveness. The pitch set gives the bright feeling of a major scale, but the melody ends in a sombre place with a minor sound. This ambivalence is in keeping with its classification as mode 1. While it uses a number of idioms of other melismatic melodies in mode 1, the configuration of these idioms gives this melody its own character. I hear not only a melodic reference to the cascading fountains of Babylon (see the words, further on), but even more a deep nostalgia, sorrow and sweet memory mixed, in the smooth and essentially beautiful melodic brightness with dark edges and ending.

*Tonal space*
A reference pitch is implied throughout; it can be heard clearly on the first pitch, *Su-(per)*, and also at the end of the first phrase on (*Babylo-)nis* (see figure 9.2). It is the reference pitch, rather than the tonal space, that is central; there is one tonal space above the reference pitch, another below it. Until *flevimus* at the end of the second phrase, the melody moves easily through both spaces. From *dum* to the end the reference pitch continues, becoming stronger, but the melody ends lower, in a seemingly offhand manner.

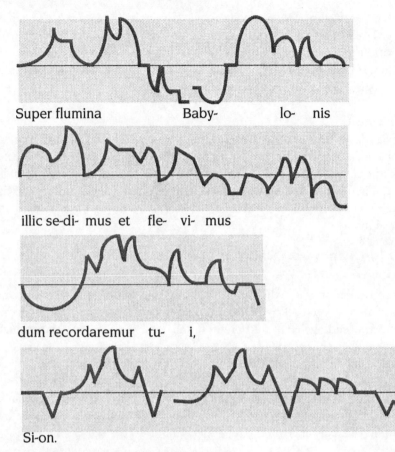

Super flumina          Baby-          lo-   nis

illic se-di- mus et    fle-  vi- mus

dum recordaremur    tu-       i,

Si-on.

Figure 9.2 *Super flumina Babylonis* (Offertory). Rather than dwelling in one central tonal space, this melody moves up and down in well-defined cycles that wind through a space above the reference pitch and another space below it.

## Words and liturgical use

| | |
|---|---|
| Super flumina Babylonis, | By the waters of Babylon |
| illic sedimus, et flevimus, | we sat down and wept, |
| dum recordaremur tui, Sion. | when we remembered thee, O Sion. |

Included in the pool of chants used after Pentecost (usually on the Twentieth Sunday after Pentecost). Also assigned to Thursday in the Fifth Week of Lent.

The first verse of Psalm 136 (137) – the topic sentence – is used in the Offertory as three short consecutive phrases. This psalm is a famous lament of the Jews that were taken captive to the fabulous city of Babylon in 586 BC. It contains the oft-quoted line about 'hanging our harps on the trees of

Babylon', as well as the poignant verse, 'How shall we sing a song in a strange land?' The words can also suggest an association of the melodic profile with the cascading fountains of the legendary hanging gardens of Babylon. (Other verses of this psalm, especially the last, are not excerpted for Christian use as liturgical sentences.)

### Technical note

Moving mostly above its ending on *D*, this melody is classed as mode 1. The optional *b* flat is used alternately with *b* natural. The motion around the reference pitch on *F* suggests a major scale, while the ending on *D* sounds minor. The relationship between the reference pitch and the ending can be heard as analogous to that between major and relative minor as used in classical music.

## 13. *Exaltabo te* (Offertory, mode 2)

This introduction and exhortation to praise repeatedly insists on the top pitch of a clear pitch set with a bright, major sound; but the bottom of the set and the ending have a different sound, and there is one spectacular departure from the central tonal space. According to its ending, the piece is classed as mode 2 (but see the technical note), while the tonal plan shares elements with mode 3.

While *Exaltabo te* may seem to lack lyricism, and has no ecstatic melisma, I sense a vibrant exaltation throughout the melody, and a passionate affirmation in the insistence on the reference pitch towards the end.

### Tonal space

A reference pitch can be heard from the first *Domine* on through to the end; it is very clear on *delectasti* and *sanasti*. This reference pitch is the upper boundary of a central tonal space marked out on *Do-mi-ne*, and also at the end of the second phrase on (*su-*)*per me*. There is an abrupt departure from the central tonal space on (*suscepisti*) *me*. The melody ends within the central tonal space, on neither the upper nor the lower boundary.

### Words and liturgical use

| | |
|---|---|
| Exaltabo te Domine, quoniam suscepisti me, | I will magnify thee, O Lord, for thou hast established me, |
| nec delectasti inimicos meos super me: | and not made my foes to triumph over me: |
| Domine clamavi ad te, et sanasti me. | O Lord, I cried unto thee, and thou hast healed me. |

Assigned to the First Day of Lent ('Ash Wednesday').

The words are from Psalm 29 (30), the first two verses. This kind of text is traditionally attributed to the king – that is, David – as a victory song after overcoming great tribulation; the king exhorts the people to join him in praising God.

Christian liturgical use places this psalm's topic sentence as an Offertory sentence for Ash Wednesday at the beginning of Lent, either as a meditation of the individual worshipper, or perhaps in the mouth of the suffering Jesus as part of the Lenten programme.

### Technical note

The reference pitch is high on *c* in the central tonal space $G-c$. The use of *E* down low is more characteristic of mode 3. The classification as mode 2, however, depends largely on the ending on *a* and the melodic movement just before it.

## 14. *Psallite Domino* (Communion antiphon, mode 1)

This short melody describes an extremely graceful arch in one phrase, with an alleluia added. It packs much melodic activity into a short space: there is inward lyric tension, very different from the exuberant, sometimes extravagant, expansion of a melismatic Gradual.

The melody begins and ends with idioms characteristic of mode 1, and sits firmly in the pitch set, which has the quality of a minor scale; but sometimes it sounds more like major. I am less aware here of modal idioms and more aware of the great refinement in the choice and succession of melodic twists and turns and the resulting expressiveness. The qualities of the individual pitches seem to be revealed with precision.

### Tonal space

The eventual ending pitch, but not the tonal space, is marked by the first words *Psallite Domino*. A reference pitch emerges only from *qui* on. The concluding alleluia, while maintaining the same reference pitch, finds a new context for it at the centre of a segment that sounds like a minor scale.

### Words and liturgical use

Psallite Domino, qui ascendit super caelos caelorum ad Orientem, alleluia.

Sing unto the Lord, who ascends to the heaven of heavens, to the Sun rising, alleluia.

Assigned to Ascension Day.

The words are from Psalm 67, part of verses 33–34 (68, verses 32–33). Psalm 67 celebrates, at length and in bloody detail, a crushing victory by Israel over the enemies of Yahweh. The beginning of the psalm, 'Let God arise, and let his enemies be scattered', was once quoted loudly at an early Christian street demonstration against the person of the emperor.

As the Christian liturgical calendar was eventually elaborated, a feast was instituted to commemorate the ascension to heaven of the Lord Jesus (after he had risen from the tomb and had been with the disciples). Among the sentences selected from Scripture were several from Psalm 67, used for this Communion antiphon as well as for other Propers of the Ascension Day Mass. In this psalm, singers are mentioned, if only in passing, as is also the ascent of the Lord on high.

A melodic reference to ascent is perfectly clear at *qui ascendit*, but the musical evocation of these words is arranged so as to be an integral part of the prevailing melodic curve. A similar reference in *ad Orientem* ('to the Sun rising') is perceptible only in the brief scale on *or-(ientem)*.

*Technical note*

With an ending on *D* and a clearly defined octave scale from *D* to the *d* above, this is a classic representative of mode 1 melodies; *b* natural is used in moving upwards, *b* flat during a generally downward trend. The low *C* is used sparingly and for a special purpose – the penultimate half-cadence.

## 15. *Qui meditabitur* (Communion antiphon, mode 3)

After an abruptly rising intonation, this melody describes a leisurely, involute descent to the end, becoming more and more meditative. I find this to be a melody of unusual beauty and expressiveness.

*Tonal space*

The pitch set as a whole is close to that of a major scale; it has a generally positive tone, without being bright. The melody seems to occupy the whole pitch set, flowing easily into all parts, so that neither a reference pitch nor a central tonal space is apparent. As the melody goes on, however, it seems to have less and less to do with a major scale, and ends in the strange place characteristic of mode 3.

*Words and liturgical use*

| | |
|---|---|
| Qui meditabitur in lege Domini die ac nocte, | He who doth meditate on the law of the Lord day and night |
| dabit fructum suum in tempore suo. | will bring forth his fruit in due season. |

Assigned to the First Day of Lent ('Ash Wednesday').

The words form one long complex clause. In *fructum suum* the Latin text provided an opportunity for rich assonance, and the singer-composer did not let it go to waste.

*Technical note*

With an ending on *E* and range up to *d*, this is classed as mode 3; *b* natural and *b* flat are used in different contexts.

## Chants for the Ordinary of the Mass

The *Ordinarium Missae*, or Ordinary of the Mass, includes all those items said regularly at Mass without variation of wording for special occasions. Some of these items are said by the celebrant, some by the congregation. Five items that were originally said by the congregation – *Kyrie, Gloria in excelsis, Credo, Sanctus, Agnus Dei* – eventually came to be treated as a group; singers came to call them '*the* Ordinary of the Mass', meaning the five invariable parts of the Mass sung by the choir. Sizable repertories of medieval chant were provided for each of these five items (but only a few chants for the Credo); at any given performance of Mass the singers would choose which settings to sing, although they could be guided by certain conventions and preferences.

In a major shift of musical style towards the end of the Middle Ages (fourteenth and fifteenth centuries) northern singers substituted polyphonic settings for the chanted Ordinary; eventually these polyphonic settings of *Kyrie, Gloria, Credo, Sanctus* and *Agnus Dei* were composed as musical sets, each set an artistic entity. Such a set is called a (polyphonic) *Mass cycle*. These cycles became the most prominent kind of music at Mass, in some cases the only kind: 'going to Mass' could mean simply entering the cathedral and listening to a polyphonic Mass cycle. After AD 1600, Mass cycles were increasingly performed with instruments – orchestras – as well as voices, and the voices, solo as well as choral, were treated by composers in increasingly dramatic ways, sounding like opera or oratorio. Bach's Mass in B minor and Beethoven's *Missa solemnis* are examples.

The revival of chant towards AD 1900 was in large part a reaction against this style of concerted Mass Ordinary (*concerted* refers to the joint contributions of voices and instruments in musical performance). The medieval chant settings of the items of the Mass Ordinary were re-edited along with the Gregorian chant for the Proper of the Mass. In some cases dedicated congregations have learned these elaborate medieval chant settings of the Mass Ordinary, and, singing them with enthusiasm, have reclaimed this part of their original liturgy at Mass.

A single setting of each of the four items – *Kyrie, Gloria, Sanctus, Agnus Dei* – has been included on the compact disc as representative of medieval musical styles. (*Credo* was too long for inclusion, and a solo voice does not give a useful demonstration of this very congregational chant anyway.)

## 16. *Kyrie eleison*

This forthright, sonorous melody presents its decorative movement in clearly defined phrases. The pitch set is only slightly different from the sound of a major scale. The melody moves with broad gestures arranged in a plan that at first shows symmetry, then at the end breaks out in a more flamboyant extension. The patterns of decoration reveal a repeating design and at the same time conceal its intricate workings. The repeated cadential idiom gives the melody a sense of closure very different from what we hear in the Gregorian style.

This is a medieval chant, probably composed in the tenth century after the Gregorian repertory was completed.

### Tonal space
There is a reference pitch, heard as the first and last pitches of the first *Kyrie eleison*; it is the lower boundary of a central tonal space. Kyries 7 and 9 move into a higher tonal space centred on a new reference pitch above the first one; the first reference pitch returns at the ends of Kyries 8 and 9. For more detail concerning this relatively complex tonal plan, see the technical note.

### Words and liturgical use

| | |
|---|---|
| 1 Kyrie eleison. | Lord, have mercy. |
| 2 Kyrie eleison. | Lord, have mercy. |
| 3 Kyrie eleison. | Lord, have mercy. |
| 4 Christe eleison. | Christ, have mercy. |
| 5 Christe eleison. | Christ, have mercy. |
| 6 Christe eleison. | Christ, have mercy. |

7 Kyrie eleison.              Lord, have mercy.
8 Kyrie eleison.              Lord, have mercy.
9 Kyrie eleison.              Lord, have mercy.

The Greek words are a token litany used in the entrance rite, the introduction to the synaxis. They are derived from ancient cultic practice, typically as the people's response to and participation in public acclaim of a god or hero, and typically involving manifold repetition – sometimes to a much greater extent than here.

The ninefold formula including thrice *Kyrie*, thrice *Christe*, and again thrice *Kyrie*, seems to be the result of the Frankish normalization of liturgical forms. The melody is the creation of the Frankish cantors of the tenth century; it effectively precludes congregational participation. Instead, the melody as sung by the choir provides a formal, celebratory mood for the beginning of Mass.

Like many other northern Kyrie melodies, this one was sung in two forms, one melismatic (as on the compact disc), the other with a set of Latin words providing a syllable for each pitch of this same melody. The words for phrase 1 of this Kyrie are these:

suavis tu Deus, rex noster verus es patiens, mitis valde in perpetuo.
(sweet thou art, O God, patient, our true king, gentle indeed for ever)

The melody could have been sung with these words, or without them; or each phrase could have been sung twice, first with its words, and then without. Taking the last option, there would have been an opportunity for antiphony between the two halves of the choir; or the choir could respond with the melismatic version after the cantor sings the words. For still another manner of performance, the soloist could sing the melody with the words while the choir could simultaneously sing the melody without the words, perhaps as a soft background.

*Technical note*
With an ending on *G* and a range up to *f* a seventh above, this melody would be classed as mode 7; but the low pitches at the start of phrases 2 and 5 would make it mode 8. Modal classification, however, is not meaningful in this case, since (1) medieval chants commonly exceed the theoretical ranges assigned to the modes, (2) medieval chants do not belong to the modal families of Gregorian chant, and (3) Kyries are not sung as antiphons to psalms, so there is no reason to look for a psalm tone corresponding to the mode of the antiphon.

The central tonal space is *G* up to *c*, with reference pitch *G*. The higher tonal space is *c* up to *f*, with reference pitch *d*. A third tonal space is suggested below, from *D* to *G*.

## 17. *Gloria in excelsis Deo*

This melody soars through its long set of words with great momentum, ranging freely over a wide pitch set. Without being melismatic it still has the quality of fantasy; and without seeming rhetorical it has great emphasis and near-extravagance. It is warmly lyric, yet on a grand scale, and is firmly rooted in a central tonal space.

### Tonal space

A reference pitch, audible at the beginning and end of the words *Gloria in excelsis Deo*, is in operation almost to the end of the whole piece; but in the last phrase, *cum Sancto Spiritu*, a slight shift accompanies the rhetorical peroration. The reference pitch is most closely associated with a central tonal space that extends downwards to the ending pitch, audible at *voluntatis*. The word *hominibus*, descending in a scale segment as if from heaven to earth, marks out the central space. There are many distractions from this central tonal space, and at the end it does not seem to define the shape of the concluding phrase.

### Words and liturgical use

| | |
|---|---|
| Gloria in excelsis Deo. | Glory be to God on high. |
| Et in terra pax hominibus bonae voluntatis. | And on earth peace to men of goodwill. |
| Laudamus te. Benedicimus te. Adoramus te. Glorificamus te. | We praise thee, we bless thee, we worship thee, we glorify thee. |
| Gratias agimus tibi propter magnam gloriam tuam. | We give thanks to thee for thy great glory. |
| Domine Deus, Rex caelestis, Deus Pater omnipotens. | O Lord God, heavenly king, God the father almighty. |
| Domine Fili unigenite, Iesu Christe. | O Lord, the only begotten Son, Jesu Christ. |
| Domine Deus, Agnus Dei, Filius Patris. | O Lord God, Lamb of God, Son of the Father, |
| Qui tollis peccata mundi, miserere nobis. | That takest away the sins of the world, have mercy upon us. |
| Qui tollis peccata mundi, suscipe deprecationem nostram. | Thou that takest away the sins of the world, receive our prayer. |
| Qui sedes ad dexteram Patris, miserere nobis. | Thou that sittest at the right hand of the Father, have mercy upon us. |
| Quoniam tu solus sanctus. Tu solus Dominus. | For thou only art holy, thou only art the Lord, |
| Tu solus altissimus, Iesu Christe. | thou only art most high, O Jesu Christ, |
| Cum Sancto Spiritu, in gloria Dei Patris. Amen. | With the Holy Ghost in the glory of God the Father. Amen. |

This is the ancient Christian morning hymn, used in the entrance rite as a festive introduction to the synaxis. The first two lines quote the angels singing to the shepherds in the fields outside Bethlehem at the Nativity of Jesus (Luke 2:14); traditionally sung as versicle and respond between bishop and people, this is followed by praises, petitions, and final doxology. After 800 the hymn was supplied with elaborate melodies such as this one. It has often been sung in an antiphonal manner.

Because of its festive nature, the *Gloria in excelsis* is used primarily during the Christmas season and after Easter, not during the more sombre times of Advent and Lent. The *Gloria in excelsis* is sometimes called the greater doxology as opposed to the *Gloria Patri*, the lesser doxology, these being the two most familiar doxologies; there are a number of others, used for various purposes.

*Technical note*

The melody ends on $D$, and extends from the $C$ below up to $f$ above the octave $d$, hence is classed as mode 1. The central tonal space is the 5th $D-a$, with the upper and lower boundaries both acting as firm reference pitches. Sections of the melody suggest other tonal spaces, such as $C-F$, $F-c$, $G-d$, $a-c$, $c-f$.

## 18. *Sanctus*

This melody is a solemn expression of the seraphic hymn: after three separate melodic gestures for the acclamations of 'Sanctus', the melody concludes with two long arches spanning the whole range (see figure 9.3).

The melody is medieval chant, probably composed after 1000 in northern France or Germany, when the Gregorian repertory had long since been completed.

This very lyric melody seems to be a most intimate musical expression of a human address to, and acknowledgement of, divinity. The frequent melodic leaps are absorbed into a smoothly continuous line in a remarkable and mysterious way.

*Tonal space*

The tonal plan is complex: there is no reference pitch nor any central tonal space. The first *Sanctus* outlines one space; the second *sanctus* outlines another, one step higher. These two spaces tend to alternate, but there is a third, still higher space on *caeli et terra gloria*.

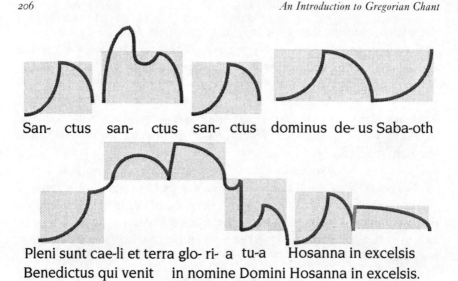

San- ctus san- ctus san- ctus dominus de- us Saba-oth

Pleni sunt cae-li et terra glo- ri- a tu-a　　Hosanna in excelsis
Benedictus qui venit　in nomine Domini Hosanna in excelsis.

Figure 9.3 *Sanctus*. The motion begins in a low tonal space, then moves immediately into a higher one. These two spaces alternate irregularly throughout. The higher one is combined with one still higher.

The words are grouped by the melody in three phrases, the third exactly repeating the second, A B B.

Starting like the first *sanctus*, *Pleni sunt* moves steadily in a longer arc that takes it into the highest space; then the line descends in a looping fashion all the way to the bottom of the range at *tua*. *Hosanna* refers to the first *sanctus* once more, then makes an ending that feels non-committal.

### Words and liturgical use

| | |
|---|---|
| Sanctus, sanctus, sanctus Dominus Deus Sabaoth. | Holy, holy, holy Lord God of hosts. |
| Pleni sunt caeli et terra gloria tua. | Heaven and earth are full of thy glory. |
| Hosanna in excelsis. | Hosanna in the highest. |
| Benedictus qui venit in nomine Domini. | Blessed is he that cometh in the name of the Lord. |
| Hosanna in excelsis. | Hosanna in the highest. |

The opening words are quoted from Isaiah's vision (Isaiah 6:3) of the six-winged seraphim singing antiphonally on either side of the Lord's throne. This Old Testament text was used by Christians, with additions and very interesting alterations, as the only congregational hymn of solemn praise in the eucharist. *Hosanna* was added as an acclamation, as was also *Benedictus*, verse 26 from Psalm 117 (118), followed by another Hosanna. The resulting plan is treated in various ways by medieval composers.

Introduced by the Preface (the opening portion of the eucharistic prayer), the *Sanctus* is sung at Mass throughout the year. Originally used with congregational intonation, the hymn was given artistic melodies by north-erners from the tenth century on, in a variety of styles. Medieval composers produced a repertory of two or three hundred *Sanctus* melodies, and con-tinued on to produce polyphonic settings of the hymn during the fourteenth and fifteenth centuries.

## Technical note

With an ending on *D*, and a range from the *C* below to the *d* at the octave, the melody is classed as mode 1, but it has its own way of sitting in the modal frame. The 5th from *C* to *G* makes a firm beginning, and the *D* at the end of the first (and third) *sanctus* seems to float; the *a* at the end of the first phrase floats even more freely, with none of the stability that might be expected.

## 19. *Agnus Dei*

Moving intricately along an expressive arch-like trajectory, this melody is a very inward musical meditation. A stable tonal space is implied, but veiled by melodic movement that begins and ends on pitches whose relationships are not clear.

This is a medieval chant, composed after 1000, when the Gregorian repertory had long since been completed.

## Tonal space

There is no reference pitch, and no central tonal space, although the melody dwells in two or three distinct tonal spaces, moving from one to the other. Together these spaces add up to – a C-major scale! This scale is expressed complete (with one more pitch above it) in the words *qui tollis pecca-(ta)*, but in typically convoluted motion.

The stable effect of a C-major scale is not apparent, however, because of the melodic motion and because of the ending. Medieval chant often used this scale with this strange ending to give veiled expression to mystical contexts.

## Words and liturgical use

| | |
|---|---|
| Agnus Dei, qui tollis peccata mundi: miserere nobis. | O Lamb of God, that takest away the sins of the world, have mercy upon us. |
| Agnus Dei, qui tollis peccata mundi: miserere nobis. | O Lamb of God, that takest away the sins of the world, have mercy upon us. |
| Agnus Dei, qui tollis peccata mundi: dona nobis pacem. | O Lamb of God, that takest away the sins of the world, grant us thy peace. |

The words are quoted from John's Gospel (John 1:29); they are said by John the Baptist when he greets Jesus. The use of these words as an acclamation at

Communion is attributed to Pope Sergius, about 680, that is, close to the time of *Ordo Romanus I*, in which the specifics of the Mass are first written down.

The words from John 1:29 may also be spoken by the celebrant at Holy Communion as if presenting Jesus to the people, just as John the Baptist did. In the *Agnus Dei* chant, on the other hand, the words are used as the people's devotional response to the consecrated bread and wine, understood to be the body and blood of the Lord Jesus.

Northern composers provided artistic melodies for the *Agnus Dei* throughout the Middle Ages, accumulating a repertory of two or three hundred different settings. The northerners stabilized the number of repetitions at three (somewhat as they did with the *Kyrie eleison* at the beginning of Mass), and later made the third repetition end with the words *dona nobis pacem*. In connection with those developments some of the earlier melodies were expanded or rebuilt to enhance the threefold repetition. The medieval melodies often seem to reflect, by their intensely inward nature, the theological mysticism implied in the words.

*Technical note*
The ending pitch *E*, together with the use of *D* and *C* below, classifies the melody as mode 4, although the firm cadence in the interval *G–c* indicates mode 3 instead.

## Chants of the Divine Office

The principal activities of the monastic Divine Office are singing psalms together, and listening to lections as they are read by solo readers. The psalms are sung to recitation formulas called psalm tones; in connection with each psalm is sung a short melody called an antiphon (usually more than once). Lections are sung to their own kind of recitation formula called a lection tone; after each lection comes a longer, more elaborate melody called a responsory, usually sung by a choir and a solo singer. There is a system of eight psalm tones; there are hundreds of responsory melodies and perhaps two thousand antiphon melodies. Antiphons and responsories are the bulk of the chant repertory for the Divine Office.

### 20. *Quare fremuerunt* (Psalm 2) *and Dominus dixit* (Antiphon)

On the compact disc, the antiphon is first heard after verse 5 of the psalm. In usual liturgical practice an antiphon is sung *before* a psalm, then during or after it.

The psalm tone for Psalm 2 was selected according to the mode of the antiphon *Dominus dixit*, which is mode 8. If sung with an antiphon of another mode, it would be sung to a psalm tone corresponding to that mode. There is a system of eight psalm tones from which the selection is made.

The antiphon *Dominus dixit* is a bright, formal presentation of the words. Like many of the antiphons used in the Divine Office, it is very short and has a relatively limited range, yet it moves intensively and continually through its set of pitches. Its reference pitch is the same as the reciting pitch of the psalm tone, and it uses the same central tonal space.

## Words and liturgical use
(The asterisk * marks the division of each verse into two parts.)

### Psalm 2

1 Quare fremuerunt gentes,

* et populi meditati sunt inania?

2 Astiterunt reges terrae, et principes convenerunt in unum,
* adversus Dominum et adversus Christum eius.
3 Dirumpamus vincula eorum:
* et proiiciamus a nobis iugum ipsorum.
4 Qui habitat in caelis, irridebit eos:

* et Dominus subsannabit eos.
5 Tunc loquetur ad eos in ira sua,

* et in furore suo conturbabit eos.
6 Ego autem constitutus sum Rex ab eo super Sion montem sanctum eius,
* praedicans praeceptum cius.
7 Dominus dixit ad me:
* Filius meus es tu, ego hodie genui te.

8 Postula a me, et dabo tibi Gentes haereditatem tuam,
* et possessionem tuam terminos terrae.

9 Reges eos in virga ferrea,

* et tamquam vas figuli confringes eos.

10 Et nunc, reges, intelligite:
* erudimini qui iudicatis terram.

1 Why do the heathen so furiously rage together?

* and why do the people imagine a vain thing?

2 The kings of the earth stand up, and the rulers take counsel together
* against the Lord, and against his anointed.
3 Let us break their bonds asunder,
* and cast away their cords from us.
4 He that dwelleth in heaven shall laugh them to scorn:

* the Lord shall have them in derision.
5 Then shall he speak unto them in his wrath,

* and vex them in his sore displeasure:
6 Yet have I set my king upon my holy hill in Sion:
*I will rehearse the decree:
7 The Lord hath said unto me
* Thou art my son, this day have I begotten thee.

8 Desire of me, and I shall give thee the nations for thine inheritance,
* and the uttermost parts of the earth for thy possession.

9 Thou shalt bruise them with a rod of iron,

* and break them in pieces like a potter's vessel.

10 Be wise now therefore, O ye kings:
* be instructed, ye that are judges of the earth.

11 Servite Domino in timore:
* et exsultate ei cum tremore.
12 Apprehendite disciplinam,
nequando irascatur Dominus,
* et pereatis de via iusta.
13 Cum exarserit in brevi ira eius,

* beati omnes qui confidunt in eo.


14 Gloria Patri, et Filio, et Spiritui
Sancto.
*Sicut erat in principio, et nunc, et
semper,
*et in saecula saeculorum. Amen.

11 Serve the Lord in fear,
* and rejoice unto him with reverence.
12 Learn obedience, lest the Lord be
angry, and so ye perish from the right
way.
13 If his wrath be kindled, yea but a
little,
* blessed are all they that put their
trust in him.

14 Glory be to the Father, and to the
Son, and to the Holy Ghost:
*as it was in the beginning, is now, and
ever shall be,
*world without end. Amen.

Psalm 2 is sung regularly in the *cursus* of the monastic Night Office for
Sunday Matins. For Matins of feasts, appropriate psalms are selected from
the Psalter; Psalm 2 seems to have been selected for the Christmas Night
Office on account of verse 7, which is used as a sentence for Christmas, here
and in other liturgical functions.

*antiphon*

Dominus dixit ad me: Filius meus es
tu,
ego hodie genui te.

The Lord said unto me, my son art
thou:
I have this day begotten thee.

The use of the words of verse 7 as antiphon has the effect of highlighting
that verse when it is sung in the course of the psalm.

The practice of psalmody has varied over the centuries, making variable
use of antiphony. An antiphon may be sung before and after the complete
psalm. In earlier practice the antiphon was sung after groups of verses, or
even after each verse; in later practice it was abbreviated before the psalm
and sung complete only after the psalm. On the compact disc, the antiphon
is not sung first, merely in order to make the psalm tone very clear; then the
antiphon is repeated after groups of verses.

There is further variety possible in the use of antiphony for the psalm
itself. Antiphonal alternation can take place verse by verse, or half-verse by
half-verse, in which case the alternation occurs at the asterisk in the middle of
each verse (see the comments on Psalm 150 in track 22, p. 214. On the compact disc, Psalm 2 is sung by one solo voice, so no antiphony is involved.

The clear phrase plan of this antiphon, with an articulation dividing into
two halves, would make possible an antiphonal alternation after *tu*; or even
an earlier alternation after *me*, both semichoirs then joining to sing *ego . . . te*.

### Technical note

Since the central tonal space of the antiphon is the 4th $G-c$, psalm tone 8 is selected because its reciting pitch is $c$. The optional ending of psalm tone 8 on $c$ leads smoothly back to the beginning on this particular antiphon, which is on the same $c$.

## 21. *O magnum mysterium* (responsory, mode 3)

The intricate decoration of this responsory, always beautifully sonorous, sometimes blossoms out with intense expressiveness. Based in a stable tonal space (sounding like part of a major scale), it drifts downwards to end inconclusively in a space much less well defined, perhaps even indeterminate.

Responsories consist of a choral respond and a solo verse. Verses are usually sung to one of a set of standard verse melodies for responsories. These are formulas, but – as used here – not formulas of *recitation*, for no reciting pitch is used. Responsory verse formulas are in general much more melodic than the formulas used for psalm singing.

### Tonal space

The intricate melody is placed in a simple central tonal space, with the upper boundary being the first reference pitch, audible on *magnum*; but the lower boundary, audible on *mysteri-um*, also functions as a reference pitch, and the melody keeps flowing on down below that. The verse stays high, in the upper part of the central tonal space or above it.

### Words and liturgical use

*respond*

| | |
|---|---|
| O magnum mysterium, et admirabile sacramentum, | O great mystery and wonderful sacrament, |
| ut animalia viderent Dominum natum, iacentum in praesepio: | that animals should see the Lord born, lying in a crib: |
| Beata Virgo, cuius viscera meruerunt portare Dominum Christum. | O blessed virgin, whose womb was deemed worthy to bear the Lord Christ. |

*verse*

| | |
|---|---|
| Ave, Maria, gratia plena: Dominus tecum. | Hail Mary, full of grace: the Lord be with you. |

*reprise*

Beata Virgo, cuius viscera meruerunt portare Dominum Christum.

Taken from an obscure source of devotional literature, the words of the respond were among various literary materials that clustered around the Infancy Narrative when it became institutionalized in the fourth century as the feast of the Nativity on 25 December. This particular set of words, used in the Night Office as a responsory, is the source of the image of the ox and ass on either side of the manger.

The image of the animals forms the first of two acclamations in the respond; the second acclamation is a direct address to the Virgin Mary. By way of focusing the piece and backing it up with a scriptural quotation, the solo verse uses the angel Gabriel's greeting to Mary from Luke's Gospel (Luke 1:28) – 'Hail, Mary'. This quote was used widely in various liturgical functions, as well as popular devotion.

The standard format for the responsories of the monastic Night Office calls for a first part, the respond, followed by a verse, followed in turn by the repetition of the last half of the respond; this repetition is sometimes called the reprise. Certain responsories were followed by a *Gloria Patri* and by another singing of the reprise, or of the whole respond.

In the Divine Office, each responsory followed a lection. Use has varied substantially over the last thousand years; originally there was more repetition of the respond, alternating between soloist and chorus.

Since responsories were not part of worship services in which congregations regularly participated (that is, Mass and Vespers), the repertory of over a thousand responsories was not made completely accessible in modern editions and revisions such as those provided by the Benedictines of Solesmes for the Propers of the Mass; for many of the melodies we have to go to monastic books or to medieval manuscripts. A few responsories, including this one, are in the *Liber Usualis*.

*Technical note*

The melody ends on *E*, and with a range from *C* below to *d* above is usually classified as mode 3. The typical focus on the central tonal space *c–G* precedes the general drift downwards to open endings on *F*, *D*, and eventually to *E* in the lower space *D–G* that is suggested at the end.

The verse is firmly located in the higher space *G–c*, insisting on the *d* above for acclamatory emphasis.

## An excerpt from Christmas Lauds

Here begins a series of items taken as a unit out of the middle of the Office of Lauds for Christmas morning; in monastic practice this Office would be sung before daybreak, so that the concluding words of the canticle, 'those that sit in darkness', would have immediate meaning, and the prayer for illumination would be answered symbolically by the first light of day.

Lauds begins with psalmody; this excerpt begins with the last psalm of Lauds, Psalm 150, with its Christmas antiphon. Then follow, in the succession of the Office, the *capitulum* and the short responsory, the Office Hymn with a concluding versicle and response, and the Canticle *Benedictus*, known as the Canticle of Zacharias, with its Christmas antiphon. In actual performance of the Office, this would be followed by certain blessings, prayers and devotions.

## 22. *Parvulus* (antiphon) *and Laudate* (Psalm 150)

Lively as well as lyric, this antiphon moves gracefully through a complex space that complements rather than matches the psalm tone. The melody is short, so even though the range of pitches is relatively narrow, the melodic motion does not settle into a central tonal space or a reference pitch. The psalm tone recites on the highest pitch of the antiphon.

*Words and liturgical use*

*antiphon*

Parvulus filius hodie natus est nobis: et vocabitur Deus, fortis, alleluia, alleluia.

A little son today is born to us: and he shall be called mighty God, alleluia, alleluia.

*Psalm 150*
1 Laudate Dominum in sanctis eius:
* laudate eum in firmamento virtutis eius.
2 Laudate eum in virtutibus eius:
* laudate eum secundum multi-tudinem magnitudinis eius.
3 Laudate eum in sono tubae:
* laudate eum in psalterio et cithara.
4 Laudate eum in tympano et choro:
* laudate eum in chordis et organo.
5 Laudate eum in cymbalis benesonantibus:
* laudate eum in cymbalis iubilationis:
* omnis spiritus laudet Dominum.

1 O praise God in his sanctuary:
* praise him in the firmament of his power.
2 Praise him in his noble acts:
* praise him according to his excellent greatness.
3 Praise him in the sound of the trumpet:
* praise him upon the lute and harp.
4 Praise him in the timbrels and dances:
* praise him upon the strings and pipe.
5 Praise him upon the well-tuned cymbals:
* praise him upon the loud cymbals:
* let every thing that hath breath praise the Lord.

6 Gloria Patri, et Filio, et Spiritui Sancto.
* Sicut erat in principio, et nunc, et semper,
* et in saecula saeculorum. Amen.

6 Glory be to the Father, and to the Son, and to the Holy Ghost:
* as it was in the beginning, is now, and ever shall be,
* world without end. Amen.

Used as an antiphon at Christmas Lauds, the words of *Parvulus* are taken from the same place, Isaiah 9:6, as the Christmas Introit *Puer natus* (and other Proper items); these words serve to give Christian as well as Christmas identity to Psalm 150, which is regularly sung at Lauds throughout the year.

When psalms are sung antiphonally, the alternation can take place between the first half of the verse and the second, or between one verse and the next. Joining the two semichoirs together at the end is also optional. The doxology *Gloria Patri*, regularly sung after psalms, consists of *three* verbal phrases; these have been adapted to the psalm tones (which all have *two* sections) in various traditional ways. The performance on the compact disc is only one way of exercising these several options.

*Technical note*

The antiphon begins in the space *F G a*, then makes a half cadence on the *D* below. It moves through the octave *C* up to *c*, and finds its way to an inconclusive ending on *G*.

With this ending and range it is classified as mode 8, and calls for psalm tone 8, which recites on *c* at the top of the tonal space of a 4th, *c–G*. This antiphon further requires the use of an optional ending on *G* for psalm tone 8; this is a different ending from the one on *c* used for Psalm 2 on track 20. The ending on *G* returns the end of the psalm down closer to the re-intonation of the antiphon on *F*; but the tonal space of the major third *F G a* at the start of the antiphon (and the turn downwards to *D*) comes as a contrast.

## 23. *Multifarium* (Capitulum) *and Verbum caro* (Short responsory)

The *capitulum* ('chapter', actually a sentence) is sung to a recitation formula that uses a reciting pitch and two pitches below.

The short responsory (as opposed to the long or 'prolix' responsory form sung in the Night Office, for example *O magnum mysterium*, track 21) functions as a response to the preceding lection, just as each of the long responsories of the Night Office follows a lection, and as the Gradual Responsory in the synaxis follows the Epistle. In the case of the short responsory this function is easier to grasp because of the limited dimensions.

*Words and liturgical use*

*chapter*
Multifarium multisque modis olim
Deus loquens patribus in prophetis:
novissime diebus istis locutus est nobis
in Filio, quem constituit haeredem
universorum, per quem fecit et
saecula.
*response*
Deo gratias.

God, who at sundry times and in divers manners spake in time past unto the fathers by the prophets, hath in the last days spoken unto us by his Son, whom he hath appointed heir of all things, by whom also he made the worlds.

Thanks be to God.

*short responsory*
*respond*

| | |
|---|---|
| Verbum caro factum est, alleluia, alleluia: | The Word was made flesh, alleluia, alleluia: |

*verse*

| | |
|---|---|
| et habitavit in nobis, alleluia, alleluia. | and dwelt among us, alleluia alleluia. |
| Gloria Patri et Filio et Spiritui Sancto. | Glory be to the Father, and to the Son, and to the Holy Spirit. |

*respond*

| | |
|---|---|
| Verbum caro factum est, alleluia, alleluia. | The Word was made flesh, alleluia, alleluia. |

As a very short lection, *Multifarium*, from the beginning of the Epistle to the Hebrews (1:1-2), gives a programme for Christmas. *Verbum caro*, used here as the responsory to the chapter, is a capsule statement of the doctrine of the Incarnation; the sentence is taken from the first paragraph of the Gospel according to John (1:14), with alleluias added for the festivity. This first chapter of John's Gospel was considered so important that it was added on as a solemn reading at the end of the medieval Mass, after everything else had been said.

Because of its multiple use, the melody for *Verbum caro* can be called a model melody; it is one of the best, a very attractive model that is used for a number of different sets of words in the Office. It focuses sharply on a reference pitch, and ends there; there is nothing to disturb the sense of tonic that a modern ear will hear.

In a short responsory we can easily hear how the solo and chorus respond to each other in repeating phrases; such repetitions were originally used in the long responsories, but were eliminated because of making each piece too long.

## 24. *A solis ortus cardine* (metrical hymn) *and Notum fecit Dominus* (versicle-and-response)

Even though it is involute and expressively detailed, the hymn tune shows a clear, simple overall plan: starting low, it rises with a terraced effect during the first half, then descends to its point of origin in the second half. But the ending is not conclusive, and the hymn tune seems to cycle through its rise and fall again and again. This repetition accommodates the words, which are cast into an unvarying succession of stanzas, each with the same number of lines and syllables. The overall effect is a microcosm of the Divine Office as a whole – an unending cycle of praise as a temporal approximation of eternity.

This type of hymn is *metrical*, in a poetic metre. This particular metre was invented by Bishop Ambrose of Milan around 370, apparently as part of his programme to involve his people in liturgical worship. The form consists of stanzas (Ambrose provided eight in his own hymns, but the form can have more or fewer), each stanza having four lines of eight syllables each.

### Tonal space

There is no reference pitch. Phrase 1 of the melody (*A solis ortus cardine*) marks out one tonal space. Phrase 2 (*ad usque terrae limitem*) marks out a higher space; this overlaps the first one slightly, yet does not sound congruent with it. Phrase 3 (*Christum canamus principem*) continues in the upper space, and phrase 4 (*natum Maria virgine*) returns to the lower one, ending the melody inconclusively inside that space.

### Words and liturgical use

| | |
|---|---|
| A solis ortus cardine | From east to west, from shore to shore, |
| ad usque terrae limitem, | Let every heart awake and sing |
| Christum canamus principem, | The Holy Child whom Mary bore, |
| natum Maria Virgine. | The Christ, the everlasting King. |
| Beatus auctor saeculi | The world's divine Creator wears |
| servile corpus induit: | The form and fashion of a slave: |
| Ut carne carnem liberans, | Our very flesh our Maker shares, |
| ne perderet quos condidit. | His fallen creature, Man, to save. |
| Castae parentis viscera | Soon as the day of grace was come, |
| caelestis intrat gratia: | A Holy Thing found place on earth, |
| Venter puellae baiulat | And in the spotless Virgin's womb |
| secreta, quae non noverat. | Was fashion'd day by day for birth. |
| Domus pudici pectoris | She bowed her to the angel's word |
| templum repente fit Dei: | declaring what the Father willed, |
| Intacta nesciens virum, | And suddenly the promised Lord |
| verbo concepit Filium. | That pure and hallowed temple filled. |
| Enixa est puerpera | She travail'd and brought forth the Son, |
| quem Gabriel praedixerat, | Announced before by Gabriel's voice, |
| Quem matrem alvo gestiens | Whose presence made the unborn John |
| clausus Ioannes senserat. | Within his mother's womb rejoice. |
| Foeno iacere pertulit, | He shrank not from the oxen's stall, |
| praesepe non abhorruit: | He lay within the manger bed, |
| Parvoque lacte pastus est, | And He whose bounty feedeth all, |
| per quem nec ales esurit. | At Mary's breast himself was fed. |
| Gaudet chorus caelestium, | While high above the silent field |
| et angeli canunt Dei: | The choirs of heav'n made festival, |
| Palamque fit pastoribus | To simple shepherds was reveal'd |
| Pastor, Creator omnium. | The Shepherd who created all. |
| Gloria tibi Domine, | All glory for this blessed morn |
| qui natus es de Virgine, | To God the Father ever be: |
| Cum Patr'et Sancto Spiritu | All praise to Thee, O Virgin-born, |
| in sempiterna saecula. | All praise, O Holy Ghost, to thee. |

In its complete form this particular poem has twenty-two stanzas, each beginning with a letter of the alphabet in order (the Latin alphabet has only twenty-two letters): this makes a famous literary form called an *abecedary*. The performance on the compact disc includes only the first seven stanzas (A to G), then adds the metrical doxology. This is like the *Gloria Patri* sung at the ends of psalms, except that the hymn doxology, sung to the hymn melody, has to be composed with the right number of lines and syllables.

## *Notum fecit Dominus* (versicle and response)

A sentence in the form of versicle and response is regularly appended to hymns and other forms in the Office. This one uses a single simple sentence out of Psalm 97, the same psalm as used for the verse in the Christmas Gradual *Viderunt*. The sentence is divided ungrammatically between the soloist and the chorus, which completes and confirms the solo part as if with a code word. The recitation formula includes a melisma on *alleluia* as a suffix.

*versicle*

| Notum fecit Dominus, alleluia, | The Lord hath made known, alleluia, |

*response*

| salutare suum, alleluia. | His salvation, alleluia. |

## *Technical note*

The hymn tune begins with the scale segment $D E F G a$. The upper tonal space is $G - c$. The ending on $E$ places it in mode 3. There is no necessary relationship between the hymn tune and the pitch of the versicle.

## 25. *Gloria in excelsis* (antiphon) *and Benedictus* (canticle)

The antiphon, quoting Luke 2:14, begins with a formal intonation lower in the range, in the same manner in which the same words would be intoned in the morning hymn as sung at Mass. Then it continues a little more brightly, rising into the tonal space to be occupied by the recitation formula for the canticle to follow.

## *Tonal space*

The antiphon is short and in a relatively narrow range, so does not have time to generate a central tonal space or a reference pitch. The reciting pitch of the canticle tone (like a psalm tone, but slightly more elaborate) matches the single high pitch of the antiphon (on *hominibus*).

## Words and liturgical use
### antiphon

Gloria in excelsis Deo, et in terra pax
hominibus bonae voluntatis.

Glory be to God on high,
and on earth peace to men of good will.

### Canticle of Zacharias

1 Benedictus Dominus Deus Israel:
* quia visitavit, et fecit redemptionem
plebis suae.
2 Et erexit cornu salutis nobis,

* in domo David pueri sui:
3 Sicut locutus est per os sanctorum,

* qui a saeculo sunt, prophetarum eius:

4 Salutem ex inimicis nostris,
* et de manu omnium qui oderunt nos:
5 Ad faciendam misericordiam cum
patribus nostris:
* et memorari testamenti sui sancti.
6 Iusiurandum, quod iuravit ad Abraham
patrem nostrum,
* daturum se nobis:
7 Ut sine timore de manu inimicorum
nostrorum liberati,
* serviamus illi:
8 In sanctitate et iustitia coram ipso,

* omnibus diebus nostris.
9 Et tu puer, Propheta Altissimi
vocaberis:
*praeibis enim ante faciem Domini parare
vias eius:
10 Ad dandam scientiam salutis plebi
eius,
* in remissionem peccatorum eorum:
11 Per viscera misericordiae Dei nostri:

* in quibus visitavit nos, oriens ex alto:

12 Illuminare his qui in tenebris et in
umbra mortis sedent:
* ad dirigendos pedes nostros in viam
pacis.
13 Gloria Patri, et Filio, et Spiritui
Sancto.
*Sicut erat in principio, et nunc, et
semper,
*et in saecula saeculorum. Amen.

1 Blessed be the Lord God of Israel:
* for he hath visited and redeemed his
people:
2 And hath raised up a mighty salvation for
us
* in the house of his servant David,
3 As he spake by the mouth of his holy
Prophets
* which have been since the world
began,
4 That we should be saved from our enemies
* and from the hand of all that hate us,
5 To perform the mercy promised to our
forefathers
* and to remember his holy covenant,
6 To perform the oath which he sware to
our forefather Abraham
* that he would give us,
7 That we being delivered out of the hand
of our enemies
* might serve him without fear
8 In holiness and righteousness before
him
* all the days of our life.
9 And thou, child, shalt be called the
prophet of the most high:
* for thou shalt go before the face of the
Lord to prepare his ways,
10 To give knowledge of salvation unto his
people
* for the remission of their sins,
11 Through the tender mercy of our
God:
* whereby the dayspring from on high hath
visited us,
12 To give light to them that sit in
darkness and in the shadow of death
* and to guide our feet into the way of
peace.
13 Glory be to the Father, and to the Son,
and to the Holy Ghost:
*as it was in the beginning, is now, and
ever shall be,
*world without end. Amen.

The angels' hymn from Luke 2:14 is quoted in this antiphon to give a Christmas identity to the canticle that is sung regularly at the end of Lauds throughout the year. This song of Zacharias, *Benedictus Dominus Deus Israel* (Luke 1:68: 'Blessed be the Lord God of Israel'), is one of three canticles from the New Testament (the other two being the *Nunc dimittis* and the *Magnificat*.

See the notes to the antiphon *Parvulus* on track 22 (p. 214) for a description of various options in the antiphonal performance of canticles.

### Technical note

The antiphon moves mostly in the space *F g a*, with a single ascent to *c*. The ending is on *G*, placing the antiphon in mode 8, and calling for psalm tone 8. The ending of the psalm tone is *G* (rather than *c* as for Psalm 2, track 20) to facilitate the return to the beginning of the antiphon.

## 26. *Salve Regina* (Antiphon, mode 1)

This is a very sombre, yet extremely expressive melody. Composed probably in the twelfth century as a post-Gregorian chant of devotion to the Virgin Mary, it became very popular in later medieval times and continued so down to the present, at least in monasteries and prayer groups. It is one of the best-known items of music inherited from the Middle Ages. At the wrenching conclusion of Poulenc's opera *Dialogue of the Carmelites* (1957), the sisters sing the words of *Salve Regina* as they march to their execution.

### Tonal space

With the exception of one important pitch (see technical note), the tonal space is very similar to a minor scale. Instead of a typical Gregorian central tonal space, one that is relatively narrow with a strong upper reference pitch, *Salve Regina* shows a wider tonal space extending upwards from a strong *lower* reference pitch first heard on '(*Sal-*)*ve*', and at the ends of phrases throughout.

### Words and liturgical use

Salve, Regina, mater misericordia:
Vita, dulcedo, et spes nostra, salve.
Ad te clamamus, exsules, filii Hevae.
Ad te suspiramus, gementes et flentes
in hac lacrimarum valle.
Eia ergo, Advocata nostra,
illos tuos misericordes oculos ad nos
converte.
Et Iesum, benedictum fructum ventris tui,
nobis post hoc exsilium ostende.
O clemens: O pia: O dulcis Virgo Maria.

Hail, queen, mother of mercy:
our life, sweetness and hope, hail.
To thee we cry, as exiles, children of Eve.
To thee we sigh, groaning and weeping
in this vale of tears.
Come, then, our counsellor,
turn those merciful eyes upon us.

And show Jesus, the blessed fruit of thy
womb, to us after this exile.
O gentle: O pious: O sweet virgin Mary.

Words and melody composed by an unknown French or German monastic poet and musician, probably in the twelfth century, as a song of devotion to be sung by the monastic community after one of the hours of the Divine Office (Vespers or Compline). One of many such songs addressed to the Virgin, *Salve regina* was given liturgical appointment for the long summer season after Pentecost.

The words of *Salve Regina* include traditional acclamations such as 'Salve' (Hail) and intensely devotional expressions of praise such as 'O clemens, O pia' (O gentle, O pious).

This and other medieval devotions to the Virgin Mary observe the traditional distinction, operative in Christian theology since its beginning, between praise for humans and worship only for God. The distinction is a fine one, and the language used is occasionally ambiguous; but the ultimate petition addressed to the Virgin (who is Blessed yet not divine) is only that she might intercede with the godhead on behalf of humankind.

In words as well as melody, *Salve Regina* seems disposed for antiphonal performance; at any rate, it can be easily sung in antiphony, the alternations becoming progressively shorter towards the end, with the concluding petition for the whole chorus in unison. In liturgical use it may be followed by a versicle-and-response.

*Technical note*

*Salve Regina* ends on D. Because of its range upwards as far as *d* the octave above, it is classed as mode 1. A central tonal space is not well defined; instead, the *whole* tonal space is clearly marked out by the fifth and octave framework *D a d*, along with the fourth below, *A D*. The melodic movement is strongly oriented towards *D*, the base of the octave framework, and this *D* becomes the ending pitch. Such use of tonal space became more and more frequent in later medieval chant, being especially characteristic of chants ending on *D*.

Hence, the scale of *Salve Regina* differs from minor only in the use of *C* instead of the leading tone *C* sharp. A European musician in the eighteenth-century tradition might identify *Salve Regina* as *modal* in the sense that it used a scale degree – *C* – heard in mode-1 chants, rather than the *C* sharp he expected in the key of *D* minor. This musician might further reflect, however, that *C* sharp is not actually present in the key *signature* of *D* minor and has to be added as an accidental. If the low *C* in *Salve Regina* is sung as *C* sharp, there is little to distinguish it from a melody in the key of *D* minor – except, of course, the chords that might accompany it; but that is another story.

# Notes

## Chapter 1: Chant, Chanting and Gregorian Chant

This book is accompanied by a compact disc with 26 tracks of Gregorian and other kinds of chant. The contents of the disc are listed on pages 173–4. The items are discussed individually in the Commentary on the compact disc, numbered according to the tracks. The specific pieces of chant referred to in the book for detailed discussion are all on the disc, and should be listened to while reading the discussion. The book as a whole is designed as commentary to Gregorian chant in general, and assumes that the reader will be listening to chant as performed on this or some other disc.

A great many recordings of Gregorian chant have been made during the twentieth century. Jerome Weber, in *A Gregorian Chant Discography* (Utica, New York: J. F. Weber, 1990), has compiled a complete listing up to 1990, including over 8,000 pieces of chant in some 800 recordings. New discs are released continually, and are reviewed by Weber in the journal *Plainsong and Medieval Music*. Compact discs currently available are listed in the standard catalogues available in stores and libraries.

Recordings vary in quality and style; over recent decades the variety of style in performance has increased, making it no easier to recommend or to select specific recordings that will suit your taste. As this book tries to show, there is no one authentic style of performance; listeners are urged to develop taste by listening to as many different styles as possible, exercising their own musical judgement at every step.

The standard handbook in English on Gregorian chant, including full bibliography, is David Hiley, *Western Plainchant: A Handbook* (Oxford: Clarendon Press, 1993).

The standard music encyclopedia in English is *The New Grove Dictionary of Music and Musicians*, edited by Stanley Sadie (London: Macmillan, 1980). It contains many entries on specific topics and several long surveys of Gregorian chant, as well as of all other kinds of chant.

A historical survey of Gregorian chant is included along with other medieval European music in *The New Oxford History of Music*, volume II (new version): *Early Medieval Music to 1300*, edited by Richard Crocker and David Hiley (Oxford: Oxford University Press, 1991).

Many useful articles on liturgy and other topics associated with Gregorian chant are in the *Dictionary of the Middle Ages*, edited by Joseph R. Strayer (New York: Charles Scribner's Sons, 1984).

Extensive use has been made in this book of current research, much of it in French or German and none of it easily accessible; adequate reference to it is not possible here. For research published before 1993, see Hiley, *Western Plainchant*.

It is hard to think of a rule of liturgy that has no exception. If the exceptions (some of them very rare) are always specified, however, the generalities become exceedingly difficult to understand on first encounter. Many generalities are made here without specifying singular exceptions.

Selected twentieth-century books containing Gregorian chant are listed on pp. 228–9.

There are several English translations of the Bible in current use. Where a specific translation is needed it will be mentioned. The use of translations for pieces of chant is described in the notes to the Commentary on the compact disc. In this volume Psalms are numbered as in the Greek Septuagint and Latin Vulgate; numbers according to the Hebrew Bible and King James Version are given in parentheses.

Thoughts on the concept of the cathedral can be found in Christopher Page, *Discarding Images: Reflections on Music and Culture in Medieval France* (Oxford: Oxford University Press, 1993).

An account of Vatican II is given in the *New Catholic Encyclopedia* (New York: McGraw-Hill, 1967); see 'Vatican, Council II'; see also 'Music, Sacred, Legislation on' for an account of episcopal supervision of music in the USA.

The revival of Gregorian chant in the nineteenth and twentieth centuries is summarized in Hiley, *Western Plainchant*, pp. 622–9.

Gregory of Tour's *History of the Franks* is translated (with an index) by Lewis Thorpe (Penguin Classics, 1974)

The role of Gregory the Great in music is summarized from recent research by James McKinnon in *Antiquity and the Middle Ages from Ancient Greece to the 15th Century* (London: Macmillan, 1990; New Jersey: Prentice Hall, 1991), chapter I, pp. 102–19.

## Chapter 2: Tone and Tonal Space

Information on scales, harmony, notation and nomenclature can be found in many introductory texts on music appreciation or musicianship as well as in encyclopaedias such as *The New Harvard Dictionary of Music*, edited by Don Michael Randel (Cambridge, Massachusetts: Harvard University Press, 1986).

The description of central tonal space and reference pitch in Gregorian chant has been prepared specially for this book, and will not be found in exactly the same form elsewhere.

Instructions for using recitation formulas of various kinds are included in the Solesmes chant book *Liber Usualis* (see the Bibliography). See also Hiley, *Western Plainchant*, part II, pp. 47–69.

For a description of MIDI see Brian Heywood and Roger Evan, *PC Music Handbook* (PC Publishing, Kent UK, 1996) or any recent handbook on computers and audio engineering.

For the development of medieval polyphony see Richard L. Crocker, *A History of Musical Style*, reprinted by Dover, 1986.

The illustration of the border is adapted from a bronze scabbard design from Treveri graves of the first century BC in Luxembourg. Cf. R. and V. Megaw, *Celtic Art* (London and New York: Thames & Hudson, 1989), p. 184.

## Chapter 3: Melodic Movement, Rhythm and Words

For the basics of appreciation of classical music see any introductory text.

For various views on Gregorian rhythm, see Hiley, *Western Plainchant*, part IV, pp. 373–85.

Instructions for using recitation formulas of various kinds are included in the Solesmes chant book *Liber Usualis* (see the Bibliography). See also Hiley, *Western Plainchant*, part II, pp. 47–69. Formula in the sense of model melody or idiom has been widely discussed in many different contexts, for instance in Crocker and Hiley, *The Early Middle Ages to 1300*, chapter 6.

The problem with the term neume is that it used to be applied in two senses: (a) it referred to a continuous mark for two or three separate pitches; (b) by transference, it was also applied to a group of several pitches that felt as if they belonged together as a melodic gesture, and so could be represented by a group of marks that might, however, include separate marks for individual pitches as well as a continuous mark as in (a). It became impossible to distinguish systematically between these two kinds of graphics, and so *neume* is better rendered by *group*. The ambiguity of neume and the difficulty of distinguishing a neume from a melisma make it preferable to use the expression *intrasyllabic melodic extension*, introduced by the Russian musicologist Izaly Zemtovsky.

The plans of all types of Gregorian chants are described in Hiley, *Western Plainchant*, part II, pp. 69–139.

For *melisma* see the article in *The New Grove Dictionary*, or *The New Harvard Dictionary of Music*.

The term mode is applied to Gregorian melody in three senses.

(1) All Gregorian antiphons are placed into eight modal classes in the following way:

(a) antiphons are first placed into four principal classes according to whether they end on the diatonic pitches *D E F G*; antiphons ending on *a, b, c* are treated as if they ended on *D, E, F*;

(b) antiphons in each of the four principal classes are then placed in two subclasses called *authentic* and *plagal*, according to whether the melody of a given antiphon spends most of its time above the ending pitch, ascending an octave or so above it; or on the other hand dwells in the 5th above the ending pitch, descending below it occasionally.

(2) All Gregorian chants are assigned to one of eight octave segments of the diatonic scale according to the following plan:

mode 1 = ending pitch *D*, higher range (authentic) = octave segment *D–d*
mode 2 = ending pitch *D*, lower range (plagal) = octave segment *A–a*
mode 3 = ending pitch *E*, higher range (authentic) = octave segment *E–e*
mode 4 = ending pitch *E*, lower range (plagal) = octave segment *B–b*
mode 5 = ending pitch *F*, higher range (authentic) = octave segment *F–f*
mode 6 = ending pitch *F*, lower range (plagal) = octave segment *C–c*
mode 7 = ending pitch *G*, higher range (authentic) = octave segment *G–g*
mode 8 = ending pitch *G*, lower range (plagal) = octave segment *D–d*

The eight octave segments are a theoretical abstraction, and rarely correspond exactly to the pitch set of any given piece of chant. Note that there are actually only seven different octave segments in the diatonic scale; the octave segment for mode 8, *D–d*, is the same as for mode 1.

(3) The chants of any given mode (as assigned by ending pitch and range) often fall into families, members of a given family being related by the use of common idioms of melody.

For a full discussion of mode see the article by Harold Powers, 'Mode', in *The New Grove Dictionary*.

The chants *Iubilate* and *Ecce quam bonum* can be found in the *Liber Usualis* or the *Graduale Triplex*, listed in the indices of those books.

## Chapter 4: Gregorian Chant, Roman Politics and European Polyphony

Some of the kinds of chant included in figure 4.1 are described in Crocker and Hiley, *The Early Middle Ages to 1300*. All are mentioned in *The New Grove Dictionary*.

Concerning documented notation for other music, such as Chinese, Egyptian or Mosaic, it is often assumed that melodies for certain sets of words identified as songs go back as far as the documents that contain the words – or even much further. This may be the case, but cannot be demonstrated.

For current appreciation of cultural life under the Roman Empire during the early centuries of Christianity, see Peter Brown, *The World of Late Antiquity* (New York and London: W. W. Norton, 1971); also Robin Lane Fox, *Pagans and Christians* (San Francisco: Harper & Row, 1986).

For non-Christian cult see Walter Burkert, *Greek Religion*, trans. John Raffan (Oxford: Basil Blackwell, 1985).

For Greek and Roman music see the comprehensive source book by Andrew Barker, *Greek Musical Writings: I. The Musician and his Art.* Cambridge University Press 1984; Martin West, *Ancient Greek Music.* Oxford: Clarendon Press 1992; volume I of *The New Oxford History of Music: Ancient and Oriental Music*, edited by Egon Wellesz (Oxford: Oxford University Press, 1957; McKinnon, *Antiquity and the Middle Ages*.

The comprehensive compilation of sources of Roman music is by Gunther Wille, *Musica Romana* (Amsterdam, 1967).

For early Christian music see the notes to chapter 5.

For the Carolingian chant project see Hiley, *Western Plainchant*, part VII, 'The Carolingian Century'. Also Rosamund McKitterick, *The Frankish Church and the Carolingian Reforms* (London, 1977).

The hymn from Oxyrhynchus was edited by Egon Wellesz in *A History of Byzantine Music and Hymnography* (2nd edition Oxford: Clarendon Press, 1961), pp. 152–5; by Egert Pöhlmann in *Denkmäler altgriechischer Musik* (Nuremberg, 1970), p. 107; and by Martin West, *Ancient Greek Music*, pp. 324–5. The pitches in these editions are virtually identical; the rhythms differ, depending on how much account is taken of the metre of the verse, which is anapaestic (except for the doxology); and to what degree the rhythmic signs are understood to apply to the pitches.

## Chapter 5: Early Christian Worship

See Hiley, *Western Plainchant*, part VI.

Current research on early liturgical history is expanding rapidly and producing new conclusions; it is published in research journals in several different languages, and is difficult of access. No adequate reference to such studies can be made here, nor is there any single listing of it.

Paul F. Bradshaw, *The Search for the Origins of Christian Worship*, New York and Oxford 1992) explores some of the new approaches to the history of liturgy. Lucien Deiss, *Springtime of the Liturgy*, translated by Matthew J. O'Connell (Collegeville, Minnesota: Liturgical Press, 1979, is an excellent collection of important early texts in translation. Other useful studies are by Edward Foley, *From Age to Age* (Chicago: Liturgy Training Publications, 1991), and also *Foundations of Christian Music* (Bramcote and Nottingham: Grove Books, 1992)

James McKinnon, *Music in Early Christian Literature* (Cambridge: Cambridge University Press, 1987), is a basic and fascinating collection of early texts and quotations about music in Christianity during the first four centuries. The Bible quotations mentioned on page 104 are McKinnon's numbers 347 (Psalm 118), 229 (Amos), 143 (Isaiah), 225 (Psalm 67).

*Dictionary of Medieval Liturgy* has an excellent account of the Divine Office. The recent but authoritative study of the Divine Office is by Robert Taft, *The Liturgy of the Hours in East and West* (Collegeville Minnesota: The Liturgical Press, 1986).

The early development of the Christian church and its doctrine is told by Henry Chadwick, *The Early Church* (Penguin Books, 1967).

The translation of *Phos hilaron* is adapted from *Hymns Ancient and Modern*, Historical Edition (1909).

## Chapter 6: Gregorian Chant in the Roman Rite

See Hiley, *Western Plainchant*, part I; Crocker and Hiley, *The Early Middle Ages to 1300*, chapter IV; McKinnon, *Antiquity and the Middle Ages*, chapter IV.

The text of *Ordo Romanus I* is edited by Michel Andrieu (*Les Ordines Romani du haut moyen âge*, Spicilegium sacrum Lovaniense 11, 23–4, 28–9; Louvain, 1931–61).

The words of six of the earliest chant books are edited by René-Jean Hesbert, *Antiphonale Missarum Sextuplex* (Brussels, 1935).

Early chant books published in facsimile, and current Roman Catholic chant books, are listed in the Bibliography.

The Roman Rite as used down to Vatican II (1964) can most easily be studied in the Introduction to the *Liber Usualis*, which includes the 'Rubrics for the chant of the Mass' from the Vatican edition, and also all the words of 'The Ordinary of the Mass', meaning everything that is said at Mass without change from one occasion to the next.

## Chapter 7: Monastic Chant in Time and Eternity

For the history of early monasticism, see 'Monasticism, Origins', in *Dictionary of the Middle Ages*; see also 'Divine Office' for an excellent account of the monastic Office; see also Taft, *Liturgy of the Hours in East and West*. McKinnon, *Music in Early Christian Literature*, especially pp. 51–74, includes maxims and attitudes of early monastic leaders.

There are several English translations of Benedict's *Rule*, for instance *RB 1980: The Rule of St Benedict in Latin and English with Notes*, edited by Timothy Fry (Collegeville, Minnesota: The Liturgical Press, 1981).

## Chapter 8: Gregorian Chant in Notation and in the Mind

Hiley, *Western Plainchant*, part IV, pp. 340–441, with eighteen plates.

Peter Wagner, *Einführung in die gregorianischen Melodien*, 3 vols (1895–1921); vol. I translated into English by Agnes Orme and E. G. P. Wyatt, *Introduction to the Gregorian Melodies* (DaCapo Press, 1986).

André Mocquereau, *Le nombre musical grégorien ou rythmique grégorienne*, 2 vols (Rome, 1908–27).

Eugène Cardine, *Gregorian Semiology*, translated by R. Fowles (Solesmes, 1982).

For Roman Catholic chant books and facsimile editions of early chant books, see the Bibliography.

Plate 1: St Gall Codex 359 (about AD 900): published in facsimile as *Paléographie musicale*, series 2, number 2: *Cantatorium IXe siècle*: no. 359 de la Bibliothèque de Saint-Gall (Solesmes 1924), p. (131) 151. At the top of the photograph is the *Alleluia De profundis clamavi ad te Domine: Domine exaudi vocem meam*. Staffless notation with adjunct letters, transcribed in *Graduale Triplex*, pp. 367–8.

Plate 2: Laon MS 239 (about AD 900), p. 39: published in facsimile in *Paléographie musicale* 10: *Antiphonale missarum sancti Gregorii*: IXe–Xe siècle: codex 239 de la Bibliothèque de

Laon (Solesmes, 1909), p. 77. At the top of the photograph is the end of the verse *(Do-)mine de gentibus iracundis, ab insurgentibus in me, exaltabis me: a viro iniquo eripies me* from the Gradual *Eripe me*. Staffless notation with adjunct letters, transcribed in *Graduale Triplex*, pp. 121–2.

Plate 3: 'Sarum Graduale': *Graduale Sarisburiense*, facsimile edition by Walter Howard Frere (London, 1894), p. 31 At the top of the photograph is the Gradual *Miserere mei Deus, miserere mei: quoniam in te confidit anima mea*. (verse) *Misit de celo et liberavit me: dedit in opprobrium conclucantes me*. Staff notation on a four-line staff with F clef on the next to top line (in the photograph, the line above the first staff is a page ruling); later there is a C clef on the top line of the staff. Compare *Graduale Triplex*, p. 63.

Plate 4: Vatican edition of the Graduale (1908), p. 295: beginning of the Gradual *Custodi me Domine*. Square notation on a four-line staff with C clef on the top line.

Plate 5: Solesmes edition of the Graduale (1945), p. 345: beginning of the Gradual *Custodi me Domine*. Square notation on a four-line staff with C clef on the top line, and Solesmes rhythmic signs.

Plate 6: *Graduale Triplex* (1979), p. 304: beginning of the Gradual *Custodi me Domine*. Square notation on a four-line staff with C clef on the top line, and Solesmes rhythmic signs; staffless notation with adjunct letters added above the staff from Laon MS 239, and below the staff from St Gall Codex 359.

Because of the development of European musical notation, carried on in close connection with musical theory over the centuries from the Middle Ages on to the present, Gregorian chant is traditionally placed on the diatonic scale so as to use no sharps at all, and only one flat as needed. It has always been understood that this notation implies no absolute pitch level – and indeed, until modern instrument construction, there was no standard to which absolute pitch could be referred.

The most obvious result is that all chant is located *by notation* in and around the octave below 'middle c', and when transcribed on a modern staff has to use the treble clef with the indication 8ve, meaning an octave lower. That corresponds roughly to the range of male singers, but women or children sing it an octave higher, corresponding to the treble clef without 8ve. Since the notation of chant pitch is completely relative in the first place, it would be less sexist to notate it all with simply the treble clef.

For purposes of performance, Gregorian chant is sometimes notated with key signatures of flats or sharps, in order to place it at an absolute level, since singers who depend on reading notation habitually identify notated pitch levels with location in their own vocal range, and may become confused in reading a melody notated at some level other than where it is sounding.

## Commentary on the compact disc: Proper and Ordinary chants for Mass, chants for the Divine Office

### List of sources for the chants on the compact disc, numbered according to the tracks

Most of these chants are in the *Graduale Triplex* (GT), for which page references are given. All are in the *Liber Usualis* (LU), but page numbers for different editions may vary; find the chants in the index, according to the type of chant. Some of these chants are only in the *Liber Usualis*; the page numbers given here may not be good for all editions. For these chant books, see the Bibliography. Offertory verses are in *Offertoires neumés avec leur verset*, edited by Rupert Fischer (Solesmes, 1978).

1. Haec dies (Gradual): GT 196.
2. Puer natus (Introit antiphon): GT 47.
3. Viderunt omnes (Gradual): GT 48.
4. Alleluia Dies sanctificatus: GT 49.
5. Tui sunt caeli (Offertory): GT 49.
    Offertory verses: *Offertoires neumés*, pp. 18–20.
6. Viderunt omnes (Communion antiphon): GT 50.
7. Laetatus sum (Gradual): GT 336.
8. Adiutor in opportunitatibus (Gradual): GT 69.
9. Custodi me (Gradual): GT 304.
10. Alleluia Dominus dixit: GT 43.
11. Alleluia Excita Domine: GT 23.
12. Super flumina (Offertory): GT 345.
13. Exaltabo te (Offertory): GT 313.
14. Psallite Domino (Communion antiphon): GT 238.
15. Qui meditabitur (Communion antiphon): GT 67.
16. Kyrie eleison: GT Kyrie IB; LU Kyrie ad libitum V, ('Conditor Kyrie omnium').
17. Gloria in excelsis Deo: GT Mass Ordinary II, p. 715; LU Mass Ordinary II.
18. Sanctus: GT Mass Ordinary II, p. 717; LU Mass Ordinary II.
19. Agnus Dei: GT Mass Ordinary IV, p. 724; LU Mass Ordinary IV.
20. Psalm 2 and Dominus dixit (antiphon): LU, The Nativity of our Lord, at Matins, in the First Nocturn (p. 371 in some editions).
21. Magnum mysterium (responsory): LU, The Nativity of our Lord, at Matins, responsory 4, in the Second Nocturn (p. 382 in some editions).
22, 23, 24, 25. Excerpt from Christmas Lauds: LU, The Nativity of our Lord, at Lauds, 5th antiphon and following (pp. 399–403 in some editions).
26. Salve Regina (antiphon): LU 276.
    For the *station* for *Laetatus sum*, see Hesbert, *Antiphonale missarum sextuplex*, p. liii.
    An edition of Kyrie eleison ad libitum V, with the verses *Suavis tu Deus*, will be included in David Bjork, *The Aquitanian Kyrie* (in press).

## English Translations

When words were used for chant from the Latin Bible, they were often excerpted as sentences or clauses, and these were arranged for singing in some modified order; in addition, details of the diction were often slightly modified. In providing English translations for the Latin Proper chants of the Mass it is often desirable to modify one of the standard translations in order to correspond more closely to the Latin word order, or to show more closely the correspondence of wording. This was done in the *Anglican Missal*, which provided the Mass in English, including English translations of all the Latin Mass Propers with a view to their being sung to adaptations of the Gregorian melodies. I have generally used these translations for the Mass Propers included on the compact disc; I have also used the English translations for the Mass Ordinary chants, which are the versions from the *Book of Common Prayer*, but with one or two slight modifications of my own, purely for correspondence with the Latin versions. The translations of the psalms and canticles are mostly not modified, however, and come straight from the Psalter in the *Book of Common Prayer*, that being the version traditionally used for singing complete psalms in English.

The translation of the Office Hymn *A solis ortus cardine* is taken from *Hymns Ancient and Modern*, Historical Edition, London, 1909, p. 71.

# Bibliography

## General reference works

*Dictionary of the Middle Ages*, edited by Joseph R. Strayer (New York: Charles Scribner's Sons, 1984).
*New Catholic Encyclopedia* (New York: McGraw-Hill, 1967).
*The New Grove Dictionary of Music and Musicians*, edited by Stanley Sadie (London: Macmillan, 1980).
*New Harvard Dictionary of Music*, edited by Don Michael Randel (Cambridge, Massachusetts: Harvard University Press, 1986).
Jerome Weber, *A Gregorian Chant Discography* (Utica, New York: J. F. Weber, 1990); see also the journal *Plainsong and Medieval Music*.

## Books on Gregorian chant

David Hiley, *Western Plainchant: A Handbook* (Oxford: Clarendon Press, 1993).
*The New Oxford History of Music*, volume II (new version): *The Early Middle Ages to 1300*, edited by Richard Crocker and David Hiley (Oxford: Oxford University Press, 1991).

## Books on liturgy and literature

Paul F. Bradshaw, *The Search for the Origins of Christian Worship* (New York and Oxford, 1992).
Lucien Deiss, *Springtime of the Liturgy*, translated by Matthew J. O'Connell (Collegeville, Minnesota: Liturgical Press, 1979).
Edward Foley, *From Age to Age* (Chicago: Liturgy Training Publications, 1991), and *Foundations of Christian Music* (Bramcote and Nottingham: Grove Books, 1992).
James McKinnon, *Antiquity and the Middle Ages from Ancient Greece to the 15th Century* (London: Macmillan, 1990; Englewood Cliffs, New Jersey: Prentice Hall, 1991).
James McKinnon, *Music in Early Christian Literature* (Cambridge: Cambridge University Press, 1987).
Robert Taft, *The Liturgy of the Hours in East and West* (Collegeville Minnesota: Liturgical Press, 1986).

## Chant books of the twentieth century

### Vatican edition of the Graduale
*Graduale sacrosanctae Romanae Ecclesiae de tempore et de sanctis SS. D. N. Pii X. pontificis maximi jussu restitutum et editum ...* (Romae: Typis Vaticanis, 1908).

## *Solesmes* Graduale

*Graduale sacrosanctae Romanae ecclesiae de tempore et de sanctis SS. D. N. Pii X. pontificis maximi jussu restitutum et editum ad exemplar editionis typicae concinnatum et rhythmicis signis a Solesmensibus monachis diligenter ornatum* (Typis Societatis S. Joannis Evangelistae: Desclée, 1945).

*The Liber Usualis*, with Introduction and Rubrics in English. Edited by the Benedictines of Solesmes (Society of St John the Evangelist, Tournai, Belgium: Desclée & Co., 1952). (Many editions were published by Desclée in Belgium between 1921 and 1963.)

*Graduale triplex, seu, Graduale Romanum Pauli PP. VI cura recognitum & rhythmicis signis a Solesmensibus monachis ornatum neumis Laudunensibus (Cod.239) et Sangallensibus (Codicum San Gallensis 359 et Einsiedelnensis 121) nunc auctum* (Solesmes: Abbaye Saint-Pierre de Solesmes, 1979.)

## *Facsimile editions of early chant books*

Laon MS 239

*Paléographie musicale* 10: *Antiphonale missarum sancti Gregorii*: IXe–Xe siecle: codex 239 de la Bibliothèque de Laon (Solesmes, 1909).

St Gall MS 359

*Paléographie musicale* series 2, number 2: *Cantatorium* IXe siècle: no.359 de la Bibliothèque de Saint-Gall (Solesmes, 1924).

*Monumenta Paleographica Gregoriana*, 3: *Die Handschrift St Gallen Stiftsbibliothek 359, Cantatorium* (Munsterschwartzach: Internationale Gesellschaft für Studien des Gregorianischen Chorals, [1984]).

Einsiedeln MS 121

*Codex Einsiedeln 121*. Graduale und Sequenzen Notkers von St Gallen, edited by Odo Lang, 2 vols (facsimile with commentary; Weinheim, 1991).

For a complete listing of the contents of the *Paléographie musicale* see Crocker and Hiley, *The Early Middle Ages to 1300*.

# Glossary

This glossary contains the technical terms of music and liturgy that are used in this book.

*mus.*: identifies special musical applications; see also Hiley, *Western Plainchant*, or *The New Harvard Dictionary of Music* (cited in the Bibliography).

*liturg.*: identifies special liturgical applications; see also the *Dictionary of the Middle Ages* or *The New Catholic Encyclopedia* (cited in the Bibliography).

*Christ.*: identifies special Christian use.

For any ordinary meanings the reader should not hesitate to consult a standard dictionary.

Music and liturgy alike often make use of common ordinary terms but give them special, sometimes far-fetched application that can only be described as jargon; such terms often resist precise definition. Musical terminology in particular is the result of centuries (in some cases, millennia) of evolution, guided or misguided by either too little or too much effort to be logical and systematic. I have tried to use the terms in ways that make sense while still conforming to customary use.

For purposes of introductory discussion, much musical terminology is unnecessary and should be replaced by commonsense language, which I have tried to do. On the other hand, readers who know some technical terms are often frustrated if those terms are not used, and such readers can be bewildered by what seems to them to be unnecessary common-language circumlocutions. I have tried to refer to such technical terms in parentheses without making obstacles for readers who do not know them.

a cappella: Music for a choir without accompanying instruments.

abbot ('father'): Head of a monastery.

absolute pitch: *mus.* Ability to recall accurately the pitches sounded by an instrument, and to reproduce them vocally at any time.

acclamation: Enthusiastic expression of public approval. In chant, such an expression is made by the congregation, usually with simple, repetitive wording and intonation, such as 'Kyrie eleison, Kyrie eleison . . .'.

acolyte: At Mass, an attendant to the celebrant.

Acts of the Apostles: One of the books of the New Testament.

Advent (Latin *adventus,* approach and arrival of the Roman emperor at a city): *liturg.* The month-long season before Christmas, spent in preparation for the coming of Jesus.

Agnus Dei: Acclamation added to the Mass by Pope Sergius, about AD 680; wording is derived from John 1:29.

altar: A raised platform where sacrifices or offerings are made to an ancestor or god. *Christ.* A table set up in front of the congregation, dedicated for use at Holy Communion.

Anglican: English; specifically pertaining to the Church of England, or churches (usually 'Episcopal') in accord with it in other countries. More specifically, members of any of these churches who emphasize continuity with the Western ('Catholic') Christian Church from before the Reformation of the sixteenth century.

Anglican chant: Formulas for singing psalms and canticles, derived originally from psalm tones, but using triadic harmony.

antiphon (antiphony): Music performed by two roughly equal groups of singers, who sing in alternation.

apostle: One who is sent. *Christ.* One of the twelve disciples appointed by Jesus.

Arian: Pertaining to the teaching of Arius ( about AD 260 –after 320) that the Son of God was in some sense subordinate to the Father. Opposed to the Catholic doctrine of the Trinity as maintained by Athanasius (about AD 295–373).

articulation: A joint, as in a finger. *mus.* Control of the sound so as to join some pitches and separate others, forming divisions between groups of pitches.

Ascension Day: A feast on Thursday of the Sixth Week after Easter; celebrates the ascension of Jesus into heaven according to the account in Acts of the Apostles 1: 9–11.

Ash Wednesday: The first day of Lent. Token ashes are placed on the heads of the people at Mass as a symbol of penitence.

augmented fourth: On the diatonic scale, the extremely dissonant interval *F–b*, which includes three adjacent whole tones, hence 'tritone'; it is larger than a perfect fourth, which has two whole tones and a semitone.

bar: *See* measure.

basilica: (Greek, 'king's house'): A very large hall; for Christians, a very large church building. Famous examples are found in Rome.

beat: *mus.* An impulse experienced by the listener at regular intervals in certain kinds of rhythm.

Benedictine: Pertaining to the monastic order built on the *Rule* of St Benedict (about AD 480–547).

Bible (Greek, 'books'): The collection of books that contains sacred writings in Hebrew from the first millennium BC, plus the Christian Gospels, Acts of the Apostles, Epistles and Revelation. Christians called the Hebrew books the Old Testament, their own books the New Testament. The list of books (the *canon*) varies slightly.

bishop: Overseer; *Christ.* Overseer of a diocese; principal pastor and administrative officer.

Book of Psalms: *See* Psalter.

cadence (a 'falling'): *mus.* An idiom that ends a section of a piece; in chant it often involves a melodic descent.

cadenza: An ornamented cadence; in a classical concerto it may be extremely extended, providing an occasion for soloistic display.

canon: A 'rule' or specification. *Christ.* A list specifying which books should be included in the Bible. *liturg.* The exact wording of the eucharistic prayer in the Roman Mass. *mus.* Metaphorically, a list of generally accepted repertory. The Gregorian Proper chants for Mass form the first canon of European music. *mus.* A rule for a procedure in counterpoint, when a second voice sings the music that was written down only for the first voice, following it either exactly or in some modified way (faster/slower, higher/lower), strictly according to a verbal direction – which is the canon.

canticle ('little song'): *Christ.* One of a number of specified Biblical songs – three in the New Testament, more than a dozen in the Old Testament; does not include psalms.

cantor (Latin for 'singer'): *Christ.* The lead singer, hence choir director and teacher, eventually, the music director of a church.

capitulum ('chapter'): *liturg.* A very short lesson read at one of the day hours; in effect, a liturgical sentence.

Carolingian: Pertaining to the family dynasty that dominated the Frankish kingdom after

AD 750. The period of Frankish culture under that family's political hegemony, roughly AD 750–900.

cathedra: Bishop's throne.

Catholic ('universal'): Name used eventually for the dominant western branch of the Christian Church.

celebrant: The bishop or priest who pronounces the eucharistic prayer at a given occasion of Mass; Mass is said to be celebrated.

censer: An ornamental container in which incense is placed.

central tonal space: *mus.* The group of pitches used most consistently in a given melody.

ceremony, ceremonial: Formal actions established for the conduct of a rite.

chant: Singing; sometimes used for singing on one note, or in a repetitive singsong manner. *mus.* Sacred monophony, as opposed to secular monophony or to polyphony.

chapter: A very short lesson read at one of the day hours; *equiv. to* capitulum; in effect, a liturgical sentence.

choir (English, *chorus*): A small, selected chorus.

Christmas: Christian feast on 25 December celebrating the birth of Jesus.

classical music: A common expression for the most admired, most frequently performed repertories of European concert and operatic music composed about 1725–1910.

clause: A syntactic unit of prose containing at least a subject, verb and predicate.

collect: *liturg.* A short prayer expressing general concerns relative to a specific occasion.

Communion: *liturg.* Partaking of bread (and wine) consecrated in the eucharistic service. Since from the beginning Christians have had a profound concern for correct doctrine, they have partaken of liturgical Communion only with those with whom they agree on certain important matters; consequently, *to be in communion* with someone is, for a Christian, to agree with them on these matters. Hence, the *Roman communion* is a way of defining membership in the group of all dioceses that agree with the diocese of Rome.

compline: *liturg.* The last service of the day hours in the monastic Office.

congregation: An assembly of people, especially for religious observance. *liturg.* The people, as distinct from the bishop or priest, assembled for Mass.

consonant: *mus.* Sounding together in a blend: certain pairs of pitches, sounding together, blend better than other pairs, which are said to be dissonant.

contrapuntal: *mus.* Relating to counterpoint.

convent: A women's monastery.

counterpoint: *mus.* Literally, music composed by setting one note against another; it has come to mean music in which two distinct series of pitches sound as two simultaneous melodic lines, but nonetheless are integral parts of one and the same harmonic context.

Credo: The first word of each of two best-known statements of Christian faith. *liturg.* The Nicene Creed (one of these two), as said at Mass after the Gospel, sung as the third chant item of the Mass Ordinary.

cult: Religious devotion.

cursus (Latin, 'course'): *liturg.* Performance of a predetermined series of psalms or readings. In the Night Office the psalms are sung in a *cursus* determined by their numerical order.

day hours: *liturg.* In the daily cycle of the Divine Office, the services appointed for the first hour (prime), the third hour (terce), the sixth hour (sext), the ninth hour (none), plus compline.

deacon: *Christ.* In the administrative hierarchy, the third level after bishop and priest. *liturg.* At Mass, the first assistant to the celebrant at the altar.

diatonic ('through the tones'): *mus.* A scale proceeding mostly through whole tones, with semitones at certain points, as on the white keys of the piano.

diminished fifth: *mus.* The interval *B–F* on the diatonic scale, which includes two whole tones and two semitones; it is a semitone smaller than a perfect fifth; it is the same size as an augmented fourth, hence an extreme dissonance.

diocese: Regional unit of administration, especially Christian.

discant: *mus.* A technique of polyphonic composition in which two voices, sounding different pitches simultaneously, produce a series of mainly consonant intervals. Used in the Middle Ages to generate music of two, three, or more voices.

dissonant: *mus.* Sounding at the same time but not in a blend: a dissonant pair of pitches does not blend as well as a consonant pair.

Divine Office: *liturg.* A prescribed daily cycle of prayer and praise, including the Night Office (= Matins), the morning and evening service (Lauds and Vespers) and the day hours. The Divine Office is usually said complete only in a monastery, where it is also called the *monastic Office.*

doubling: *mus.* Making a single pitch stronger by duplicating it higher or lower, usually at the octave, in which case the added pitch, being a strong overtone of the original one, sounds 'the same'. Doubling can be applied to a melody or other configuration of pitches, and can be done at other intervals, such as thirds.

doxology: *liturg.* An expression of praise, specifically one addressed to the Trinity of Father, Son and Holy Ghost.

Easter: *Christ.* The spring festival that celebrates the resurrection of Jesus; refers to a specific Sunday and also to the season following.

epic: A long story of heroic adventure. In antiquity such stories were sung in a particular kind of verse (dactylic hexameter).

episcopal: *Christ.* Pertaining to the bishop (Latin, *episcopus*).

episema: *mus.* Dom Mocquereau's term for a short horizontal line added to a note in square notation, indicating that the pitch should be lengthened.

epistle: *Christ.* A type of open letter included in the New Testament. *liturg.* A selection from one of those letters read at Mass as a lesson, hence called the *Epistle.*

ethnomusicology: The study of music in society; so far the societies studied have been mostly non-European.

eucharist: *liturg.* The Christian ritual service of thanksgiving.

eucharistic prayer: *liturg.* The main thanksgiving said by the celebrant at the eucharist.

evangelist: *Christ.* A preacher of the Gospel. Specifically, the putative authors of the four canonical Gospels included in the New Testament – Matthew, Mark, Luke and John.

falsobordone: *mus.* Italian term for French *fauxbourdon* ('false bass') used in the sixteenth century for a technique of singing harmonies in parts (soprano, alto, tenor, bass) with the effect of a psalm tone.

feast (festal): *Christ.* One of the occasions for celebration appointed in the ecclesiastical calendar. The five principal feasts are Christmas, Epiphany, Easter, Ascension and Pentecost.

feria (ferial): *liturg.* A day of the week, or a day without a feast appointed to it; distinct from Sunday (*Dominica*, the Lord's day), since that is always considered a feast.

fifth: *mus.* In the diatonic scale, any interval that includes five consecutive pitches, as *A* (*B C D*) *E*. All such fifths are 'perfect', that is, are consonant and have a low-number frequency ratio of 2:3, except for *B* to *F*, which is a diminished fifth, an extreme dissonance, ratio 512:729.

figure: *mus.* A series of pitches that is clearly perceptible yet abstract, not identified with a melody, theme or motive.

formula: *mus.* A pattern of pitches used with only slight changes in many different contexts. In chant, formulas are found especially in psalm tones, and also in verses of certain responsorial forms. Some scholars use formula to mean *idiom* or *model melody*.

fourth: *mus.* In the diatonic scale, any interval that includes four consecutive pitches, as *A* (*B C*) *D*. All such fourths are 'perfect', that is, are consonant and have a low-number frequency ratio of 3:4, except for *F* to *B*, which is an augmented fourth, an extreme dissonance, ratio 512:729.

fraction: *liturg.* The breaking of the consecrated bread on the altar at Holy Communion.

Franks (Frankish): A tribe from northwest Germany that crossed the Rhine and dominated northern France from the sixth century on.

frequency: *mus.* The number of cycles per second of longitudinal vibration in air, producing a given pitch; audible frequencies range from 20 to 20,000 cycles per second.

functional harmony: *mus.* A system of relationships among harmonic triads and chords derived from them; the system was developed by European musicians and used extensively from AD 1600 to the present.

fundamental: *mus.* The component (usually the lowest) most representative of a complex musical sound; has the frequency (in cycles per second) of which the overtones are multiples; hence, it is the prime, with overtones at double, triple, and so forth.

Gallican: Pertaining to Gaul.

Gallo-Roman: The culture developed in Gaul as a province of the Roman Empire.

Gloria in excelsis: *Christ.* The best-known early prose hymn, used as a morning hymn and also at Mass after the *Kyrie*, as the second item of the Mass Ordinary. For wording see the Commentary to track 17; also called the 'greater doxology'.

Gloria Patri: *Christ.* An expression of praise addressed to the Trinity of Father, Son and Holy Ghost; for wording see *Puer natus*, in the Commentary to track 2; also called the 'little doxology'.

glossolalia: An ecstatic utterance of unintelligible speechlike sounds.

Gospel: *Christ.* One of the four canonical accounts of the life and death of Jesus, included in the New Testament; *liturg.* A selection from one of the Gospels read as a lesson at Mass and referred to as the *Gospel*.

Gothic: In the history of architecture, a style that developed in northern France around AD 1150 and spread throughout Europe; characterized by the pointed arch, but more importantly by thoroughgoing use of modular design, producing lofty effects.

Gradual: *liturg.* A melismatic responsorial chant sung after the Epistle at Mass.

greater doxology: *See* Gloria in excelsis.

Greco-Latin: The literary and artistic culture of Greece as diffused through Latin-speaking parts of the Roman empire. The more common term 'Greco-Roman' would apply to political aspects of culture.

Greek: The language and culture of the people who dominated what is now Greece, along with the western coast of Turkey, from circa 1600 BC until the Roman empire.

Gregorian chant: *mus.* As used in this book, specifically the Proper chants at Mass, that is, the repertory of melodies for the variable sentences assigned to be sung at the Roman Mass throughout the yearly ecclesiastical calendar; the term can also include related repertories sung in the Divine Office.

half step: *equiv. to* semitone; The smallest interval in the diatonic scale.

harmonic triad: *mus.* Three pitches forming the interval of a fifth with a third in between, as *C E G*, a major triad, or *D F a*, a minor triad. The major triad has special acoustic and mathematical properties that make the pitches blend in a unique way; also called the 'common chord' or the 'perfect chord', or simply 'the triad'.

harmony: *mus.* The special blend of sound heard in certain combinations of three or more pitches (harmonic triads); also, music made by using such combinations; also, the systematic study and use of such combinations, specifically by European musicians AD 1600 to the present.

Hebrew: The language used especially for sacred writings of the Semitic peoples who called themselves 'Israelites' and eventually 'Jews'; *see* Bible.

Holy Scripture: Sacred writings; the term used by Christians to identify the Bible as opposed to other writings sacred or secular.

homily: A sermon.

hours: *See* day hours.

hymn: Specifically, performance of a word or words of praise. *Christ.* A sung piece of prose or verse incorporating praise of God.

hymn tune: *mus.* A melody used for a stanzaic hymn.

Iberia: The peninsula containing Spain and Portugal.

ictus: *mus.* Dom Mocquereau's term for a short vertical mark that he used for the beginning of a rhythmic group.

idiom: *mus.* A short bit of melody used as a stylistic convention; can also apply to rhythm or harmony.

Infancy Narrative: A term for the Gospel accounts of the birth and infancy of Jesus, especially the accounts in Luke 1 and 2.

inflection: *mus.* The bending of a reciting pitch or a melodic line up or down by tones and semitones.

interval: *mus.* The distance from one pitch of a scale to another; the two pitches can be taken successively or simultaneously; the scale can be diatonic or some other scale.

intonation ('putting into tone'): Generally, chanting or singing as distinct from speaking; also, the first few pitches of a chant as sung by a soloist to start a chorus. It can also refer to the accuracy with which a pitch is sounded.

intrasyllabic melodic expansion: *mus.* Singing more than one pitch on a syllable before going on to the next syllable. The term, introduced by Izaly Zemtsovsky, successfully avoids the difficulty of distinguishing between neume and melisma.

Introit: *liturg.* The entrance song at Mass; the first item of the Gregorian Mass Propers.

iubilus: *mus.* A Latin term for the melisma performed on the last syllable of 'Alleluia' when sung before the Gospel at Mass.

John: The *Gospel according to St John*, the fourth canonical Gospel of the New Testament.

Kiss of Peace: *liturg.* A ceremonial greeting given by the celebrant at Mass to his assistants (who may pass it on to the congregation), usually in preparation for Holy Communion.

Kyrie (Greek, 'Lord'): *liturg.* The chant with the words *Kyrie eleison* (Lord, have mercy), as sung at the start of Mass. *mus.* The first item of the Mass Ordinary.

Latin: The language spoken by ancient tribes in central Italy, made into a literary language after the third century BC (drawing on Greek literary technique), then eventually the official language of the Roman empire and of Christian Roman liturgy; later, the language of medieval European philosophy and scholarship; still used for Roman Catholic doctrine and sometimes liturgy.

Lauds ('praises'): *liturg.* The name of the morning prayer service as integrated into the daily cycle of the Divine Office.

leap: *mus.* An interval larger than a whole step, such as a major or minor third, a perfect fourth or fifth.

lection: *liturg.* A lesson or reading, often a selection from the Bible.

lector: *liturg.* A reader appointed to read lessons at Mass or in the Divine Office.

Lent ('spring season'): A season of penitence in preparation for Easter; nominally forty days long, and called in the Latin liturgy *quadragesima.*

lesser (little) doxology: *See* Gloria Patri.

lesson: *equiv. to* lection; a reading.

liquescent: *mus.* A symbol in early chant notation used for pitches sung to liquid consonants and semivowels such as *l, r, m.*

litany: *liturg.* A ritual series of petitions addessed to God; the petitions are all sung in call-and-response format that can include praises. A litany is usually sung in procession around the church or through the city.

liturgy: Assigned ritual actions; more generally, ritual worship.

Luke: The *Gospel according to St Luke*, the third canonical Gospel of the New Testament.

Lutheran: *Christ.* Pertaining to the teaching of Martin Luther (1483–1546), who began the Protestant Reformation in AD 1517; applied to the some of the churches that were established in Germany and Scandinavia as a result of the Reformation.

lyric: *mus.* Originally, poetry sung to the accompaniment of the lyre, as first attributed by the Greeks to Sappho (seventh century BC). More generally applied to melody, meaning 'song-like'; in modern popular music, however, the term can have its original meaning, as in 'the lyrics of a song'.

major scale: *mus.* In the diatonic scale, the octave segment *C D E F G a b c*; called major because above its first note *C* is a major third *E*, a major sixth *a*, a major seventh *b*. It is the primary scale in use in classical and popular music.

major third: *mus.* The interval of the diatonic scale that includes two whole tones, as *C* to *E*, or *F* to *a*, or *G* to *b*; as a simultaneity it usually has a bright, joyful sound.

Mass: *liturg.* A worship service that includes the synaxis and the eucharist, both in specific traditional formats; *equiv. to* Catholic Mass.

Mass Ordinary: *liturg.* All the words said or sung at Mass without change from one occasion to the next; *mus.* The items Kyrie, Gloria in excelsis, Credo, Sanctus, Agnus Dei.

Mass Propers: *liturg.* Variable items appointed for a particular occasion for Mass. *mus.* The items Introit, Gradual, Alleluia, (Tract), Offertory, Communion.

Matins: *liturg.* A worship service consisting mainly of psalms and readings, said or sung daily between midnight and first light; *equiv. to* Night Office. Matins is in the form of one, two, or three nocturns (*see* nocturn).

measure: *mus.* The unit of duration and number of pulses specified by the meter for a given piece; also called bar.

medieval chant: *mus.* Sacred Latin chant composed later than the canonical repertory of Gregorian chant, beginning around AD 850.

melisma: *mus.* A stretch of melody with many pitches sung to one syllable; the number of pitches can range from half-a-dozen up to dozens.

melismatic: *mus.* Pertaining to chant that contains one or more melismas.

melody: *mus.* Originally a sweet rendering of a poem (Greek, *mel-ode*); now specifically a succession of single pitches heard as a 'line', usually with the implication that it seems like a song.

melody type: *See* model melody.

Merovingian: Pertaining to the family dynasty and culture (named for Merovaeus, a legendary king) dominant in France circa AD 500–700.

metre: *mus.* A system for measuring durations against the background of a basic unit (the *measure* or *bar*); usually divided regularly into two parts (*duple*), three parts (*triple*), or some multiple or combination of two and three.

metric grid: a specific system of metre as used in a given piece, to which all the notes in the piece are referred.

metrical hymn: *mus.* A hymnic poem set in stanza form so that it can be sung to a repeating melody (the hymn tune).

Middle Ages: The historical period between antiquity and the European Renaissance, roughly AD 500–1400.

MIDI ('musical instrument digital interface'): An electronic device that connects a musical instrument to digital processing and recording equipmment.

minister: *liturg.* The celebrant or one of his assistants in their function of administering at Mass.

minor scale: *mus.* In the diatonic scale, an octave segment such as *A B C D E F G a*, so called because it has a minor third above the first note; the upper part is usually altered by flats or sharps for purposes of functional harmony.

minor third: *mus.* In the diatonic scale, an interval that includes a whole tone plus a semitone, as *A* to *C*, *B* to *D*; as a simultaneity, it is sometimes used for a sombre sound, whereby it characterizes a minor scale.

missal: *lit.* A book containing all the words said at Mass, including Proper and Ordinary items.

modal scale: *mus.* An imprecise expression for any octave segment that lacks the distinguishing features of a major scale, particularly a semitone below the top note (the *leading tone*, an essential ingredient in functional harmony).

mode ('way' or 'manner'): A family of melodic idioms; a classification of chant by the ending pitch; or, with closer specification of range, a classification in one of eight modes (see endnote to chapter 3); thence, also a classification of melodies according to which octave segment of the diatonic scale they characteristically employ.

model melody: *mus.* A melody adapted for use with several alternate sets of words, making minor adjustments for the differing number of syllables but maintaining the overall profile.

monastic (monasticism, monastery, monk): Pertaining to solitude for the purpose of meditation. In European monasticism the solitude is not as prominent a feature as are the very well defined *rules* or *orders* of communal life, still separate (*cloistered*) from society.

motive: *mus.* A short pattern of a few pitches that returns frequently in changing but recognizable form within a piece.

Nativity: *liturg.* Usually refers to the celebration of the birth of Jesus on 25 December; also, the theme of many saints' days.

nave: The largest part of a cathedral or other church, in which the congregation stands or sits.

neumatic: *mus.* Using groups of two to six pitches per syllable; from *neume*.

neume: *mus.* A term sometimes used in chant for a notational sign for several pitches written as a group.

New Testament: *Christ.* The set of books of the Bible that includes the four canonical Gospels, the Acts of the Apostles, Epistles and Revelations.

Night Office: *See* Matins.

nocturn: The format of a unit of Matins: a nocturn contains a specified number of psalms with antiphons, and lessons with responsories; there can be one, two or three nocturns in one night's service.

none: *liturg.* One of the day hours, the short office at the ninth hour.

note: *mus.* A musical sound of a single frequency, hence *equiv. to* pitch. Also, a mark in music notation indicating such a sound.

nuance: *mus.* A detail of rhythmic movement, as indicated in the early notation of certain tenth-century chantbooks.

octave: *mus.* The interval that includes eight adjacent pitches of the diatonic scale, as *A* to *a*; the simplest, most consonant interval, with frequency ratio 1:2; because the higher pitch is equivalent to the first overtone of the lower, the two pitches resonate strongly, and while they are distinguishable, they can be said to sound 'the same' in pitch.

octave segment: *mus.* A segment (section) of the diatonic scale, consisting of the eight pitches bounded by an octave, as *A B C D E F G a*.

ode: A sung poem; a song.

Offertory: *mus.* The chant sung at Mass while the gifts of the congregation are collected and brought to the altar.

Old Testament: *Christ.* The books of the Bible containing the sacred Hebrew writings.

Ordinary of the Mass: *See* Mass Ordinary.

orthodox ('correct praise' or 'correct doctrine'): *Christ.* Designation of certain eastern churches, such as the Greek Orthodox Church.

overtones: *mus.* The additional pitches produced by a basic pitch (the *fundamental*) at multiples of the basic frequency (twice, three times, four times, etc.); both the fundamental and the overtones, which together make up the complex sound, are also called *partials*. The audibility and number of the overtones depends on the nature of the sound source and the acoustic environment; their configuration determines the tone quality (*timbre*) of a given sound.

pagan: In Mediterranean antiquity, a perjorative term used by Christians to designate non-Christians; applied especially to traditions of civic cult.

papyrus: A standard writing surface used in antiquity, made from reeds.

Passiontide: The period of two weeks before Easter, commemorating the 'passion' or suffering of Jesus.

Pentecost (Greek, 'the fiftieth'): A Jewish feast fifty days after Passover. *Christ.* A commemoration of the day when the disciples of Jesus received the Holy Spirit.

perfect pitch: *See* absolute pitch.

phrase: *mus.* The basic unit of musical discourse, comparable to a sentence of prose or a verse of poetry.

pitch: *mus.* A musical sound of a single frequency; *equiv. to* tone or note.

pitch set: *mus.* The set of pitches used in a given piece or section of a piece.

poetic metre: The length of a given verse or line of a poem, measured by the number of syllables, or by the configuration of long and short syllables, or by the pattern of accented and unaccented syllables, or by some combination of such factors.

polyphony (Greek,'many sounds'): Usually designates styles of medieval and Renaissance music in which more than one voice or melodic line is heard at the same time, as opposed to chant or *monophony*. In principle, the term applies equally well to classical and popular music, and to any music in which more than one pitch is sounding at once – or even to any music that uses more than one sound source at once.

pontiff: High priest; *Christ.* Bishop.

pope: The bishop of Rome, acknowledged as primate by the bishops of the *Roman Communion*.

popular music: In twentieth-century Europe and America, a group of musical repertories developed as the confluence of European styles of song, dance, and march music with African-American styles of performance.

Preface: *liturg.* The opening portion of the eucharistic prayer, leading into the *Sanctus.*

priest: *Christ.* One designated by a bishop as an assistant, delegated to celebrate Mass in the bishop's stead.

prime: *liturg.* One of the day hours, the short service at the first hour of the day.

Proper chant: *liturg.* A chant appointed to be sung at a particular occasion of Mass on a feast or saint's day.

Proper Chants of the Mass: *mus.* The items Introit, Gradual, Alleluia, (Tract), Offertory, Communion.

prophet: One who proclaims for all to hear; or, one who foretells publicly. *liturg.* As the *prophecy*, a selection from one of the books of the Old Testament prophets might be read at Mass as the first lesson.

psalm (from Greek, 'to pluck with the finger'): Originally, a song accompanied on a plucked stringed instrument. *Christ.* Generally, an unaccompanied song (since early Christians did not use instruments). Hence, specifically one of 150 sacred Hebrew poems in the Old Testament Book of Psalms (the Psalter).

**psalm** tone: *mus.* A melodic formula used for singing a psalm.

Psalter: One of the books of the Old Testament, containing 150 sacred poems in Hebrew.

pulpit: A raised platform, small but high, with a railing, used for preaching to a congregation at Mass or on other occasions.


range: *mus.* The span of pitches ranging from low to high in a given piece.

recitation formula: *mus.* A melodic formula used for reciting words, mostly on one pitch (the *reciting pitch*), plus a few other pitches to mark punctuation. Used for psalms, lections, prayers.

reciting pitch: *mus.* The single pitch repeated as often as needed in reciting words to a recitation formula.

reference pitch: *mus.* A pitch in a given piece to which the other pitches can be compared as being higher or lower, or related by interval; the reference pitch may be distinguished by some factor such as prominence, central location in the range, or reiteration.

Reformation: *Christ.* In the sixteenth century, the independent reorganization of most German and Scandinavian dioceses (and in England the Church as a whole) following their refusal to acknowledge the authority or leadership of the pope.

reprise: *mus.* Repetition of a section of a piece, usually after a different section intervenes.

resonance ('re-sounding'): The accumulation of force in acoustic vibration.

response: *liturg.* The answer, typically made by the congregation, to an utterance by the bishop, deacon, or solo singer; both call and response may be intoned in a recitation formula or sung to a melody.

responsorial: *mus.* Performance involving alternation between a solo singer and a chorus.

responsory: *mus.* A melody for a response. The most important and elaborate responsories are for the Gradual at Mass, and following each lesson at Matins.

reverberation: Echo.

rhythm: *mus.* Flow; periodicity. See pages 41–4.

rite (ritual): Prescribed forms of cult or worship.

Roman Catholic: Catholic rite and doctrine that acknowledges the authority and leadership of the bishop of Rome.

Roman Mass: Mass said according to the traditions of the diocese of Rome.

sacramentary: *liturg.* A book containing prayers said at Mass by the bishop. Sacramentaries are the principal type of book on which the early history of the Roman rite has been reconstructed.

Sacrifice of the Mass: *liturg.* The doctrine that at Mass a sacrifice (variously described, but in any case not made by mere human hands) is re-presented; it is a central mystery of the Christian faith.

sanctuary: *liturg.* The part of a church building around the altar, in Catholic practice dedicated to the Sacrifice of the Mass.

Sanctus: The acclamation 'Holy', addressed to God, said or sung by the congregation during the eucharistic prayer.

scale: The display in ascending or descending order of the set of pitches used in a given musical system or style.

Scripture: *See* Holy Scripture.

segment: *mus.* A section of a scale.

semichoir: *mus.* One of two roughly equal divisions of a choir.

semiology: The study of signs; used by Dom Eugène Cardine for the study of early chant notation in its meaning for performance.

semitone: One of two roughly equal divisions of a (whole) tone.

sentence: A clause, or group of two or three clauses, related in sense and suitably connected. *liturg.* Such a grammatical unit used as an independent pronouncement in a worship service.

Septuagesima ('the seventieth'): A Sunday at the start of a pre-Lenten season of preparation, nominally seventy days before Easter.

sequence: *mus.* An early medieval type of chant (not Gregorian) with the distinctive musical form *a, bb, cc, dd*, etc. (There is another meaning, unrelated, concerning a device of melodic or harmonic construction in classical music.)

sermon ('word'): *liturg.* Instruction by a preacher to the congregation at Mass or on another occasion, typically explaining the meaning of the words said at Mass, especially the Gospel reading.

sext: One of the day hours, the short service said at the sixth hour.

simultaneity: *mus.* Two or more pitches sounding at the same time.

singing in parallel: *mus.* A medieval practice of doubling a chant recitation formula or melody with octaves, fifths and fourths.

Solesmes: The location in France of the Benedictine Abbey of St Pierre, where much of the revival of Gregorian chant took place.

square notation: *mus.* The type of musical notation used in modern chant books for Gregorian chant, modelled on a medieval style that developed in France from the twelfth century on.

staff: *mus.* In standard European musical notation, the set of five closely spaced horizontal lines on which the musical notes are placed.

stanza: In poetic verse, a pattern of lines of words (for instance, four lines of equal length). The pattern is repeated consistently through the poem a number of times, and thus can be sung each time to the same melody.

step: *mus.* Motion from one pitch of a scale to the next adjacent pitch; if that is a semitone away, the step is a *half step*.

strophe: In poetry and music, often used for *stanza*.

subdeacon: *liturg.* At Mass, the second assistant to the celebrant, after the deacon.

synagogue: A congregation (or place of assembly) of Jews for instruction and worship.

synaxis (synax): *liturg.* A worship service involving readings, prayers, and songs; usually the first half of Mass, before the eucharist.

tonal: Pertaining to tone. Also used, in an incorrect and misleading way, in opposition to 'modal', presuming that 'tonal' music must be in a key and have a 'tonic', that is, must use major and minor scales and functional harmony.

tone: A sound heard as a single steady frequency, a single pitch or note; also, the basic interval between two such tones on the diatonic scale, as the *whole tone*. *See also* psalm tone.

triad: Commonly used for *harmonic triad*.

una voce (Latin, 'with one voice'): A phrase commonly used by early Christian writers for *unison* singing.

Unison ('one sound'): *mus.* The pitch relationship between two sound sources performing the same pitch.

verse: A line of poetry. In the Bible, a numbered sentence. In Gregorian chant, a secondary section comparable to a *bridge* in popular music; *verse* is also sometimes used for *stanza*.

whole step (whole tone): The distance from one pitch of the diatonic scale to the next, except for the half steps (semitones) *B–C* and *E–F*.

# Index